SACRED SOUND
Music in Religious Thought and Practice

Edited by
Joyce Irwin

Journal of the American Academy of Religion Studies

Volume L, Number 1

Scholars Press
Chico, California

☐ The Cover _____

The intersecting lines in the graphic sign represent the action of religious reality (the vertical line) upon the world of ideas (the horizontal line) by going back to the origin (the dot) from which reality and ideas come. In a general way, this is the intention of the Journal's thematic series in religious studies.

Library of Congress Cataloging in Publication Data
Main entry under title:

Sacred sound.

(Journal of the American Academy of Religion thematic studies ; v. 50, no. 1)
1. Religion and music. I. Irwin, Joyce L. II. Series.
ML3865.S2 1983   291.3'8   83-15390
ISBN 0-89130-655-2

Manufactured in the United States of America

Contents

Preface

The articles in this volume approach a common theme—music in religion—from different starting points. The approaches of the authors are determined partly by the particular religious tradition under consideration, partly by the particular materials the authors have chosen, and partly by the discipline and training of the author. Most contributors are scholars of religion, but some hold a primary or strong secondary allegiance to music, while one is explicitly interdisciplinary in training and approach.

The resulting volume is therefore more a mélange than a cohesive examination of a single issue. Whereas all essays deal with some aspect of the juncture of music and religion, some place greater weight on music, some on religion. Some focus on the theoretical writings of respected religious leaders; others begin with actual devotional or liturgical practice. Some restrict their consideration to music designed for worship, some define religious music more broadly to include devotional song, while the first writer, even more inclusively, finds a religious element in all music.

In spite of a lack of uniformity of approach and the diversity of religious traditions, the similarities which emerge are striking. All the religions studied affirm music in some form and under some circumstances as positive. Yet those circumstances are generally well defined, hinging upon the type of music, the ritual setting, and often the spiritual status of the performer. There is usually a form of music considered acceptable for worship, while other forms may be considered appropriate for nonliturgical gatherings, private devotion, or—even more problematically—secular occasions. If these latter forms are introduced into formal worship, conflicts arise and debates ensue. It is at these times that we find most of the explicit reflection on the value of music and its propriety in the life of faith. Different views are expressed on the relationship of the sacred to the secular and, accordingly, on the definition of sacred music. Many perceive sensual elements even in music considered religious by others. Whether music's appeal to the senses detracts from or contributes to devotion is an important question for all traditions. To consider this question is to open up fundamental issues about human nature and human access to the divine.

Hence, several of the articles reveal that controversies about religious music have coincided with controversies over the means of salvation. When either mysticism or a conversion experience is regarded as a better or even essential path to salvation, institutional worship and its traditional musical forms are often found to be insufficient and superficial. New forms of worship and music arise to express more intense religious experiences. Whether these more expressive forms can or should be appropriated by the larger congregation is a question which opens up reflection on the nature of the religious institution as an aggregate of persons at different levels of faith.

The present volume is only a first step in the direction of a phenomenology of religious music. The obscurity of primary sources, the scarcity of secondary analyses, and the absence of a common body of theory push a truly comparative study of music as a religious phenomenon well into the future. If the essays presented here serve to demonstrate the viability of such a project, they will have accomplished their purpose.

Music and Theology:
A Systematic Approach

Oskar Söhngen[*]

In a dialogue between the composer Adrian Leverkuehn and the devil in Thomas Mann's novel *Doktor Faustus*, we find the remark: "Music—a highly theological concern" (374). This description may appear surprising to us moderns; we are prepared to concede to music an aesthetic, perhaps even a philosophy, but we react with initial surprise to the idea of a theology of music. By contrast, people of earlier times—into the Renaissance period—took this for granted. Music was considered by them not primarily as *ars* but rather as *scientia*. Even Martin Luther could bemoan the deaths of renowned composers in his time with the comment that so many "learned people" had been swept away./1/ But when a modern writer such as Thomas Mann claims a theological dimension for music in his key novel—whose hero bears resemblance to the composer Arnold Schoenberg—the question of the contemporaneity of such a mode of thinking cannot be discarded.

All those who are familiar with the history of music know that theological decisions have frequently influenced music's development. For example, the most musically gifted of the Reformers, Ulrich Zwingli of Zurich, removed from the church service all music—congregational singing as well as choir and organ music—because it disturbed devotion. The result was, among other things, a rapid flourishing of chamber music for the home (cf. Nef). Conversely, Martin Luther, convinced that the community of the universal priesthood of believers (I Peter 2:9) was the bearer of the liturgy, tried to engage the congregation in the service primarily through singing. That God speaks with us through His Word, and we in response speak with Him through prayer and praise is Luther's famous formulation in the sermon for the dedication of the castle church in Torgau from the year 1544 (WA:XLIX, 588). Thus he set himself to the task of writing hymns and setting them to music, urging friends and those so gifted to do likewise. In this way he created the basis for the great flourishing of evangelical church music which soon revealed its first impulses in multiple adaptation of hymns./2/

---

[*]Translated by Joyce Irwin

But more is intended by the assertion that music is a highly theological concern than that intellectual–historical influences from the realm of theology have occasionally given the development of music another, a new direction. The assertion claims no less than that the strange occurrences which have their basis in ordered vibrations of air—which are transmitted through our hearing organs and registered in our consciousness as musical processes of experience and knowledge—have in substance theological content and belong in the comprehensive system of theology.

If I am correct, we can distinguish in music history three forms of the relationship of music and theology. While they overlap from time to time, their distinct structures can be clearly discerned.

I

The first goes back to a mathematical discovery ascribed to the Greek philosopher Pythagoras in the sixth century B.C. According to the legend, one day he passed a smithy and heard how the hammers on the anvil resulted in paired harmonies. Thereupon he went into the smithy and tested the weight of the hammers on the scale in order to disclose the basic musical intervals of octave, fifth, and fourth from the proportion of weights. Overpowered by the recognition that the musical intervals could be mathematicized, he hurried home to continue his experiments on proportionally stretched strings. These revealed the relationship of 2 to 1 for the octave, 3 to 2 for the fifth, and 4 to 3 for the fourth. However doubtful the details of this legend, nevertheless they make convincingly clear the primal scientific experience of *thaumazein*, of amazement. With the discovery of a numerical order in the world of sound, music moved into the universe of the sciences. And indeed the musician who was familiar with the natural reality of sounding numbers belonged as scholar to the mathematical disciplines. Together with geometry, arithmetic, and astronomy, music from now on forms the classical quadrivium. The realm of sound is a universe of firm, numerically structured order, and the interval is an *audible* law. One must not misunderstand this process in the manner of our modern scientific division of labor, as if the discovery of the physical basis of music were only an incidental aspect of the knowledge of its essence. The Pythagoreans were convinced that the essence of music was grasped in its arithmetic proportions. Numbers were for them the foundations of the musical arts. The Pythagorean law of sound and number signifies the correspondence of the basic relationships of simple, small, finite whole numbers to the basic musical relationships of the octave, fifth, and fourth: $2{:}1=(4{:}3)\text{x}(3{:}2)$.

The same mathematical laws, however, which determine the structure of music, also determine the order of the cosmos up to the movements of the stars. Whoever occupied himself with music also stood in the workshop of the secrets of the structure of the world. Music unfolded itself in all three areas of the world picture of the time: as inaudible music of the spheres (*musica mundana*); as well-ordered interrelationship of the human body and soul (*musica humana*), and as its own realm of sounding *musica instrumentalis*, which ontologically binds heaven and earth.

The conception remained determinative also for the early Christian Church. Augustine's *Six Books on Music* stand in the tradition of Pythagorean music theory. The resounding order of the cosmos, however, no longer rests in itself but is the work of the Divine Creator. It is God who has created the harmony and consonance in microcosm and macrocosm. From now on the verse from the Wisdom of Solomon (11:20), "Thou hast arranged all things by number and weight" (RSV), becomes the cantus firmus for the praise of God out of creation. If earthly music thereby becomes an image of the heavenly, its worth and honor are not lessened but rather infinitely heightened. Unity, number, and order rule everywhere in material nature, in the roots of the plants, in their budding, growing, unfolding of leaves and bearing of fruits. Even more is this true in the bodies of living beings. "Whence, I ask, can all this come, if not from that highest eternal origin of numbers, of resemblance, of equality and of order? And when you take this away from the earth, it is nothing. Only thus has the almighty God created the world, and out of nothing has it come" (Bk. VI, ch. 17)./3/

To be sure, Augustine's concept of music cannot be placed entirely on the side of *musica speculativa*. Influenced by Neoplatonic thought, he sees in music, by which God created the world, also a means of intellectual ascent to God, of *anagogē*, and of the mystical return of the soul into God. This will be further discussed in part II.

The music theory of the Middle Ages is even more one-sidedly determined by the idea of *musica mathematica*, which is transmitted primarily through the Roman philosopher and statesman Boethius (d. about 425) and his work *De institutione musica*. As Isidor of Seville (d. 636) wrote in his main work *Etymologiarum sive Originum libri XX* (Bk. III, before I,1), "Music is a discipline which speaks of numbers which are found in sounds." In music we touch the mystery of creation, for *Deus artifex* created the world according to the laws of music. According to Isidor, "Without music no discipline can be perfect, for nothing is without it. Indeed the world itself seems to be composed by a certain harmony of sounds, and heaven itself revolves with an accompanying change of harmony" (Bk. III, ch. iii).

Again and again in the music treatises of the Middle Ages we meet the idea that music as art is the practical application of the teachings and rules of music as science. To this extent *musica practica* is subordinated to *musica speculativa* or *theoretica*. Johannes de Grocheo, in the second half of the thirteenth century, designates music as *scientia* "insofar as it treats the knowledge of principles," and as *ars* "insofar as it rules the practical intellect in performing" (10). The *materia propria* to be used is the *sonus harmonicus*.

In addition there appears another thought highly characteristic of the

Middle Ages. If God created the world according to the rules of music and the audible music of humans therefore has only representative significance in the hierarchy of creation, the musician, who is initiated into the mathematical mystery of music, has the task of imitating divine laws. Proceeding from them deductively, he determines and establishes the legitimacy of audible music. It is important to clarify this deductive process through an example from the music treatise of Johannes de Grocheo:

> We also agree . . . that man, as Plato and Aristotle say, is like a cosmos, hence he is called by them a microcosmos, that is, a small world. Hence, his laws and operations ought to imitate divine law as completely as possible. For the diversity of generating and corrupting forces of all the universe seven stars with their virtues have sufficed. Likewise it was rational to place in human art seven principles which have been the causes of all the diversities of sound with harmony. . . . We call these unison, tone, semitone, ditone, semitritone or diatesseron, diapente and diapason. (7–8)

To compose and to make music is, therefore, a work of devotion, for it concerns the reverent reflection on and imitation of God's ideas of creation: "Truly the author of nature and not man made the consonances which are implanted in nature, for the consonances existed before they appeared to men. For this reason we take great pains to inquire into these consonances" (Adam of Fulda:III,368). The glance of the musician is directed immediately to God—not toward himself and not toward the listener. (Music of the time was as little concerned with the listener as art before the discovery of perspective was concerned with the observer.) This explains the composers' mode of musical construction, working solely from the laws of music itself and prior to the distinction between vocal and instrumental music. Their works are absolute music *supra voces vocales*. When in the thirteenth century the motet arose as one of the early forms of polyphony, a new syllabic text was placed under the upper voice, generally as a commentary on the tenor text of the vox principalis. In the double and triple motet more voices were added. But since only the continual stream of voices and the laws of counterpoint determined the musical structure, the placement of the text up to the turn of the sixteenth century was generally somewhat accidental. Frequently the cantus firmus could not be perceived by the ear as a musical unity, as constructional framework, but rather figured only as symbol bearer. In Perotin's famous "Sederunt principes" for the feast of St. Stephan, for example, the individual notes of the cantus firmus are drawn out so far from each other in organ point manner that a single note (in modern transcription) often stretches over fifty to sixty beats.

Thus, it is important to make clear that at that time—that is, into the fifteenth century—music was heard wholly horizontally. Next to numerical order the element of movement was important to medieval music theory, so that music could also be described as "moved order" or as "ordered movement." The linear-melodic occurrences were the essential aspect, and the harmonic context (in our sense) represented a rather accidental secondary result. At the beginning of the modern age, this view of music is subordinated and suppressed by another, which makes humans with their affections the measure of musical things.

Nevertheless, it is noteworthy that the thread of *musica mathematica*— admittedly in connection with other elements of order and new intellectual forces—continues even over the rift of the Renaissance and remains important up to the period of Johann Sebastian Bach. The astronomer Johannes Kepler (1571–1630), for example, can claim in his *Weltharmonik* of 1619 that all harmonies which occur in music are found in heaven. Max Bense has pointed out that the study of music theory was for a man like Kepler an outright prerequisite to the mathematical natural sciences (192). And in the *Syntagma musicum* of his contemporary, the great composer Michael Praetorius, there is the statement, "Equality of measure is also to be preserved, lest the harmony be spoiled or confused; for to sing without rule and measure is to offend God himself, who arranged all things by number, weight, and measure, as Plato [!] said" (III,59). Here a new, powerful breakthrough of natural philosophy asserts itself, taking up the ideas and themes of the old natural philosophy. In Galileo's *Dialogue concerning the two chief world systems* of 1632, the thought is developed which is decisive for all later natural science, namely, that nature is in agreement with mathematics. Mathematical music theory and mathematical nature theory fertilized each other. Music was grounded on a firm cosmic foundation. Because God is a "harmonic being" (Andreas Werckmeister, d. 1706), music appears as divine order perceivable in the visible world; because "the order and wisdom of [man's] gracious creator are led through such *numeros sonores* into the hearing and successively into the heart and mind," music may be understood not only as art but also as science (Werckmeister:24f.; see also Dammann). Kepler, though not only he, concluded from this that human beings, in setting up the tone system, actually "are doing nothing else in this business except to play the apes of God the Creator and to act out, as it were, a certain drama of the ordination of the celestial movements" (1038 [V,5]). The definition of music coined by the philosopher Gottfried Wilhelm Leibniz (1646–1716) for the "praise of the order from which all beauty comes" has become famous: "Music is the secret exercise of arithmetic of a soul which does not know it is counting" (240). The work of Johann Sebastian Bach also belongs in this intellectual context. Since the sensational publication by Martin Jansen in the *Bach-Jahrbuch* of 1937 we are aware how extensive is the number symbolism in Bach's work.

But also in our time the numerical–theological evaluation of music has celebrated a resurrection. This happened most vividly in the *Unterweisung im Tonsatz* (1937) of Paul Hindemith (1895–1964), in which he sought to develop out of the natural acoustical phenomenon of overtones a grouped row of sounds and values of all twelve chromatic tones within the octave. He professes the enduring insights of the Pythagorean view of music as well the belief in music's relationship to the transcendent through the material of sound:

> With this attitude toward the mechanical aspect of the phrase, I recognize my agreement with the views which were long valid before the time of the great classical masters. We find their representatives in the early ancient period; far-sighted artists of the Middle Ages and the modern era preserve the teaching and pass it on. What was the material of sound for them? The intervals were witnesses from the original days of the world's creation: mysterious as numbers, of the same substance as the basic concepts of surface and space, the standard for both the audible and the visible world. They are parts of the universe, which extends in the same relationships as the distances of the overtone row, so that measure, music, and cosmos blend into one. And the art of composing itself? To devout musicians it was a means of praising God and letting the congregation of listeners participate in the praise. That the work is created to the honor of the highest being we sense with many composers, but seldom so forcefully as with Bach, to whom the "Jesu juva" in his partiturs was no empty formula. (27)

Hindemith, whom I have cited here, belongs to the musical avant-garde of the first half of our century. This raises the question of the contemporary significance and validity of this theology of music. I will seek to answer briefly.

Music, the art of sound, is commonly regarded by modern thought as one of the highest creations of the human spirit, and, in contrast to other arts, as a creation which so to speak the human spirit has brought forth out of nothing and always brings forth anew. In face of such a spiritualistic mode of consideration, the theology of music seeks to remind us that music in its elemental foundations is a gift of God in creation. As the givenness of language is a prerequisite of all speech, so the ontical quality of music is the given prerequisite of all music-making. "The realm of sound is not chaotic matter from which the art of sound brings forth order. Music is not only 'art of sound' but also kingdom of sound, not only historical spirit but also ideal Logos" (Wiora:15). This order of the world of sound as given in nature corresponds to the musical receiving apparatus of humans (and in corresponding variations also of many animals). The musical ear is not an empty vessel from which one can "expect complicated no less than simple arithmetical relationships, aharmonic no less than concordant" (Wiora:153). Through experimental research it has been determined that all intervals produced by proportions of whole numbers are registered especially purely and markedly in the psycho-physical experience of hearing. It has been said that physiological hearing processes have a built-in "consonance sieve" which is tuned to the proportion of intervals (cf. Husmann). This means that sensation is able to control thinking; the ear is in a position through hearing to ascertain intellectual relations, such as the mathematical relationship 1:2 in the octave.

The knowledge of the—in a literal sense—foundational significance of the order of numbers not only for music but also for the structure of the elements of the world has retained its claim to truth up to the present day. In particular Hans Kayser has shown in his book *Akroasis: Die Lehre von der Marmonik der Welt* (1946) that the same laws which determine the relationship of sounds to one another establish order in chemistry, crystallography, botany, and astronomy—even in atomic theory. The physicist Werner Heisenberg has identified the belief in the meaningfulness of mathematical structures as one of the great fundamental ideas which the exact sciences of our time have taken over from the ancient world. "This discovery belongs to the strongest of all stimuli of human knowledge, and whoever has sharpened his eye to the formative power of mathematical order recognizes its effects in nature and in art at every step" (38). Similarly, the philosopher and physicist Carl Friedrich von Weiszäcker: "Nature is not subjectively intellectual; she does not think mathematically. But she is objectively intellectual; she can be conceived mathematically. That is perhaps the most profound thing that we know about her" (17f.). The timeliness of this thought is demonstrated in the conviction, underlying Heisenberg's *Weltformel*, that the structure of the world is profoundly mathematical and comprehensible through an all-encompassing formula.

The observation that music is developed out of and upon the basis of the sounding order of creation suggests that God himself wanted to arrange his praise in this manner. This thought—that heaven and earth proclaim the glory of God—has found many expressions in the Psalms (especially 19, 103, 104, 148, and 150). The more primitively we experience the wonders of creation, the more devoutly we will join in the 148th Psalm, in which the constellations of the heavens unite with the animals, plants, and powers of earth in praise of the divine creator. The Silesian poet Angelus Silesius banishes the secret that creatures are God's echo in the lovely couplet of his "Cherubinischer Wandersmann" (I,264):

> Nichts weset ohne Stimm: Gott höret überall
> in allen Kreaturn sein Lob und Widerhall.

Creation's music-making is an expression of its order and success: the morning stars (Job 38:7), day and night (Psalm 19:2), winds, fire, and flame (Psalm 104:4), babes and infants (Psalm 8:2), birds of the air (Psalm 104:12), and the sons of God and angels in heaven (Job 38:7; Psalm 103:20f.; Psalm 148:2). All these can do nothing but praise God together and shout to him. They praise through their *Dasein* and *Sosein, objective et realiter*—to speak with the formulas of the old scholastic dogmatics—whereas it is reserved to humans to praise God *effective et verbaliter* (Gerhard:483 [III,12])./4/

The fundamental experience that the world is cosmos—that is, ornament, decoration, order, and harmony—underlies creation's song of praise. Just as the bird sings his song unconcernedly next to the abyss, so creation's simple, primitive song of praise is not aware of the reality of sin as enmity toward God, which is the characteristic mark of the concept "cosmos" particularly in the Johannine writings. Human music joins in the praise of the creator, *objective et realiter*, even when that is not its explicit intention. Wolfgang Amadeus Mozart, for example, in Karl Barth's words, "does not intend to proclaim the praise of God. He just does so in fact; precisely in the humility in which he—himself to a certain extent only as an instrument—lets be heard what he apparently hears, that which impresses itself on him from God's creation, which rises up in him and demands to proceed out of him" (27).

II

A second point of juncture between music and theology occurs where music is connected to the believer's intention to enter into immediate relationship with God. When music is put to use in worship (in the broadest sense), it is with the expectation that either in and of itself or under certain conditions it contributes toward fulfilling the purpose of worship (of adoration or submission) and perhaps even makes a contribution specific only to it. Here we confront the conception of *church* music, one of the grandest conceptions of intellectual history, consisting of the transformation of worship into music. Wherever we look in the wide world of religion, cultic activity is presented everywhere in the language of song. How is this to be explained?

In worship the human being is confronted with God as the Wholly Other, who qualitatively is infinitely superior to the human creature. The collective primal fears and primal raptures of the creature, however, cannot be articulated in the words of secular colloquial speech; only the elevated language of tones is fitted for speaking with God. And the death zone of speechlessness, through which one passes in the encounter with the holy God, can be endured if need be with sounding tones resembling stuttering and whispering. Contributing thereto may also be the fact that sound is the vehicle for a primal sensation and a likeness of secret powers; to this extent it is the demonstrated means of communication in the encounter with the sacred Godhead. The role of "liturgical" music is limited at this level of religious history mostly to the audible envelopment of the cultic ritual. At the higher levels of religious history, also, the impulse to clothe the liturgical word in music continues. To rabbinic tradition belongs the conviction that any who approach God other than through singing commit blasphemy. In the message of Christian faith the hymn in worship was displayed grandly already in the New Testament (Deichgräber). Still today the *Gloria in excelsis Deo* (Luke 2:14), in conjunction with the early church *Laudamus te*, forms a high point of the service. The hymn, the doxology, speaks in the liturgical form of adoration directly to God.

> Because God, who reigns on high, has shown mercy on the insignifi-
> cant in his historical work of salvation, he is praised as the Lord who
> without end looks down graciously from the heights, who indeed is
> without end majestically elevated and mercifully, graciously, amica-
> bly condescending. Adoration lives from the recognition of God's
> historical deed. It is in a real sense the theological display of thanks
> for God's deed, in which the thanks moves over into the praise of the
> eternal God himself. [Therefore the hymn is] the reflection of God's
> eternal glory in the praise of human beings. (Schlink:254)

The musicologist Johannes Angenvoort is able to designate the hymnic element as so essential to many places of the liturgy "that in case of necessity
the dimension intended here should be reached through a textless music
rather than through a musicless text" (57).

Liturgical praise is also the most important root of the formation of confessions and thus of theological assertions. It is no coincidence that the Greek
word *homologia* designates the hymn in the worship service as well as the
confession of faith. As the immediate reflex to worship encounter with the
mystery of God and Christ, doctrine appears in the hymn in a still glowing,
fluid state and not yet cold and rigid as dogma often later becomes. For this
reason, to speak theologically about God as about a substance is designated
by Wilhelm Stählin as an abuse of the divine name and therefore an offence
against the Second Commandment, saying, "If God exists, I must fall on my
knees and adore him" (150). He considers it the function of hymns to preserve theology from this linguistic "fall into sin"—and we can go further to
include liturgical music in general.

The most venerable form of liturgical singing in the Christian Church is
Gregorian, or more properly Roman, chant. It is *cantus ecclesiasticus* in the
original sense. The musicologist Thrasybulos Georgiades points out correctly
that such a form of liturgical singing cannot be designated as a "serving art";
rather, it is a necessary side of the cult. In contrast to *musica mensurata* the
chant is *cantus planus*; it does not intend to interpret the text musically but
merely to adapt itself to the Latin speech patterns and structure, which are
made clearer through musical punctuation. "In its essence chant is liturgical
prayer" (Stäblein:col. 1267).

If monophonic chant is no more than the audible envelopment of the
"sacred word," the development of Western polyphony from the early forms
of organum results in a profound and far-reaching process of translating liturgical pieces into musical forms. Karl Gustav Fellerer therefore divides church
music, in his *Geschichte der katholischen Kirchenmusik*, into the following
three epochs: "music of worship," "music in worship," and "music for worship"
(6f.). With this differentiation the various stages of the retreat of liturgical
elements behind the musical should be made clear. Correspondingly, Fellerer

limits music *of* worship to the *cantus ecclesiasticus* of Roman chant, hymns in
the vernacular, and the earliest forms of polyphony in parallel organum. With
the development of compositions for the ordinary, proper, and daily offices in
the age of classical polyphony, there begins, according to Fellerer, the epoch of
music *in* worship. By contrast, the entire period of Tridentine church music,
from the early Baroque to J. S. Bach, is liturgically downgraded as music *for*
worship. With its musically autonomous development and its subjective affec-
tivity it grew out of ground alien to liturgy and thereby effected the separation
of liturgy and music.

We cannot here debate Fellerer's thesis. Important in connection with
our theme is solely the assertion that the transition from the musical envelopment of the liturgical text to its translation into music marks a fundamental break. While the original liturgical songs, similar to the folk song, are of
anonymous origin, there begins now the history of the composer of liturgical
music.

The goal which is set for worship determines the theological yardstick
by which the appropriateness of music for worship is measured. The orgias-
tic character of certain instruments, as for example, cymbals, tympany, and
the Phrygian double flute—with which in pagan cults demons were to be
warded off and ecstatic states of frenzy effected—was the reason for exclud-
ing instrumental music in principle from Christian worship as *pompa
diaboli*. Canon 12 of the *Canones Hippolyti*, stemming from the end of the
fourth century, even banned music teachers from the church community.
Next to the general purpose of glorifying God, of *laudatio* and *glorificatio
Dei*, for which music is especially fitted on the basis of its *modus emphat-
icus*, its special anthropological ability to raise hearts to devotion becomes
important to Christian theologians. This theological line can be traced from
Augustine through Thomas Aquinas, the young Martin Luther and John
Calvin, up to the present, though the accents and devotional–psychological
goals vary in details. In accordance with the Neoplatonic motto, "A cor-
poreis ad incorporea transeamus," Augustine sees in music an excellent
means of elevating the soul to God and to its return into God. The sacred
words when sung move the mind "more devoutly and ardently in the flames
of piety" (*Confessions*, X,33). But at the same time Augustine, influenced by
Neoplatonic ideas, can combine the *anagogē* to God with Pythagorean number theory. Thus, the caption to the fourteenth chapter of book VI of his *De
musica* reads: "The soul, through the principle of numbers and of order—
which it loves in matter—is called to the love of God." Thomas Aquinas
draws explicitly on Augustine: "The harmonies of music change the affections of men . . . whence it is . . . that in every cult some harmonies are
used in order that the mind of man may be aroused toward God" (*In
psalmos expositio*, 32,2). For him, however, it is primarily the weak whose
hearts must be moved to devotion through music (*Summa theologiae*, pt.
II,2, qu. 91). The young Luther, the monk before his tower experience, also

has a high opinion of the innervating power of music. Thus he wants to see it in the service of devotion and of the elevation to God; as *calcar spiritus*, as *stimulus* and *hortarium*, it provides the best prerequisites for this (WA III,40 and V,89). For the Genevan reformer John Calvin the main point of departure for music is the lukewarmness of human nature during liturgical prayer, which offends God. Music should remedy such coldness of heart. For this reason such words and images as *enflammer, inciter, emouvoir,* and *ardeur* recur again and again in Calvin's description of the *vertu* of music. Even in the *Motu proprio* of Pope Pius X from November 22, 1903, the demand is placed on church music "to add greater efficacy to the text in order that by means of it the faithful may be the more easily moved to devotion and better disposed to receive the fruits of grace associated with the celebration of the most holy mysteries" (I,1 [p. 18]).

Although theology directed toward devotional psychology generally esteems music as a gift of God, it often does not overcome a deeply rooted mistrust of music as such. Augustine struggles with the temptation of paying more attention to the pleasures of the ear, the *cantilena suavis,* than to the sung words. The monk Luther wants to allow only spiritual songs and sees in secular music only decline. Thomas Aquinas and Calvin fundamentally reject instrumental music in worship. Only in connection with the Word of God can music take on the character of worship, according to Calvin, for God can be glorified only through his Word. Calvin also bans polyphonic music from worship because it endangers the clarity of the scriptural text. Anxiety in face of the dangers of a worldly or even lascivious effect of music sometimes leads to the attempt to "domesticate" it and to exclude a certain stylistic sphere of sacred music. For Calvin, it belongs to the essence of *chants ecclésiastiques* that not only their texts but also their music be "saints"; their melodies should therefore possess "poids et majesté": "And there is a great difference between the music which serves to give pleasure to people at home and at table and the psalms which are sung in church in the presence of God and his angels." The *Constitutio de sacra liturgia,* resolved by the Second Vatican Council in 1964, takes a similar position when it declares church music to be the more holy the more closely it is connected with the liturgical action: "Therefore sacred music increases in holiness to the degree that it is intimately linked with liturgical action, winningly expresses prayerfulness, promotes solidarity, and enriches sacred rites with heightened solemnity" (VI,112 [p. 171]). To be sure, in contrast to earlier papal pronouncements, this is no longer a one-sided preference of Roman chant and the Palestrina style. The *Constitutio* aims at a music not only of the Western church but of the universal Roman church.

We cannot conclude this section without returning to one of the strangest processes in the history of music. At the beginning of the section we said, "When music is put to use in worship (in the broadest sense), it is in the expectation that as such it is able to contribute toward fulfilling the purpose

of worship." This expectation was not shared but instead passionately con-
tested by one of the three major Reformers, and paradoxically by precisely
the man who was the most musical among them. Ulrich Zwingli in Zurich
banned from worship all music of any form; even congregational singing
was silenced in Zurich for seventy-five years. At the same time Zwingli was
regarded by his contemporaries as a sensitive musician and gifted composer
who had mastered a dozen instruments, especially wind instruments. But
music was not compatible with his understanding of worship, which was
determined by meditation and inward prayer: "True worshippers call to
God in spirit and truth without any howling before men," he wrote in his
Schlussreden of 1523 (art. 44). Because music brings the danger of diverting
the congregation from the immediate encounter with God, Zwingli excludes
it from worship. Worship is one thing, music another. Zwingli is aware of
the temptation of music, to which precisely the musically gifted person is
susceptible. It is amazing to see how Zwingli's relation to music is exclusively
determined by aesthetic points of view; nowhere in his writings does one
find a remark (of which there are many by Luther) to the effect that music
is a divine present, a gift of God. Here Zwingli shows himself completely a
disciple of his humanistic teachers, even in music. The humanistic temper
strove to release all thought from its dependence on theology and pushed to
justify systems and institutions from within themselves; similarly, humanism
as a world view attempted to place the arts on their own feet by proclaim-
ing the aesthetic and artistic an end in itself. The arts were considered fundamentally secular from their roots up. This had far-reaching consequences
for the fate of church music in Reformed German-speaking Switzerland. To
be sure, there resulted also the possibility of taking up the connection with
folk instrumental music which—often arrogantly misjudged and regarded
with suspicion—had been a secular secondary current alongside the art
music intended for church (cf. Söhngen, 1897:32–53 and 250–53).

As an addendum it may be noted that after the apparent end of the
history of great church music with the death of J. S. Bach—or, by a more
generous interpretation, with the deaths of Mozart and Haydn—liturgical
music experienced a surprising rebirth in the first half of our century. The
driving forces were above all the movement for liturgical renewal, the redis-
covery of the church after the end of World War I, the resistance struggle
against National Socialism and the shift of "secular" music away from fin-
de-siècle style (cf. Söhngen, 1978).

III

Over against the Pythagorean–medieval *musica speculativa* and the
pragmatic approach to "church" music, the Reformer Martin Luther represents a fully new point of view. He proceeds from the question, "What does
music as a form of sound signify from a theological standpoint?" All his

utterances about music reveal that he was profoundly open to its audible mysteries. Whether he is marveling over the resounding vibrations of air, rejoicing at the song of birds, or reflecting on the "round-dance" artistry of a polyphonic motet, the primal reverence before the miracle of creation, music, is evident. This primal musical experience, however, is incorporated into a characteristic theological view. Music is *creatura*, creature of God, and counts for Luther among the miraculous things which come to us through hearing. But that which comes to us is also that upon which it alone decisively depends: "Ocularia miracula longe minora sunt quam auricularia," that is, "The miracles which our eyes offer us are far smaller than the miracles we perceive with the ears" (WA:XLIV,352 on Gen 39:5–6a).

The kerygma of God's miraculous deed in Jesus Christ is also *akoē*, hearing. That music stems from the realm of *auricularia*, audible things—as does the Gospel—that it has a heavenly origin, and that it comes to us in the same way, namely, through the voice—these likenesses to the Word cause Luther again and again to marvel. Gospel and music, theology and music, point to one another: the Gospel is an advanced school of singing, just as music, for its part, leads quite close to the Gospel. Indeed, it knows more of the mystery of the Gospel than many a highly learned theologian. Luther's musical co-worker Johann Walter tried to describe the organic unity of theology and music: music, which "actually and hereditarily" belongs to sacred theology, is "entwined and locked up in theology so that whoever desires, inquires, and learns theology thereby captures the art of music, even if he doesn't see, feel or understand it" (Preface to *Lob und Preis der löblichen Kunst Musica*).

Thereby all weight falls on what I would like to call the specifically declarative character of music. The composer Heinrich Kaminski (d. 1946) was of the opinion that the word *Kunst* (art) was not to be derived from *können* (to be able) but rather from *kunden* (to make known). However questionable it may be from an etymological standpoint, such an interpretation harbors a kernel of truth. According to ancient Greek conceptions, the poet-musician is above all the "one who hears"; with his singing and reciting he reveals the being and depth of things (W. Otto). And, indeed, music makes known the realities of creation which cannot appropriately be mediated through the Word, or through the Word alone. Arnold Schoenberg said once very significantly about Anton Webern's "Bagatelles for String Quartet" (Op. 9): "This piece will be understood only by those who believe that sound can express something which can *only be said through sounds*." For Luther all music is "spiritual," i.e., theologically relevant. There is for him no secular music in the strict sense, only degenerate music.

This designation of music is made more concrete when music is bound to the Word, supplying the latter with elements beyond itself. Music no longer needs to be satisfied with "objective" and "real" praise of God; its singing and sounding can now, through the accompanying word, be unmistakably recognized as praise of God. It gains the ability to become aware of the action, namely, of glorifying God. But above all music is capable of seizing and spreading the message of the Gospel. The musicologist Leo Schrade—one of the first to point to the importance of the prefaces to the great musical collections of the Wittenberg publisher Georg Rhaw, in which not only Martin Luther but also Philipp Melanchthon, Johannes Bugenhagen, Johann Walter, Sixt Dietrich, and Georg Rhaw are represented— believes that, in spite of all the differences in the individual conceptions, the common constant and new aspect of the Reformation view of music is the self-evident manner in which music is here placed in the service of the spread of the Gospel (Schrade:34ff.). According to the opinion of the Lutheran Reformers, it is especially suited to this for four reasons: it can be combined with the Word, it enters the ears sweetly and enticingly, it moves the spirit, and it causes the texts with which it is connected to be retained more firmly by the memory than texts which are only spoken. The composer Sixt Dietrich, for example, uses the Latin concept *decantare* in this sense as a technical expression. Music is given to the human race mainly in order that the message of the Gospel be proclaimed in singing (*decantetur*); likewise it is said of the blessings of God which are reported in the Bible that they are made known through singing. In particular, God's marvelous deed in Jesus Christ should be *decantiert* by all, that is, spread through singing.

That music's service in the spread of the Gospel is here taken as self-evident reveals a new theological dimension of music. The kerygmatic function as a sounding image of the wisdom of God the Creator appears here on a level equal to the liturgical function and the pursuit of music for its own sake. The original task of music—to glorify God—is by no means abandoned, but the making of music now receives a second pole in the task of proclamation. Music is "an organ through which the name of God is celebrated and doctrine about God is sung to humankind" (Dietrich).

The status and task of music herewith become the same as those of the sermon. Luther's friend, the Württemberg Reformer Johannes Brenz, expresses his esteem in his sermon on hymnody explicitly also for the musical side of hymns. Congregational singing represents for him a piece and a form of the sermon. Just as the sermon is a *praecipuum organon spiritus sancti*, so also is music its means and tool. Music is endowed by God with special power. If that is true for singing in general, how much greater must be the efficacy of spiritual music! For that which is sung in church consists of the words of Holy Scripture; but the words of Scripture or the Gospel of Christ are a power of God toward salvation for every believer. If music is then added over and above this, the songs will have a still much greater efficacy (Müller). This conviction of the extra faith-evoking power of the combination of music with the Word of God is precisely also Luther's conviction.

It will not be surprising to note that the setting of this new goal resulted in the creation of a significant Word or sermon music, the greatest masters of which on German territory were Heinrich Schütz and J. S. Bach. Also, in the surprising renaissance of church music in the first half of our century, kerygmatic music plays an important role. Hence the judgment of a great circle of artists in Alsace after hearing the motet "Jesus and Nicodemus" by Ernst Pepping (1901–1981): "Never before have we had such a strong impression that the Gospel has moved right into the body as in this music." To be sure, we cannot overlook the fact that with the free development of kerygmatic music in the worship service a new element is introduced which in the long run brings with it the risk of bursting open the liturgical order and unity. In the famous Lübeck *Abendmusiken* of Dietrich Buxtehude around the turn of the eighteenth century, church music as "religious music" steps outside the realm of the worship service for the first time.

It would be intriguing to develop the three forms of a theology of music in trinitarian fashion, according to the following areas: (1) music in the realm of creation; (2) the Christ hymn and the *musica crucis*, cultic music as contrasted with religious music; (3) music as work and instrument of the Holy Spirit, instrumental music and the phases of music as stations on the way to the eschaton. I have pursued this elsewhere (Söhngen, 1967:262–340); here it would take us too far.

The German pavilion at the 1970 World Exposition in Osaka, at which for months literally millions of people from all parts of the earth listened to the music of Karlheinz Stockhausen, offered a new impressive example of music's power to bind people together. A related phenomenon has been less noticed up to now: the ecumenical character of music, its ability to unite people of different confessions in the praise of God. That is by no means an unintended side effect, a mere anthropological fact. Rather, both medieval and Lutheran theology saw therein the actual destiny of music. To this extent, music even after the division of Christendom represents to some degree the paradisiacal original condition of ecumenical unity among rival churches and confessions.

This assertion receives special weight through the high spiritual value which Martin Luther ascribes to music. To him music was a likeness of the freedom of the Gospel. When music is rejected because of a lack of receptivity to its evangelical character, its likeness to the Word, theology cannot be in order. The more sovereign a composition makes itself over the firmly laid rules and the more securely the musical discovery goes its own way, the closer such music stands to the Gospel. For this reason, Luther felt himself so closely bound to the gifted Catholic court composer in Munich, Ludwig Senfl, that, when he feared death at the Feste Coburg during the Diet of Augsburg, he asked Senfl rather than his coworker Johann Walter to write his funeral motet on Psalm 4:8: "In peace I will both lie down and sleep; for thou alone, O Lord, makest me dwell in safety." One must read Luther's letter to Senfl only once to sense how deep the ecumenical bond in the spirit of music reaches. Luther includes in this community even the inimically inclined Bavarian princes, because "they so honor and foster music." Senfl fulfilled Luther's wish and sent—a beautiful gesture—in addition to the desired funeral motet another on Psalm 118:17: "I shall not die, but live, and declare the works of the Lord."

NOTES

/1/ Tischrede 3516: "Prima Januarii anni 1537 egregias cantilenas post coenam cecinerunt. Quas cum admiraretur Doctor Martinus, dixit cum singultu: Ach, wie feine musici sind in 10 Jahren gestorben! Josquin, Petrus Loroe [Pierre de la Rue], Finck et multi alii excellentes. Die Welt ist gelehter Leute nimmer wert, sed vult habere rudissimos asinos" (WA: *Tischreden*, III:371).

/2/ Luther's position on congregational hymns and hymnals is documented in volume 35 of the Weimar edition and volume 53 of the American edition.

/3/ The sixth book of *De Musica*, in contrast to the first five, was written after Augustine's conversion and is therefore of particular importance.

/4/ Different in character but similar in its roots is the old Greek concept that at the end of his work of creation Zeus, at the request of the Gods, created another voice to praise his great deeds in word and tone. This was the origin of the Muses (Otto:28).

REFERENCES

Translator's note: Where no English-language edition is cited, the translations appearing in the article are mine.

Adam of Fulda
1490   *De musica.* In M. Gerbert, *Scriptores ecclesiastici de musica sacra potissimum.* St. Blasien, 1784. Reprint: Hildesheim, 1963.

Angenvoort, Johannes
1969   "Warum Musik im Gottesdienst?" *Musik und Altar.*

Augustine, Aurelius
1947   "On Music." Tr. Robert Catesby Taliaferro. In *Writings of Saint Augustine*, II (*The Fathers of the Church*, IV). New York.

Barth, Karl
1956   *Wolfgang Amadeus Mozart 1756/1956.* Zurich.

Bense, Max
1949   *Konturen einer Geistesgeschichte der Mathematik II: Die Mathematik in der Kunst.* Hamburg.

Calvin, Jean
1542   "Epistre au lecteur." Preface to *La forme des prières et chants ecclésiastiques*. Geneva.

Constitutio de sacra liturgia
1964   *The Documents of Vatican II*. Tr. by Joseph Gallagher. London, 1967.

Dammann, Rolf
1954   "Zur Musiklehre des Andreas Werckmeister." *Archiv für Musikwissenschaft* XI, 204–237.

Deichgräber, Reinhard
1967   *Gotteshymnus und Christushymnus in der frühen Christenheit*. Göttingen.

Dietrich, Sixt
1545   Preface to the *Hymnen*. Ed. H. Zenck. St. Louis, 1960.

Fellerer, Karl Gustav
1949   *Geschichte der katholischen Kirchenmusik*. 2nd ed. Düsseldorf.

Georgiades, Thrasybulos
1960   *Sakral und profan in der Musik*. Münchener Universitätsreden, Neue Folge, Heft 28. Munich.

Gerhard, Johann
1649   *Schola pietatis*. 4th ed. Jena.

Grocheo, Johannes de
1974   *Concerning Music (De Musica)*. Tr. by Albert Seay. Colorado College Music Press Translations, I. Colorado Springs.

Heisenberg, Werner
1938   "Die mathematische Gesetzmässigkeit in der Natur." In Eberhard Dennert, ed., *Die Natur, das Wunder Gottes*. Berlin.

Hindemith, Paul
1937   *Unterweisung im Tonsatz*. Mainz.

Husmann, Heinrich
1953   *Vom Wesen der Konsonanz*. Heidelberg.

Kepler, Johannes
1619   *Weltharmonik*. Linz in Austria. Eng. trans. by Charles Glenn Wallis, *The Harmonies of the World* (*Great Books of the Western World*, 16). Chicago, 1952.

Leibniz, Gottfried Wilhelm
1734–1742   *Epistolae ad diversos*. Ed. by Chr. Kortholt. Leipzig.

Luther, Martin
WA   *Weimarer Ausgabe* of Luther's Works. Ed by J. C. F. Knaake et al. Weimar, 1883ff. American edition, St. Louis and Philadelphia, 1955ff.

Mann, Thomas
1947   *Doktor Faustus.* Gesamtausgabe. Stockholm.

Müller, Christa
1934   "Die Lehre des Johannes Brenz von Kirchendienst und Kirch-
               engesang." *Monatsschrift für Gottesdienst und kirchliche
               Kunst.*

Nef, Karl
1869   "Die Collegia musica in der deutschen reformierten Schweiz."
               Diss. St. Gallen. Reprint: Walluf bei Wiesbaden, 1973.

Otto, Walter F.
1956   *Die Musen und der göttliche Ursprung des Singens und
               Sagens.* 2nd. ed. Darmstadt.

Pius XI
1903   "Motu proprio." In *Official Catholic Teachings: Worship &
               Liturgy.* Wilmington, North Carolina, 1978.

Praetorius, Michael
1619   *Syntagma musicum.* Wolfenbüttel.

Schlink, Edmund
1957   "Die Struktur der dogmatischen Aussage als ökumenisches
               Problem." *Kerygma und Dogma.*

Schrade, Leo
1954   "The editional practice of Georg Rhaw." In Theodor Hoelty-
               Nickel, ed., *The Musical Heritage of the Church.* Valparaiso,
               Indiana.

Silesius, Angelus
1924   *Sämtliche poetische Werke in 3 Bänden.* Ed. by Hans Ludwig
               Held. Munich.

Söhngen, Oskar
1967   *Theologie der Musik.* Kassel.
1978   "Die Renaissance der Kirchenmusik in der ersten Hälfte des 20.
               Jahrhunderts." In *Religiöse Musik in nicht-liturgischen Werken
               von Beethoven bis Reger.* Ed. by Walter Wiora with Günther
               Massenkeil and Klaus Wolfgang Niemöller. Regensburg.

Stäblein, Bruno
1952   Art. "Choral." In *Musik in Geschichte und Gegenwart,* II.
               Kassel and Basel.

Stählin, Wilhelm
1958   "Das Lied der Kirche." *Music und Gottesdienst.*

Walter, Johann
1538   *Lob und Preis der löblichen Kunst Musica.* Facs. repr. Kassel:
               Bärenreiter Verlag, 1938.

Weizsäcker, Carl Friedrich von
1954   *Die Geschichte der Natur.* 2nd ed. Göttingen.

Werckmeister, Andreas
     1707   *Musicalische Paradoxal-Discourse usw.* Quedlinburg.
Wiora, Walter
     1951   "Der tonale Logos." *Die Musikforschung*, IV, 1–35, 153–75.

What Makes "Religious Music" Religious?

Lois Ibsen al Faruqi

Introduction

From very early times, even in the most primitive civilizations, music has been closely connected with religious activities. Long before the Greek philosophers made the study of music a branch of metaphysics and subjected it to moral judgment, people had been aware of its tremendous power on the minds and emotions of men. Plato felt that its power for good and evil in men made control and censorship of music by the state a recommended policy. He added that music serves various specific needs and that to take modes, instruments, and other sound characteristics that apply to one particular mood and utilize them in a different context was a serious and dangerous breach of practice that should be prohibited. Although Aristotle was less authoritarian, he confirmed Plato's belief in music's vital connection with morality, the power of its emotional effect, and also the need to prevent secular musical characteristics from corrupting the music used for religious observances. Evidently, even at that early time, the incursions of elements considered incompatible with the religious experience were regarded as a danger, and the idea of a properly "religious" music was discussed by writers and thinkers. Again among the fathers and authorities of early and medieval Christianity, we read numerous pleas for preserving the proper form of religious music and for isolating it from aspects of secular musical practice. Muslim thinkers have been equally concerned with this problem. Each period of Islamic history has brought forth treatises on the subject, treated from different viewpoints./1/ It is obvious then that our question: What makes "religious music" religious? is not a new question. It must have been asked, either explicitly or implicitly, for millenia.

Some writers, most prominently Schopenhauer, have maintained that in a sense *all* music is religious since it is an aural expression of man's idea about Existence—about the Will. In fact, Schopenhauer treats music as the aesthetic experience *par excellence* since it objectifies the Will or the transcendent, ontological reality directly, and not indirectly as the visual arts and literature do. Others maintain that *no* music *per se* can be religious—in short, that music is only functionally religious. The proponents of this latter view are no more helpful than the followers of the former in answering our question. If we argue that all or any music is suitable for religious use, we would be forced to espouse the relativist's claim that the latest rock and roll tune, with its thumping, brutal rhythm and its sexually oriented words, the fiddle music of the hillbilly hoedown, or an antiphon from the Gregorian chant literature are all equally suitable for being used by the Christian, the Hindu, or the Buddhist to enhance religious contemplation. This view contends that all share equal claim to a legitimate place in any religious service. This might be considered by some as a "scientific" and "empirical" response to the question since it takes into consideration every possible human opinion and experience. But does not such empiricism actually risk being less scientific than one would at first imagine? Is it not actually a way of dodging the question?

The truth is that in any particular culture and time, one can discern a societal consensus regarding the musical style or styles that the civilization in question considers suitable for religious purposes. Other styles, just as surely, are rejected. Our purpose is to try to determine why certain characteristics arouse acceptance within a particular context, while others arouse rejection. Subsequently, it should be determined if any of these characteristics are universally significant, or if they vary so sharply that the attempt to describe the "religious" in music becomes impossible.

A Comparative Study of Two Forms of Religious Music

Two categories of musical performance which have been consistently regarded as religious have been chosen for comparison. They are the Gregorian chant of the Christian tradition and Qur'ānic recitation (or qirā'ah) of the Islamic tradition.

A. Melodic Characteristics

Both Gregorian chant and qirā'ah are based on a limited range of tonal materials. Phrases are often confined to four or five contiguous notes, and they rarely extend beyond an octave. Small intervals and stepwise progressions abound, while ornaments and repetitions of tones increase the emphasis on contiguous melodic movement in both literatures. Musical phrases in Qur'ānic chant are prone to start at the upper extremity of a four- or five-tone scalar segment, or with a leap to its upper tones. In the melodic progression, there are few if any downward leaps and only occasional upward skips of a second or third to protract the descending progression. In the Gregorian literature, the musical phrase may take various shapes, but descending passages are the most prevalent (Reese:169). In both types of chant there is a marked preference for upward-leading openings and downward-leading terminations (Apel:249–250; Lois al Faruqi, 1978:57).

B. Durational Features

Gregorian chant and *qirā'ah* are both free of that characteristic commonly known as "meter," i.e., the regular recurrence of a durational "measure" characterized by a specific number of beats and consistent placement of accents. Instead, both can be described as being rhythmically "free." Accent as a rhythmic feature is a matter of little concern in both literatures. Emphasis is achieved more through the use of repetitive motifs than through alterations of intensity. Note values in both Christian and Muslim religions chant shun the long and short extremes of duration. A regular pulse is seldom recognizable in *qirā'ah*. Although authorities on Gregorian chant disagree about the matter of pulse in the medieval performance of the chants (Reese:140ff.), tempos are generally consistent, being neither changed abruptly nor subjected to extravagant accelerations or retardations.

C. Relationship of Music to Words

Religious chant, whether in Islamic or Christian culture, reveals little attempt to match musical features programmatically with the words (Lois al Faruqi, 1974:chap. 7; 1978:54–56; Apel:301–3). Though there have been attempts to characterize the Gregorian chant as a word-bound or dramatic music (e.g., Gevaert:153; Ferretti:97, 99; Pierik, 1963), even the authors of such claims are compelled to admit that "certainly all liturgical plainchant does not embody the melodic symbolism that the texts portray. In fact, some melodic lines do just the contrary" (Pierik:54). Also absent from these two types of religious music is that technique called "tone painting," which attempts to employ musical elements physically imitative of precise objects, feelings, or ideas simultaneously expressed in the words. The same lyrics are often treated with quite different musical settings, and similar musical treatments are utilized for a variety of textual passages.

This does not mean that the music of Christian or Islamic chant does not "fit" the words it accompanies, but the "fitting" is based on other considerations than programmatic and imitative ones. The relation of music to words, in these examples of abstract music, is one of the structural matching of musical phrase to literary phrase, and of the musical emphasis of important literary syllables through the repetitive use of rhythmic and melodic motifs. Such emphasis includes few extremes of duration or pitch. Instead, there are returns to a particularly important note on the more significant syllables or words, repetition of melodic or durational motifs at points of literary stress, slight prolongations on an important word or syllable, or strategically placed melodic ornamentation.

D. Form

As has been noted above, both religious chant literatures under consideration are composed of a series of musical phrases of limited pitch and volume range, of generally descending movement and evidencing few if any abrupt tonal or durational changes. Instead of thematic development and

variation techniques, return of motifs are the most important unifying element in the chants of both cultures, and they provide the audible perimeters
for their structural units.

Since programmatic elements play such an unimportant role in these
genres of music, structural characteristics reveal correspondence to physical
segments (i.e., poetic lines and groups of lines) but little determination by
narrative or dramatic partitioning or progression.

E. Performance Practice

Gregorian chant is principally antiphonal, i.e., sung by two groups of
singers performing alternatively; or responsorial, i.e., an alternation between
one or more soloists and a choir or group of vocalists. Qur'ānic chant, on the
other hand, is generally rendered by a single vocalist. Both kinds of chant,
being vocally performed, maintain a continuity of timbre or tone color.
There has been a consistent rejection of instrumental accompaniment for
these chants. For the early Church, the association of most instruments with
pagan activities kept them from being utilized. It has been suggested that to
have introduced a flute into the church "would have had the effect on the
fourth century Christian conscience which would be produced on our own
by the introduction of a dance-band into Westminster Abbey" (Routley:52).
This feeling was to persist for centuries. The Islamic tradition has been
equally uncompromising on the use of musical instruments in the religious
service./2/ Vocal techniques for both literatures shunned the expression of
sensuality and sentimentality. Toward this end, vibrato (i.e., performing
tones with slight fluctuations in pitch which are felt to render greater
sensuousness) as well as harmony (i.e., the accompaniment of a single
melodic line by a chordal structure) has been avoided.

The Historical Development

Since Gregorian and Qur'ānic chant reveal such a conformance of characteristics, are we justified in believing that Aha! we have put our fingers on
the characteristics of religious music? By analyzing the elements of these
two religious genres which have so much in common, can we pin down the
musical stimuli which induce a religious mood? Can we isolate some universal characteristics of religious music? In other words, can we prove that
these same characteristics are suitable for religious worship at all times and
in all cultures? The answer to this question is an emphatic No. Even a quick
perusal of the development of religious music in history makes any other
answer impossible.

Gregorian chant as described above was, for centuries, the music of the
Christian Church in Western Europe. Gradually, however, new elements
were accepted as religious music. Additional literary texts were added to the
scriptural. The legacy attributed to Pope Gregory was supplemented with

the composed music of later periods./3/ Despite the individual and official efforts to limit musical innovations, rhythmed music, rapid tempos and proliferation of wide leaps, accents, modulations, abrupt changes of intensity all became noticeable characteristics of subsequent examples of Christian religious music./4/ Many varieties of religious music came to be accepted by the different Christian denominations which developed after the Reformation. Today, not only the traditional forms of religious music are heard; spirituals, gospel music, and even folk, rock and jazz elements from the secular musical field have all made their way into the services of some Western European and American churches.

In the Islamic tradition, on the contrary, little if any change has taken place over the centuries. The Qur'ān is still the only literary text used in the prayer service, and the manner in which it is chanted has been carefully guarded from intrusions from the secular musical world, or from any other source that would have changed its style (Lois al Faruqi, 1974:chap. 7; al Sa'īd:345–48). It is in fact agreed by most scholars (Boubakeur:393; Shiloah:417) that the *qirā'ah* chant accepted by the religious scholars and community today is not radically different from that acceptable in other periods of Islamic history. Geographic dispersion has had amazingly little effect on the chant. The *qirā'ah* of southeast Asia evidences characteristics strikingly similar to those heard in any center of the Middle East.

Music and Meaning

It is apparent that in the Islamic religious ritual those musical characteristics found in Gregorian and Islamic chant have been maintained over the centuries. Despite a near identity with that expression in earlier times, the history of music in the Christian church reveals subsequent development of widely variant musical styles. Given these facts, must we reject the possibility of discovering the nature of a correspondence of musical sounds and their organization with religious meanings or qualities? Must we view the similarities of the chant styles of Islam and early Christianity as purely coincidental, as totally unrelated to meanings conveyed through musical sound? Again, my answer is No.

In order to explain this answer and to arrive at a solution for the problem posed by this paper, the relationship of musical sound patterns to ideas, values, and emotional expressions should be reviewed. Let us explore briefly how nonmusical "meanings" can be communicated through and by music. This function of music has been much debated./5/ Most writers would agree that musical notes and series of notes do not comprise a precise musical vocabulary or language, as has been claimed by Deryck Cooke. Generally, music is not considered to be expressive of definite or specific ideas. To be sure, there are some genres of music commonly designated as "programme music" which are expressly and obviously imitative of certain actions, objects or beings; but the sensory materials out of which most music is made have only subtle connections with the world of objects and concepts. This makes the question raised by this paper even more difficult to answer than it might be if it were asked in regard to literature or the visual arts. Despite the fact that a separation of music from the phenomenal world makes music difficult to describe in concepts, it is such probing that may lead us to understand why two varieties of religious chant are so remarkably similar and yet other forms of religious music have varied considerably from each other.

Many studies have been made to determine how certain connotations and images are related to the sound elements of music. Some of these base their conclusions on psychological testing which proves that any such imparting of nonmusical meaning by music is not just haphazard. The argument is that there are correspondences which exist between our experience of the musical sounds and their organization, on the one hand, and the concepts, images, objects, qualities, and states of mind of our nonmusical experience, on the other.

Other scholars have tried to explain these correspondences between musical sounds and nonmusical experiences by pointing out that musical elements like pitch, tempo, intensity, timbre, mode of emission of sound, and accent have a kinesthetic effect on the listener (Pratt:228ff.). When listening to different pitches, for instance, the listener is affected by the physical adjustments, the tensions and relaxations, necessary to produce such variations. His body responds to the musical stimuli as if he were himself producing them. The psychophysical effect of a piece of music which jumps around rhythmically or tonally can actually give the listener a measurable impression of tension, strain, or even fatigue, while another with the opposite sound characteristics and dynamism level will have a calm, restful effect. These effects, in turn, are either related to or disparate from many nonmusical matters. It is easy to see that such relationships might be judged either compatible or incompatible with the religious mood.

Still another view is presented by Leonard B. Meyer, who has linked his ideas of how music conveys meaning to the conflict theory of emotion (14ff.). He adopts the position that emotion and meaning are not resident in the single tone or series of tones themselves. However, neither is that meaning a hallucination in the mind of the listener. Meyer contends that music is a succession of sound events which, to the culturally knowledgeable listener, provide a series of tendencies or expectations. These are in turn followed by other musical stimuli which may either inhibit or fulfill the psychological demand for resolution or satisfaction. A consequent emotional activity is aroused by such interplay of inhibition and resolution, of tension and release. This activity is in itself of an indifferentiated nature. But Meyer argues convincingly that, since musical experiences are "continuous with and similar to our experience of other kinds of stimuli" (260), the individual as well as the cultural group will either consciously or unconsciously relate those sound stimuli to many nonmusical concepts, images, objects, qualities and states of mind.

A Theological Explanation

Regardless of which of these theories or which combination of theories is espoused, it is obvious that musical stimuli can be related to nonmusical experiences and therefore to religious ideas. Religious ideas and religious experience, however, when considered in their global dimensions, are "many-splendored things." They have many meanings and modes, as well as many external patterns, in the different religious traditions. They may also vary appreciably within the same religion at different periods of history. One set of such religious beliefs predicates one kind of religious experience and, by extension, a particular notion of suitable religious music. Another set of religious beliefs gives rise to a different kind of religious experience and accordant religious music. Just as "religious" is an adjective applied to quite different gods, different prayers, different rites and different moral codes, "religious" also refers to a number of quite different bodies of musical expression. The examples of religious music are then but reflections and expressions of the complex of religious ideas held in a given culture at a particular time.

Let us examine just one of the factors which combine to make up that complex of ideas and beliefs which we designate as the religion of a people, and then see how it might affect the religious music associated with that religion's rites and services. The chosen factor is one which is at the very core of every religion, but its content varies from one tradition to another. It is the tradition's idea of the nature of divinity, its emphasis on transcendence or immanence. At one end of a continuum would stand those religions or those periods in the historical development of a religion in which divinity is understood as identifiable with nature itself. At the other end of the continuum stand those religions or periods of a religious tradition which hold a view of God and of the transcendent realm which rejects any confusion or absorption of the divine with the nondivine. Religious adherents at both poles of the continuum, as well as at all midpoints on that spectrum of ideas, believe in a God or gods; but their views of the cosmos, of humanity and its relation to the Creator and creation, are drastically altered by their varying conceptions of the nature of divinity. Such views affect not only the theology; they have consequences as well for a vast complex of human activities and thought patterns. Among these are certainly the aesthetic products which are created to enhance and deepen the religious experience.

Those who believe in a transcendent realm which is absolutely distinct from this world find little in the natural world which can serve as an adequate vehicle for expressing divinity. In fact, although it is impossible to avoid using sensory materials, such persons or societies choose aesthetic "raw materials" which express the inexpressibility, the other-than-nature-ness, the other-than-human-ness of the Transcendent (Isma'īl al Fārūqī). At the other end of the continuum is the religious adherent who views the transcendent realm as immanent and integrally identifiable with this world. His religious art and music are consequently replete with obvious relationships to phenomenal life. His art may present an idealized form of nature; or, on the other hand, it may present themes from nature in their imperfect raw form. But it will always be grounded in nature and nature's objects, creatures, and activities.

Since the "religious" for the Muslims as well as for the early Christians was that which concentrated on nonphenomenal and transcendent aspects of divinity, it could not be expressed in musical terms which were imitative or suggestive of the physical world, with its extremes of joy, of pain and sorrow, and of swift changes between the two. Ideally, the "religious" for them was divorced from everyday existence. It was improper for the worshipers of such a God to be involved during the religious service with kinesthetic impulses, whether psychologically felt or physically expressed, which reminded of the rough and tumble of everyday life. Religious music, therefore, avoided the emotive, the frivolous, the unfettered responses either to great joy or great sorrow. The limited range and contiguity of notes in Gregorian and Qur'ānic chant, the prevalence of stepwise progression, the avoidance of large melodic leaps—all these contributed to this demand. The relaxed tempos, the calm and continuous movement, the rejection of strong accents and changes of intensity or volume were likewise conducive to an attitude of contemplation and departure from worldly involvement. The use of regularly repeated metric units would have tended to arouse associations, kinesthetic movements and emotions incompatible with the notion of religiosity among Muslims and early Christians. These were therefore avoided.

The religious experience for Muslims and early Christians was meant to draw the worshiper away from this world in order to concentrate on another, spiritual, realm. Music could better support this desire if it contributed little or nothing to dramatic/programmatic content or tone painting imitating the objects, events, ideas or feelings of this world. Hence, abstract quality has been a marked feature in both chant traditions. Formal characteristics accorded with this tendency, making elements of unity and change dependent upon correspondence with poetic units rather than with narrative or descriptive factors. Performance practice, relying on the human voice, has avoided the secular associations which instruments might bring, as well as the chordal harmonies which could be suggestive of emotional or dramatic effects. Even the use of the human voice or voices in these genres of religious music has avoided the sensual and imitative in order to enhance the spiritual effect on the listener.

While there was much in early Christianity's notion of transcendence that resembled that of the Islamic tradition, by the fourteenth century the Renaissance had begun, and sweeping changes of thought and practice were initiated in Christian Europe. The doors were opened to the ancient world of Greece and Rome, and nothing in the secular or religious world escaped being affected in the centuries to follow. Responding to that influence of the classical world, Christianity and Christians turned their concentration toward humanism and this world, in contrast to the medieval concentration on the afterlife and the transcendent nature of God. More personalism and naturalism were to come in later centuries with the advent of the Reformation, the Counter Reformation of the Catholic Church and the establishment of the various national Protestant churches. The Romantic Movement brought a further drift toward humanism and the importance of man and nature as opposed to the transcendent realm. In more recent times, the influence of relativism and logical positivism has created a sense of fear and insecurity in man that is revealed in skepticism along with a proclaimed doctrine of antitranscendence. For many of our contemporaries in the twentieth century, the discovery of the nature of a transcendent realm is no longer a valid quest; they in fact recognize no transcendent aspect to existence./6/

The changes of religious thought and practice, in general, and of the notion of transcendence, in particular, in Christian Europe over the centuries brought concomitant revolutions in what the Christians considered to be proper religious music. As the Western Christian world espoused different national and sectarian bodies of doctrine, some forms of music came to be judged suitable for the Catholic service, others for the Protestant service generally, and still others for particular groups within Protestantism./7/ The religious music of each group varied according to the differences in the correspondent belief system of its participants. The wider the divergence from the belief system of the early Church, the wider the musical differences that resulted. Even the contemporary denial of divinity has its expression in the religious music of our time. We see this evidenced in the abolition of any hint of boundary between the sacred and the secular, a development which has taken place in recent decades in many religious contexts in the Western world.

Since the notion of transcendence has changed little in Islam over the centuries, one would expect comparable stability in the related religious experiences and in the music which has formed part of the congregational worship. This, in fact, has been the case. Muslim authors of all periods have condemned and opposed any incursions of musical elements which would have altered the original qualities of the chant, and no new genres were allowed to be added to the ritual. Labīb al Saʻīd is a contemporary spokesman for the Muslim community in this matter. His book on the chant includes a list of linguistic and vocal practices which have been prohibited in qirā'ah to the present time (see esp. 345–48).

The transcendence/immanence dichotomy is not the only one which could be explored in an attempt to understand the nature of a religion and of the "religious" in music. It is also possible to discover shades of meaning along a theistic/atheistic continuum, between a personal and impersonal god, between world affirmation and world denial, between a religion of individualism and one of societism. These are a few of the many theological issues which determine the characteristics and identity of any religion./8/ Having determined these in regard to a particular religion, it should be possible to investigate which musical elements, which styles, and which forms best symbolize the subtle elements of that religious ideology. As a corollary, those characteristics which are least suitable for providing musical accompaniment for the religious ceremony or experience under investigation should become evident.

Are there then any universals for "religious" music? Or must every tradition express itself in religious sound patterns of a totally unique idiom? The answers to such questions are still to be worked out in full; but from the study thus far made, certain principles have crystallized. Just as there are certain theological premises which different religious traditions hold in common,/9/ there must be some analogous musical characteristics which pertain to all or a large number of the examples of religious music. But these universal characteristics of religious music are limited since the common features in religious thought which they symbolize are few.

At the same time, there are other theological premises which differ from religion to religion./10/ These generate the different sets of musical characteristics which make one religious musical tradition distinguishable from another. These premises and musical characteristics, as well as those universal religious factors, must be investigated before it will be possible to draw the perimeters of the "universally religious" and the "specifically religious" in music.

The problem is big, and the materials are diverse. But the rewards of the study are manifold. Studies of interrelations between religious beliefs and music can only increase our knowledge, not only of the music in question, but also of the religious ideas which guide its development and that of the concomitant culture. Thus a contribution could be made to intercultural/interreligious understanding.

This is not the only benefit to be derived from answering such questions as "What makes 'religious music' religious?" Such a study would also alleviate many practical problems which contemporary religious communities and leaders face. In the Christian community it could assist in the proper upgrading of the artistic value of religious music (as well as religious art in general) in contemporary churches, without distorting or corrupting the message conveyed. It could provide guidelines for solving the problems caused by cultural diversity, the revolt against established norms, and the controversy between conservative and liberal elements within the congregation.

An investigation of recordings of the religious music of some contemporary Ṣūfī (Muslim mystical) groups/11/ reveals that the definition of "religious music" is equally important for Muslims if a compatibility and coherence with the Islamic ideology is to be maintained in the new environments brought about by conversions in Europe and America and wholesale emigrations to those lands from the Muslim World. The effect of alien musical standards has often been considerable, and one would wonder if these are digestible and absorbable to a degree that would make them suitable for the "religious music" of these Muslims living in a Western environment. Ṣūfī groups, in general, have been more lenient in the incorporation of diverse musical materials for their religious ceremonies known as *dhikr*,/12/ though they have never deviated from the mainstream of the community in restricting themselves to Qur'ānic chant in the prayer service. The mystics have often been criticized for their musical practices, which, to most Muslims, have seemed unsuited to the religious experience. A proper definition of "religious music" in an Islamic context might help resolve this controversy as well as help Muslims in alien environments choose wisely from the many musical elements to which they are exposed.

The study of what makes "religious music" religious could also throw light on the often hotly debated issue within Islamic society of the legitimacy of certain types of secular musical performance. Few Muslims or scholars of Islamic culture are aware of the importance of the relationship between theology and music which that controversy evidences, or of the influence on the secular music of the Muslim World which religious beliefs have sustained (Lois al Faruqi, 1981; forthcoming). Substantial work in these fields must be done if the Muslim community is to resolve its differences in these matters.

The issues raised by the question, What makes "religious music" religious? are therefore wide reaching and significant. They can only be resolved when theologians, historians of religion, and comparative religionists combine their research and knowledge with that of aestheticians, music historians, and music theorists. It is hoped that scholars as well as institutions will encourage and support such efforts for cooperation in future scholarly activities. It may be the only way to cope with the need, felt profoundly in our steadily more complex world community, to bridge the gaps which separate each of us from other branches of knowledge, as well as from our counterparts in other religious communities.

NOTES

/1/   For quotations on this subject from Christian writers who lived from the second to the fourteenth centuries, see Routley:232–50. For writers on religious music in the Islamic tradition, consult Boubakeur; al Ghazālī; Robson.

/2/   In many cases, it was even considered suspect in a nonritual context. See al

Ghazālī, 1901:238; Robson:31–32,96.

/3/   In the twelfth century, Johannes Cotto wrote in his *De musica*: "The most blessed Pope Gregory, acting, we are told, under the direct influence and at the dictation of the Holy Spirit, composed songs, and gave to the Roman church hymns for the celebration of all the offices of the Church's year. . . . Well then, seeing that these hymns for the church's offices which we have mentioned were thus composed, and that we may add to them the compositions of certain others who have lived nearer to our own time, I see nothing to prevent the musicians of our own day making their contribution" (quoted in Routley:247).

/4/   The Edict of Pope John XXII in 1325 argued against a "new school" of composers in the following way: "But there is a new school, whose disciples, observing with care the regularity of musical time-values, concern themselves with new devices, preferring their new inventions to the ancient songs of the church; by their practices the music of the liturgies is disordered with semibreves, minims, and even shorter notes. They break up the melodies with hockets, they embellish them with discants; sometimes they so force them out of shape with 'triples' and other music proper to profane occasions that the principles of the antiphonary and the gradual are wholly neglected. . . . Indeed the multitude of notes is so confusing that the seemly rise and decorous fall of the plainsong melody, which should be the distinguishing feature of the music, is entirely obscured. They run and will not rest, they inebriate the ears without soothing them; the conduct of the singers is so appropriate to their matter that decent devotion is held in contempt and reprehensible frivolity is paraded for admiration. . . . We hasten to banish and eradicate this thing from the church of God" (quoted in Routley:249–50).

/5/   There is a so-called "heteronomist" or "symbolist" view which maintains that music carries a statement of ideas and communicates values. This was espoused by Hegel, Schelling, Schopenhauer, Wagner, and others. It contrasts with the "autonomist" view of writers who argued that music should present an aesthetic statement free of any connection with nonmusical ideas and values (see Hanslick).

/6/   Nathan A. Scott, Jr., laments over the philosophical and religious situation of contemporary Western society in which there is no longer a central god-view or stance from which the individual can mold his life.

/7/   For a discussion of Protestant variations in liturgical music from ardent espousal (Luther) to total rejection (Zwingli), see the article by Söhngen in the present volume, as well as those of Irwin and Marini.

/8/   See Wach for other theological issues that govern the nature of a religious tradition.

/9/   These premises are the ones designated by Frithjof Schuon as the "esoteric" or essential and spiritual.

/10/   These premises, according to Schuon, are the "exoteric," or formal and exterior ones.

/11/   For example, see *An Introduction to Sufism*, a recording issued in Toronto by the Society for Understanding the Finite and the Infinite, n.d., a Ṣūfī organization headed by an immigrant from the Indian subcontinent.

/12/   *Dhikr* is the name given to the various "remembrance" (of God and the Prophet Muḥammad) sessions for inducing the mystical experience. They involve Qur'ānic and poetry recitation, group chanting and singing, instrumental music, and in some cases movement and dance.

REFERENCES

Apel, Willi
    1959   *Gregorian Chant*. London: Burns and Oates.

Boubakeur, Si Hamza
    1968   "Psalmodie coranique." In *Encyclopédie de Musiques sacrées*, ed. by Jacques Porte, 1:388–403. Paris: Labergerie.

Cooke, Deryck
    1959   *The Language of Music*. London: Oxford University Press.

al Fārūqī, Ismaʿīl
    1973   "Islam and Art." *Studia Islamica* 37:81–109.

al Faruqi, Lois Ibsen
    1974   "The Nature of the Musical Art of Islamic Culture: A Theoretical and Empirical Study of Arabian Music." Diss.: Syracuse University.

    1978   "Accentuation in Qur'ānic Chant: A Study in Musical *Tawāzun*." *Yearbook of the International Folk Music Council* 10:53–68.

    1981   "The Status of Music in Muslim Nations: Evidence from the Arab World." *Asian Music* 1:56–84.

    1982   "The *Shariʿah* on Music and Musicians." In *Islamic Thought and Culture*, pp. 27–52. Herndon, Virginia: International Institute of Islamic Thought.

Ferretti, Paolo
    1938   *Esthétique grégorienne*. Tournai.

Gevaert, François Auguste
    1917   *La Mélopée antique dans le chant de l'église latine*. Paris.

al Ghazālī, Abu Hāmid
    1901–2   "Emotional Religion in Islam as Affected by Music and Singing." Tr. from *Ihyā' ʿUlūm al Dīn* by Duncan B. MacDonald. *Journal of the Royal Asiatic Society*, part 1: 195–252; part 2: 705–48 (1901); part 3: 1–28 (1902).

Hanslick, Eduard
    1957   *The Beautiful in Music*. Tr. by Gustave Cohen. Indianapolis: The Bobbs-Merrill Co.

Meyer, Leonard B.
1961   *Emotion and Meaning in Music*. Chicago: University of Chicago Press.

Pierik, Marie
1963   *Dramatic and Symbolic Elements in Gregorian Chant*. New York: Deselee Co.

Pratt, Carroll C.
1931   *The Meaning of Music: A Study in Psychological Aesthetics*. New York and London: McGraw-Hill Book Co.

Reese, Gustave
1940   *Music in the Middle Ages*. New York: W. W. Norton and Co.

Robson, James
1938   *Tracts on Listening to Music*. London: The Royal Asiatic Society.

Routley, Erik
1967   *The Church and Music*. Boston: Crescendo Publishing Co.

al Sa'īd, Labīb
1967   *Al Jam' al Ṣawtī al Awwal lil Qur'ān al Karīm*. Cairo: Dār al Kātib al'Arabī lil Ṭibā'ah wal Nashr.

Schuon, Frithjof
1975   *The Transcendent Unity of Religions*. Tr. by Peter Townsend. New York: Harper & Row, Harper Torchbooks.

Scott, Nathan A., Jr.
1969   "Religious Symbolism in Contemporary Literature." In *Religious Symbolism*, ed. by F. Ernest Johnson, pp. 159–84. Port Washington, N.Y.: Kennikat Press, Inc.

Shiloah, Amnon
1968   "L'Islam et la Musique." In *Encyclopédie des Musiques sacrées*, ed. by Jacques Porte, 1:414–21. Paris: Labergerie.

Wach, Joachim
1961   *The Comparative Study of Religions*. New York: Columbia University Press.

The Mystical Strain in Jewish Liturgical Music

Judith K. Eisenstein

The literary influence of mysticism on the Jewish liturgy has been well identified and amply documented. The canon is admittedly replete with complete poems from mystical sources, as well as with interpolations within larger texts. The musical influence of mysticism is less easily recognized, for at least three reasons: (1) the musical liturgy is far less uniform in the numerous scattered communities than is the text; (2) there is an almost total lack of notation of musical tradition in the earlier centuries of the synagogue;/1/ (3) there is some confusion between the contributions of mystics to the sung liturgy and the reflection of mystical thought in the form and style of the music. This study will draw principally on evidence from the Ashkenazic tradition which has been the most dynamic musically, to a smaller extent on that of the Sephardic and Yemenite tradition. It relies, for the most part, on notations of the nineteenth and twentieth centuries. It will consider both the identifiable contributions of mystics and, where possible, elements which actually grew out of mystical theory.

The music of the Jewish liturgy in all communities of the dispersion is essentially an oral tradition—a stylized folk art./2/ As in the folksong of all peoples, two main styles coexist, and establish a certain tension. To use Curt Sachs's terminology, the logogenic and the pathogenic song are both present in it (Sachs:41ff.). It is this writer's contention that the former represents the Rabbinic, intellectual and didactic strain: chanting of scripture, whether in lesson or in quotations in the prayer text, psalmody, and specific petition for specific benefits such as crops, rain, health, long life, etc. The pathogenic style would then represent the mystical strain: the striving for identification with the divine through abandonment of self, and through rapture to ecstasy. Both these strains obtain in every worship service, their proportions varying from time to time and from place to place.

Our concern here is with the post-biblical period, from the time that the synagogue had its beginnings, in the latter days of the Second Temple, developing, indeed, within the very gates of the Temple. The synagogue service at first took over the liturgy which had been constructed around the sacrificial order: the call to prayer, the benedictions, the psalmody/3/ associated with the various sacrifices. The music of the Temple service had been

performed by the Levitic choir and orchestra, made up of hereditary profes-
sionals. In the synagogue, the liturgical song was carried on for some centuries by educated leaders of the congregation, called "Representatives of the
Community," *shelihey tzibbur*, together with the congregations, who would
respond with refrains, with repetitions of the text, and with acclamations.
Subsequently (probably in the Geonic period in Babylonia, seventh century
and after) a professional cantor, who was also a poet and sometimes a sort of
sexton as well, took over the responsibility for leading the congregation in
prayer. What we know of the earliest period is of "logogenic" chanting,
psalmody or prayer texts sung syllabically, with the tune and rhythm determined entirely by the words.

However, there are evidences that, parallel to this early development
within the synagogue, there existed pockets of pathogenic worship. The first
such evidence appears in the description of Philo of the practice of the
Therapeutae, an ancient mystical sect of Jews in northern Egypt. The following is a portion of his text:

> After the supper they hold the sacred vigil which is conducted in the
> following way. They rise up all together and standing in the middle
> of the refectory form themselves first into two choirs, one of men and
> one of women, the leader and precentor chosen for each being the
> most honoured amongst them and also the most musical. Then they
> sing hymns to God composed of many measures and set to many
> melodies, sometimes chanting together, sometimes taking up the
> harmony antiphonally, hands and feet keeping time in accompani-
> ment, and rapt with enthusiasm reproduce sometimes the lyrics of
> the procession, sometimes of the halt and of the wheeling and
> counter-wheeling of a choric dance. (165)

Similarly, the discovery of the Dead Sea Scrolls has brought to light the
practice of singing new (nonscriptural) hymns, together with movement
(dance would be too precise a description for it) accompanying the song of
choirs, male and female, in the communities of the Essenes. So far as we
know, these practices were not carried over into the mainstream of the
synagogue.

Only some centuries later did written evidence of the tension between
Rabbinic and mystical trends begin to appear. Almost the first nonpsalmodic
poetry comes down to us in the form of the hymns of the *Hekhalot Rabbati*
(the Greater Palaces), produced by some of the oldest mystics in Jewish
history, the followers of *Merkavah* mysticism, the mysticism of the Chariot-
Throne. The approximate dating is between the fourth and sixth centuries,
in either Palestine or Babylonia. The poems are anonymous, attributed by
legend to the angels who inhabit the passages leading to the Heavenly
Throne-Chariot and surrounding it. Gershom Scholem regards them as good
examples of what Rudolf Otto called "numinous hymns" (Scholem:57;
Otto:ch. 6). Though no trace of melody exists, the assertion in the texts that

the angelic choir sang these poems seems to indicate that they were sung, rather than simply recited. The utterance of them, in any case, would have had a hypnotic effect, calculated to result in a state of ecstasy. They consist of a series of solemn utterances, repeated exaltation of God's Being—many sonorous but almost meaningless phrases following each other in a driving, mechanical rhythm. The following transliteration may give some impression of the style:

> *Panim na'im, panim hadurim*
> *Panim shel yofi, panim shel lehavah*
> *Penei adonai elohei yisra'el*
> *Keshehu yoshev al kisei khevodo,* etc.
>
> (Lovely face, majestic face,
> face of beauty, face of flame
> The face of the Lord God of Israel?
> When He sits upon His Throne of Glory, etc.)/4/

By and large, these hymns did not find their way into the mainstream of Jewish liturgy. Several Talmudic passages voice strong disapproval of their exaggerated type of praise, of their "multiplying the praise of God to excess."/5/ Nevertheless, there is one hymn, *ha'aderet veha'emunah*, which has been preserved in the traditional liturgy for the morning of the Day of Atonement. Some centuries after its composition, it was given the appellation "Hymn of the Angels." The following excerpted translation, though it makes no attempt to reproduce the alphabetical acrostic of the Hebrew or to preserve its insistent pairings of phrases, does give some sense of the effect of the poem:

> Steadfast glory, blessed insight, great majesty
> Appertain to Thee who dost live forevermore.
> Knowledge and speech, sublime grandeur, true constancy
> Appertain to Thee who dost live forevermore.
> Radiant purity, mighty valor, stainless beauty
> Appertain to Thee who livest forever, etc. (Birnbaum:658)

The Sephardim of the Levant sing this hymn in a very simple responsive intonation, the cantor alternating with the congregation. In Ashkenazic congregations it is most likely to be chanted freely in the mode of the prayer-chant.

A later hymn, in the style of the *Hekhalot*, written by the Palestinian poet Eleazar Kallir (early seventh century) has found its way into the liturgy of the Day of Atonement. This poem is a triple acrostic, and is broken up by the refrain, "The Lord is King, the Lord was King, the Lord will be King forever and ever." The following is selected from the translation by Bathya Bayer, cited by Hanoch Avenary in his monograph *Hebrew Hymn Tunes*:

> All powerful in Awe shall their Anthems resound,
> The Lord is King!
> Begot of the Blasts shall their Blessings resound,
> The Lord was King!
> The Firmament Fastnesses Full-voiced resound,
> The Lord will be King! (11)

The complete refrain is taken from the *Hekhalot*, where it is stated that it was proclaimed aloud by the leader of the Angelic choir. It became a fixed item occurring at many points in the liturgy throughout the year, in a variety of settings (ex. 1) taking its place as one of a number of acclamations./6/ While responses such as *Halleluyah, Amen, Hoshanah*, were already in practice, as the Bible testifies, in Temple days, they increased and took on new significance in the synagogue. The *Trisagion* (Holy, Holy, Holy) quoted from Ezekiel, the acclamation "Blessed be the Name of the Glory of His Kingdom," the interpolations into the numerous benedictions, "Blessed be He, and blessed be His Name!," "The Lord is God!," etc., all have their distinctive musical equivalents in all the communities. It is possible to surmise, but not yet to document, that it was those earliest *Merkavah* mystics and their immediate successors who introduced acclamations into the liturgy, injecting a note of drama and elation.

The next great epoch of Jewish mysticism, the Hasidism of the twelfth and thirteenth centuries in Germany (not to be confused with the eighteenth-century Hasidism of Eastern Europe) was widespread and helped to sustain the Jews in the bitter days of Crusades, exiles, and massacres in Northern France and Germany of the time. Some hymn texts composed by a great leader of the time, Judah the Pious (Yehudah he-Hasid), and his son, were admitted quite early into the canon of the prayer book. The Hymn of Unity (*Shir ha-Yihud*), which stresses the idea of the immanence of God, and his omnipresence, contains passages like the following:

> Nothing exists outside Your existence.
> You contain all things, and there is nothing besides You,
> Before anything existed, You were all of existence,
> And when all things came into existence, You filled all of them.

This hymn was frowned upon by later Rabbinic authorities. It seemed to open the way to pagan forms of worship. Similarly, the Hymn of Glory (*Shir ha-Kavod*), written by the same authors and containing vivid descriptions of the beauty and brightness of God, was considered too boldly anthropomorphic and was opposed by eighteenth-century Rabbinic leaders such as Jacob Emden and the Gaon of Vilna. Nevertheless, the text remained in the canon. The original melodies for this poem have been lost. The Hymn of Glory is currently sung in most Ashkenazic synagogues to a simple metrical hymn which could well fit into Idelsohn's table of archetypical melodies such as *Yigdal, ha-Tikvah*, and some Spanish *canciones* (1929:222ff.). It has even found its way into the *Union Hymnal* of the Reform movement, set to an English paraphrase by Alice Lucas. (It should be noted that even in traditional prayer books the text has been abbreviated and the most blatant anthropomorphisms omitted.)

Thus far we have discussed the remnants only of texts from the period of medieval German mysticism. It seems reasonable to speculate that there are a number of melodies which were introduced into the liturgy by individuals—possibly cantors—who were part of the movement of German Hasidism. I refer now to the group of *Mi-Sinai* melodies ("From Sinai" melodies, given that appellation by later generations because of their age and the reverence they commanded). The texts of these songs are, in some cases, considerably older than the tunes. Those tunes have been dated and their provenance pretty well established by Idelsohn, Werner, and others through careful comparison with songs of the Minnesingers, with Gregorian chant, and with folksongs of which the later German chorales were contrafacts. It must be that the Jewish tunesmiths of the time were exposed to such German song, sacred and secular (there was constant interchange between the two), in the market place and at outdoor festivals, rather than in the confines of either Church or court.

The melodies are applied to important prayers of the liturgy, particularly to those of the High Holy Days and the three Pilgrimage Festivals. They are sung at the climactic and dramatic moments of the ritual. What is more, they subsequently served as *leitmotifs* throughout the services in which they first appeared and as such persist in the practice of the Ashkenazim. (The same and equivalent texts have other melodies in other communities—melodies which did not become a pervasive influence in their respective traditions.)

Among these songs is the most widely known of all, the *Kol Nidre*, whose text derives from Geonic days in Babylonia. Others are the *Avodah* (the reenactment of the Confession of the High Priest in the ancient Temple), the Prayer for Rain, the Prayer for Dew, and many others. Space does not permit their discussion here. In his definitive book on the music of the Jews of Germany, *A Voice Still Heard*, Eric Werner has a chapter on the *Mi-Sinai* tunes, all given in notation and analyzed in detail (ch. 3). However, Werner makes no connection between them and the German Hasidim. The connection is suggested, rather, by Scholem, who indicates that the influence of the earlier Merkavah mysticism on many of the Talmudists and tosafists of Germany and Northern France was profound, and that the Hasidism of the time was dominant in the various north European communities (84).

This is not to say that there is identifiable mysticism in the melodies themselves. It is rather that a process was set in motion which was not necessarily conscious at that period. The process of making the secular holy seems to have its roots in mysticism, becoming a conscious process in later times. It is not unique to Judaism. The "conversion of song," to use Luther's phrase, admitted music to the liturgy from very mundane sources. The *Mi-Sinai*

tunes stand out as quite different from the logogenic cantillation of Bible
and prayer text, that chant which is largely syllabic and narrow in tonal
range, consisting of arrangements and rearrangements of tonal formulae.
These songs are melismatic (ex. 2) and wide in tonal range; and in some
instances, they fall within the prevalent forms of lai, bar, strophe, and
refrain and thus are autonomous, independent of the word.

Almost at the same time as German Hasidism flourished in Northern
Europe, Kabbalistic mysticism was burgeoning in Spain. Here we find that
music was expected to play a vital role, as part of the discipline of contemplation. In particular, the great mystical philosopher Abraham Abulafia
considered the combination of musical tones equivalent to the concentration
on combinations of the letters of the alphabet (tseruf) the ultimate abstrac-
tion capable of leading to the final aim, prophetic ecstasy.

Abulafia seems to have been dealing with music theoretically, rather
than practically. Like most of the Judeo-Arabic writers, he seems to have
been dealing with mathematical aspects of music, rather than with actual
performance, vocal or instrumental, and most certainly not with liturgy.
(They dealt also with the ethos doctrine of modes, and with the "harmony
of the spheres" [cf. Werner and Sonne].) Perhaps the exception is his positing
music as the final stage in the progression toward the goal of prophetic
ecstasy, the progression moving from the cleansing of the body, to seclusion
in a quiet house, to decorating the house with fresh greens, and finally to
praying and singing psalms in a pleasant and melodious voice (Scholem:151).

What sort of melodies Abulafia had in mind we do not know. No surviving song has been recognized as the outcome of his mathematical manipula-
tions. His manuscript which deals specifically with music, in its original
Arabic, has been lost, and extant is only a highly defective Hebrew translation so obscure that it has not been rendered in English (Werner and
Sonne:17:553). However, many hymns have survived from this era in the
liturgy of the Sephardic Jews, and their melodies, like those of their North
European contemporaries, seem to be influenced by the music of their
environment—in their case, the songs of troubadours, sequences and laudes,
and cantigas of the court of Alphonso the Wise.

To this category belongs a penitential hymn (selihah) for the morning of
Rosh ha-Shanah whose text was written by one Abraham he-Hazzan (ex. 3).
He was a member of the group of Kabbalists who surrounded Moses
Nahmanides in the Catalonian town of Gerona. His poem opens with the
words "little sister," quoted from the Song of Songs and used here as an
appellation for the Jewish people. Its form, meter, and rhyme scheme
closely resemble the verses of the Cantiga Ave Madre Dolorosa, and at least
one of the many melodic variants to which it is sung throughout the
Sephardic diaspora bears an equally strong resemblance to the Christian
melody.

In the latter days of the Jews of Spain, the Zohar became the focus of mystical study, and after the Exile (1492) that study was carried across the Mediterranean to the whole Spanish dispersion. It was in Safed, in the northern hills of Palestine, that Isaac Luria established the next important center of mysticism. One of the features of Lurianic mysticism was the creation of a specifically Kabbalistic type of song, a song that was supposed to lose itself in infinity, called *En Sof* (without end) (Idelsohn, 1929:411). A very small congregation of descendants of the Safed mystics persisted in Jerusalem until at least the thirties of this century, when Idelsohn recorded their songs, presumably preserved from the days of their ancestors.

One of those songs (ex. 4) is a setting of a poem by Eleazar Azkari of Safed, a disciple of Luria (1510–1600). The poem is in strictly syllabic meter, and contains the Tetragrammaton (the four-lettered name of the Deity) in its acrostic (Carmi:126). The melody, meandering and melismatic, is not related to the form of the poem at all. To the modern ear this may not suggest infinity, but to the mind of the Kabbalists the act of meditating intensely on the meaning of every word is exemplified by the extension of the word tonally in time, through elaborate melodic twists and turns. Thus, the song represents a deliberate, if somewhat naive, attempt to incorporate mystical theory in song. It has not survived in the general practice, any more than have its fellow *en sof* melodies. However, the poem remained a favorite among the later Hasidim and is sung to a variety of folk melodies, all in rather doggerel duple or triple meter, and equally independent of the form and meter of the poem.

Another sample of this rather literal-minded application of mystical theory appears at a somewhat later date in Germany. Lurianic mysticism seeped into the continent, largely through the workings of the Sabbatian movement, that thoroughly discredited outbreak of false Messianism, which shook the Jewish world in the sixties of the seventeenth century. In the wake of this movement, and in spite of severe opposition by Rabbinic authorities, traces of the Messianic Kabbala lingered in the thinking and practices of many communities. Musically, perhaps the only recognizable effect was the incorporation of trumpet calls into liturgical tunes. What might appear to be simply Germanic influences can be viewed as carrying out the Kabbalistic notion that trumpet calls symbolized *d'vekut*, closeness to the Divine. Werner cites examples of this practice in *A Voice Still Heard*, attributing the interpretation to a verbal suggestion by Abraham Heschel (122 and 309, n.48). These songs, like the *en sof* songs, have not endured in synagogue practice.

What has remained in the liturgy is a generous spate of poetry introduced by Luria and his followers (fondly dubbed "The Lion and his Cubs"), along with a number of new rituals and ceremonies, in particular, the greeting of the Sabbath at sundown with Psalms and hymns and the singing of family songs to accompany the Sabbath meals on Friday night, Sabbath noon, and the "third meal" before sundown on the Sabbath day. These songs are called *Zemirot*. (Space does not permit the discussion of a number of other rituals with their accompanying music.) Perhaps no text in the whole liturgical literature has been more widely sung and more variously set to music than the poem of Solomon Alkabetz, *Lekha Dodi*, "Come my beloved to greet the Bride (the Sabbath)." Anonymous folk composers have left a vast heritage of musical settings. Example 5 is an eastern Sephardic setting (Idelsohn, 1914:I,182). At the other end of the spectrum would be the long through-composed work, with solo, chorus, and organ accompaniment, by the twentieth-century composer, Castelnuovo-Tedesco (Putterman:418ff.).

The full impact of Safed mysticism came after the center itself had disintegrated. The influence was felt throughout the Middle East during the late seventeenth and early eighteenth centuries. The Yemenite community, in particular, produced a new type of wedding song, using excerpts from the *Zohar*, couched in Arabic verse forms, and the Arabic melodic form of a long introduction in recitative, followed by highly metrical passages sung to the accompaniment of some sort of drum. (In latter days, the Jews of San'a in Yemen were forbidden by the Moslems to use drums, and substituted anything at hand, especially Shell oil cans!) Some of the authors of the poems are known by name, e.g., Sa'adiah (sixteenth century) and Shabazi (seventeenth century). The poems are in Hebrew, Aramaic and Arabic, frequently with stanzas alternating from one to the other. The melodies are anonymous. They are sung at the Yemenite wedding by men only, who hold books from which they read the words of the many stanzas (ex. 6).

The impact of Lurianic mysticism was felt less immediately in the Western world. It seemed to carry on underground, and its musical expression—if it existed—did not flourish. It was the rise of East European Hasidism that brought music very much to the foregound of religious ritual. The founder was Israel ben Eliezer of the Ukraine, better known as the *Baal Shem Tov* (Master of the Good Name). He, and his successors to this date, regarded song as essential to the achievement of *kavanah* (sincere meaningfulness) and *d'vekut* (closeness to the Divine). Sometimes their melodies were meditative, highly melismatic, and deeply emotional. At other times they were vigorously rhythmic, impelling the clapping of hands, snapping of fingers, stamping, and dancelike movement. Frequently, they combined both in one song. Some of their melodies were derived from the liturgical chant, but many were frankly contrafacts on popular folksongs, gypsy tunes, drinking songs, even soldier songs. Again we observe the process of redeeming secular song and making it holy.

Later, under the leadership of Shneor Zalman of Ladi, a new system was built of songs freed from the shackles of words, melodies sung to meaningless syllables such as "lei di Dei" or "yaba bam." Their form was based on the presumed passage of the soul through a corridor toward complete communion with God. This form is seen in example 7, a melody presumably composed by Schneor Zalman himself, and dubbed *Dem Rebbes Niggun*

(The Rebbe's tune). It begins slowly—meditatively—and increases in tempo and intensity to ecstatic joyousness (Idelsohn, 1929:82ff.).

This form remained outside the synagogue service itself. Hasidism preached that God could be worshiped at any time in any place. It is our purpose here to discuss only the influence of such music on that of the liturgy. In their own synagogues the Hasidim carried over three characteristics which might be considered the hallmarks of mystical worship: concentration by means of melisma on each word of a text; autonomous melody, sung without text to meaningless syllables; highly motoric metrical song impelling bodily responses. In the last of these, prose texts are frequently forced into metrical forms by means of repetitions of words, breaking up of words into repeated syllables, and untexted dance melodies interpolated into the written words. Example 8 is a rhapsodical Hasidic setting of a passage from the closing service of the Day of Atonement, the highly emotional ending of a long day of fasting. The motoric element is present, together with interpolations of meaningless syllables in example 9, the ecstatic joyous limning of the wondrous appearance of the High Priest which follows the *Avodah* (see example 2).

Followers of so-called "normative" Rabbinic Judaism opposed Hasidism strenuously, and sometimes even viciously; however, the music of the Hasidim found its way quite early into the liturgy of the *mitnagdim* (the opponents). The majority of the cantor-composers of the East European synagogue grew up in Hasidic circles and carried the style, with all its components, into general practice. Untutored in music, they could not write down their own tunes. As they became more popular and were called on to officiate in various synagogues, they engaged "singers," usually a boy, or a high tenor, and a bass, to interpolate chordal responses. Subsequently, they found assistants who had learned musical notation and were able to write down their melodies. Throughout the nineteenth century this kind of folk-composing persisted, and spread even into the more sophisticated and Westernized communities of Bohemia, Austria, Germany, France, England, and the New World. The compositions became "traditional" alongside the totally Western compositions of such musically educated men as Solomon Sulzer of Vienna and Louis Lewandowski of Berlin (Idelsohn, 1929:432–34).

In the twentieth century, and particularly in America, Hasidic song entered the liturgy more as a vehicle for congregational singing than as an expression of mysticism. A dearth of hymnody in the Ashkenazic tradition was compensated for by adapting Hasidic melodies, particularly those without words, to prose texts. The rise of neo-Hasidism and of the youth culture brought forth a spate of new so-called Hasidic songs, imitations of the older songs. These are largely settings of biblical verses and excerpts of texts, all of the metrical, hand-clapping variety, but lacking in the hallmarks noted above: no melisma, no contemplative or rhapsodic passages, and little, if any, autonomous melody, music without words. These songs serve not only as highly oversimplified congregational hymns, but also as mnemonic devices for the memorization of many brief biblical quotations in Hebrew. They are neither composed nor sung by mystics.

The continuation of mystical trends in music of the synagogue may be perceived, rather, in a few of the sophisticated compositions for the synagogue by contemporary composers. Perhaps a prime example of this would be the "*Adon Olam*"—the penultimate section of Ernest Bloch's *Sacred Service*. The text is a strophic poem and is usually sung as a hymn by the congregation. Many composers have set it as a hymn. Darius Milhaud, for example, fashioned it as a lilting Provençal song. But Bloch wrote a through-composed piece, with each word given its interpretation (*kavanah*, indeed!). Instead of melismas in the vocal parts, Bloch uses his orchestra to supply the autonomous musical elements. They are highly atmospheric passages, which suggest the mystery of the spheres. Others, before and after Bloch, have dealt this way with the liturgy: Joseph Achron, in the Psalm 92 which opens his *Evening Service for the Sabbath*, and his *Adon Olam* in the same *Service*; Arnold Schoenberg in his *Kol Nidre* and his *De Profundis*; Yehudi Wyner in his music for the High Holy Days.

It may be that the mysticism of our day is finding its artistic apotheosis in the work of the sensitive and talented individual, rather than in spontaneous folk-outpouring. Some of this contemporary music makes demands on the ears and the minds of the congregation. But then, so, too, does genuine mysticism.

NOTES

/1/   Some scattered exceptions to this have been discovered in recent decades from scraps of twelfth-century manuscript to early baroque compositions. The notations of biblical chant by German humanists of the sixteenth century provide source material for study and comparison, but were largely unknown to synagogue musicians until recently. The compositions of Salomone Rossi (ca. 1600) have been known.

/2/   Art music in the Western sense appeared sporadically, beginning with the late Renaissance. It began to develop only in the nineteenth century. It continues side by side with the now more or less notated oral tradition.

/3/   In the first Temple, the singing of psalms may have been pathogenic, but in the second Temple, it is presumed, psalmody became a totally word-oriented intonation, which continued into the ancient synagogue.

/4/   This reading and translation of the Hebrew text is taken from Carmi (196). There are several examples of *Hekhalot* hymns in this anthology.

/5/   Scholem (59) cites examples of this disapproval from *Megillot* 18a and *Berakhot* 33b.

/6/   This melody bears great similarity to the Frankish Christian acclamation *"Christus vincit, Christus regnat, Christus imperat"* which appears in manuscripts as early as the eighth century, punctuating some *laudes*. Our melody may therefore be of medieval North European origin.

REFERENCES

Achron, Joseph
    1932   *Evening Service for the Sabbath*. New York: Bloch Publishing Co.

Avenary, Hanoch
    1971   *Hebrew Hymn Tunes*. Tel Aviv.

Birnbaum, Philip, ed.
    1951   *High Holyday Prayer Book*. New York.

Bloch, Ernest
    1934   *Avodat ha-Kodesh (Sacred Service)*. Boston. Recorded by New York Philharmonic Orchestra, Leonard Bernstein, conductor, Robert Merrill, cantor. Columbia MS 5221.

Carmi, T., ed. and tr.
    1981   *The Penguin Book of Hebrew Verse*. New York: Viking Press.

Idelsohn, Abraham Z.
    1929   *Jewish Music in its Historical Development*. New York: H. Holt and Co.
    1914–33   *Thesaurus of Oriental Hebrew Melodies*. Leipzig, New York, and Jerusalem.

Philo Judaeus
    1941   "On the Contemplative Life or Suppliants." *Philo* IX, trans. by F. H. Colson. Loeb Classical Library. Cambridge, Massachusetts.

Putterman, David, ed.
    1951   *Synagogue Music by Contemporary Composers*. New York: G. Schirmer.

Sachs, Curt
    1943   *The Rise of Music in the Ancient World, East and West*. New York: W. W. Norton and Co.

Schoenberg, Arnold
    1938   *Kol Nidre*, op. 39. Associated Music Press, Inc. BMI. Recording
    (first   in *The Music of Arnold Schoenberg*. Vol. 3. Columbia M2S–
    performance)   709.

1955   "Psalm 130, A Song of Ascents." In *Anthology of Jewish
                        Music*, ed. by H. Vinaver. New York. Recording in *The Music
                        of Arnold Schoenberg*, vol. 8, under the title "De Profundis"
                        (sung in Hebrew). Columbia M2S–780.

Scholem, Gershom
1941   *Major Trends in Jewish Mysticism*. Jerusalem: Schocken
                        Publishing House.

Werner, Eric
1976   *A Voice Still Heard*. University Park, Pa.: Pennsylvania State
                        University Press.

Werner, Eric, and Sonne, Isaiah
1941–43   "The Philosophy and Theory of Music in Judaeo-Arabic Liter-
                        ature." *Hebrew Union College Annual* 16:251–319 and
                        17:511–73.

Wyner, Yehudi
                        Kodosh Ato/R'tzei (High Holy Day Liturgy). Unpublished MS.
                        Recording on "A concert by the American Conference of
                        Cantors." 18/Chai Life.

Zalmanoff, Rabbi Samuel, ed.
1979–80   *Sefer Ha-niqunim*. Vol. 3. New York.

EXAMPLES

Example 1   Trad.

A - do - nai _____ me-lekh, A
do - nai _____ ma-lakh, A-do -
nai yim - lokh _____ le-o- lam va - ed.

The Lord is King, the Lord was King
The Lord shall be King forever and ever.

Example 2   Notated by Gerovitsch, from Vinaver, *Anthology*, p. 150

Recit. Solo.

And the priests and the people who stood
in the court, when they heard the glorious
venerated and Ineffable Name proceed from
the mouth of the High Priest, in sanctity
and purity, kneeled and prostrated themselves,
falling on their faces and saying: Blessed
be the name of His sovereign majesty
forever and ever.

Example 3   Idelsohn, *Thesaurus*, Vol. 4, No. 187

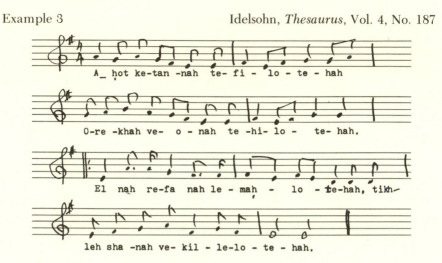

A_ hot ke-tan -nah te- fi - lo - te - hah

O-re -khah ve- o - nah te -hi- lo - te- hah.

El nah re-fa nah le - mah - lo - te-hah, tikh-

leh sha -nah ve- kil - le-lo - te - hah.

Little Sister, oh hear her plea!
Her Prayers she orders all weeping to Thee.
May all her wounds now healed be.
Avert the stern decree!

(Trans. J. K. E.)

Example 4   Idelsohn, *Jewish Music*, p. 421

Beloved of my soul, merciful Father
Draw Your servant after You to do
Your will. He would run, swift as a
deer, to kneel before Your majesty . . . etc.
                    (Trans. Carmi)

Example 5   Idelsohn, *Thesaurus*, Vol. 4, No. 8

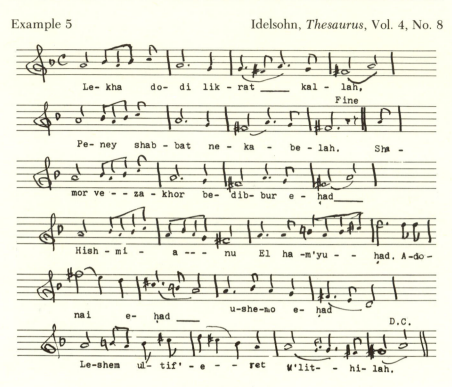

Le- kha   do- di lik - rat ____ kal - lah,

Pe- ney shab - bat ne - ka - be - lah.   Sha -

mor ve - - za - khor be- dib- bur e - had ____

Hish - mi -   a - - - nu El ha -m'yu - - had. A-do -

nai   e- had ____   u-she-mo e- had

Le-shem ul- tif' - e - - ret w'lit- - hi- lah.

Come my friend, to greet the bride,
    Let us welcome the Sabbath.
'Observe' and 'remember' in a single commandment
    God the Only One gave us to hear,
The Lord is one, and His name is one
    For fame, for glory and for praise,

Come my friend, etc.

Example 6

If the doors of princes are closed to me
the doors of Heaven are not closed. The
living God will lift us on the wings of
kheruvim. All of us shall rise on the
strength of His spirit.

Example 7   Idelsohn, *Music*, p. 422, No. 5

Example 8   Notated by S. Silbermintz in *Sefer ha-Niggunim*,
                                    ed. Zalmanoff, Vol. 3, No. 249

From the beginning, Thou hast distinguished
man by endowing him with reason and filled
him with the desire to seek Thy Presence.
Yet who shall say to Thee: "What doest Thou?" etc.
                    (Trans. Ph. Birnbaum)

Example 9   Notated by S. Silbermintz in *Sefer ha-Niggunim*,
                                              ed. Zalmanoff, Vol. 3, No. 248

Like the clearest canopy of heaven
    Was the countenance of the priest.
Like lightnings flashing from benign angels
    Was the countenance of the priest.
Like the purest blue from the four fringes
    Was the countenance of the priest.
Like the wondrous rainbow in the bright cloud
    Was the countenance of the priest. Etc.

(Trans. Ph. Birnbaum)

Shifting Alliances: The Struggle for a Lutheran Theology of Music

Joyce Irwin

In the face of changing tastes in church music in recent decades, perhaps no style or period of music has remained so universally acceptable as German Baroque. Romantic music of the nineteenth century may be thought too sentimental, twentieth-century music too abstract or dissonant, Renaissance music too difficult or distant. Few question the appropriateness of the baroque style represented by the three S's—Schütz, Schein, and Scheidt—and the church musician par excellence, Johann Sebastian Bach. The theologian who provided the foundation for such musical expression, Martin Luther, is therefore accorded high praise for his artistic sensitivity and encouragement of choral as well as congregational singing.

Less well known is the fact that simultaneous with the "golden age of church music," there raged a debate among theologians regarding the appropriateness of the choral and instrumental music which was being practiced in the Lutheran churches. Isolated criticisms uttered in the 1640s and 1650s broke into full-fledged controversy with the Rostock pastor Theophilus Grossgebauer's *Wächterstimme aus dem verwüsteten Zion* in 1661. The introduction of Italian operatic style singing and the expanded role of the organ in Lutheran worship deprived the congregation, according to Grossgebauer, of its rightful role in the singing of chorales. The situation as he saw it was similar to that under the papacy where the people were awed into silence: "Whoever it may have been who invented organs and music-making in the church, it has certainly been a great advantage for the Roman clergy: along with the Latin Psalms this put a bit in the mouth of the church and makes it mute so that only the Pope can speak and say what he wants. And the church is so enraptured by the sound that it marvels over the animal's power and glory" (225).

Similar criticisms of organ music had long been heard in Calvinist circles. Indeed Grossgebauer recognized that he would probably be accused of Calvinism because of his views. At least since the colloquy of Mompelgard (1586), the Lutheran position on music in worship had been formulated more in opposition to Calvinists than in opposition to Roman Catholics. Because

Calvinists generally opposed organ music in worship, it was important for Lutherans to defend it. For Grossgebauer the opposition of Calvinist and Lutheran is of less concern than the distance between musicians and congregation.

The music sung by choirs is for this reason as problematic as organ music. If organ music is meaningless noise which does nothing more than tickle the ears, the music of the singers is no better. Though words are sung, they are incomprehensible either because they are in a foreign tongue or because they are obscured by distracting ornamentations. "So songs are sent to us in Germany from Italy wherein the biblical texts are torn apart and chopped into small pieces through fast runs in the throat. . . . Sometimes it's Latin, sometimes German; very few can understand the words" (227).

Even worse perhaps than the meaninglessness or the incomprehensibility of the music is the sacrilege committed by the performance of inappropriate music. Grossgebauer is particularly offended by communion music which ignores the fact that the death of Christ is being commemorated. Here again a social critique is combined with a theological point: the usual occasion for grandiose music during communion is the approach of an important person or a bride to the altar. "And when the death of the Lord is supposed to be proclaimed, what is proclaimed is . . . that a distinguished person is going to communion or that a bride is among the communicants. Thus one idolatry follows another" (234).

Just as communion should, in Grossgebauer's view, result in brotherly love, so the music of worship should be a communal effort. Interaction among members of the congregation is best accomplished through antiphonal singing. "But when with Augustine I can sing in the congregation in such a manner that for a little while I keep still, catch my breath, and listen to the other words of the other choir, my spirit is even more enflamed through the beautiful words. Thus is fulfilled what Paul demanded: Speak to one another through Psalms" (221).

Although Grossgebauer was not the originator of any of these ideas, the abrasiveness of his style of writing made his book the focus of the heated debate which ensued. An impartial reader might note that Grossgebauer had quite persuasively defended the value of music; nevertheless, he was labeled a hater of music and treated as an insensitive boor. The "defenders of music" now saw the enemy within their own ranks. The criticism which reminded them so much of Calvinist error must be recognized as such and attacked with all possible force. No longer was moderation possible.

Yet the cause of the controversy lay not only in the passions aroused by Grossgebauer's attack. Whatever Reformed influence may have come to the surface in his work, he also expressed some fundamental concerns of Luther's reform. The fact that both sides could draw on the same sources indicates not that one was spuriously and the other genuinely Lutheran but rather that within Luther's theology there were unresolved tensions which had finally pulled apart. Standing midway between Roman Catholics and other Protestants, Luther was destined to be pulled in both directions by his successors, depending on their perception of the greater danger./1/

Luther's views on music have been well presented in Oskar Söhngen's article. What is necessary here is not to reiterate his fundamental position but to point up some of the complexities or ambiguities which were potentially problematic. To the extent that music, like the sermon, served as an instrument of the Word for Luther, the sung text is primary, perhaps even indispensable. Luther was less enthusiastic about organ music than about choirs for this very reason. Yet to the extent that music works psychological benefits, the text is less important than the sound. Finally, the affirmation of music as part of the goodness of God's creation allows for pure sound not limited even by pragmatic judgments concerning its effects. Music was regarded as a gift so sacred that its pursuit necessarily brought morally beneficial results. Scarcely could an unfaithful person make music. Yet there was a kind of music which was produced by sinful people, such as tavern or dance music.

The liturgical result of Luther's multifaceted view of music was also multifaceted. Congregations were encouraged to sing chorales in their own languages that the Word of God might be engrained in their hearts and minds. Choirs were retained for their essentially pedagogical value: boys received moral and educational benefits from singing good music. Latin texts were even desirable as an encouragement to learning the language. Organs were a nonessential, yet potentially useful, means of supporting congregational singing./2/ They, as many other elements of liturgical ceremony, fell under the category of *adiaphora*, neutral elements which might be used to good ends in public worship. Thus Luther maintained flexibility and openness in liturgical form and musical expression while at the same time making clear that the spiritual text was of primary importance in church music.

In this, as in other issues, Luther's followers were not long content with ambiguity. The question of adiaphora, in particular, was subjected to scrutiny during the time of the Leipzig Interim (1549). While some considered the liturgical compromises imposed by the Catholics not worth disputing, others maintained that persecution brought ceremonies into the realm of doctrine. Incorporated into the Formula of Concord (1580), therefore, was the principle that ceremonies which were by nature indifferent were no longer neutral if persecutors considered them matters of faith. Though the problem had arisen in relation to Catholics, it came to be applied to Calvinists after the Formula of Concord. Because Calvinists had silenced organs in worship out of principle and often by the forceful removal of organs from churches, Lutherans became equally belligerent in their defense of instrumental music. At the colloquy of Mompelgard, where the Calvinist Theodore Beza was prepared to admit the possibility of a beneficial use of organs, the Lutheran Jakob Andreae pressed toward a stronger endorsement, almost to a claim of their necessity: "So indeed it is apparent to everyone, also on the basis of your confession, that they (adiaphora) are neither commanded nor forbidden by God and thus in themselves are not only permitted but also a gracious ornament of the church if only they are used for the praise and glory of the name of God. In this manner they are not only not forbidden but rather expressly commanded in order that one praise God therewith, as it is written in Psalm 150" (*Colloquium*:735).

When the Calvinists made inroads into Saxony at the end of the century, animosities peaked and likewise the controversy over organs. The Reformed theologians of Zerbst-Anhalt were far more adamant in their rejection of organs than Beza had been (*Erinnerungsschrift*:70–75). They left no room for adiaphora, teaching that anything not commanded in the New Testament had no place in Christian worship. Organs and Latin singing are human inventions which work against the requirement of comprehensibility, as expressed in I Corinthians 14:9: "Except ye utter by the tongue words easy to be understood, how shall it be known what is spoken?" (KJV).

In reaction to this potentially persuasive argument, the Wittenberg theologians who defended Lutheran practice developed an argument which opened the door to problems later in the century (*Notwendige Antwort*:1073–77, esp. 1076). Music can communicate its meaning, they argued, even when no text is sung. As long as the genus of the music is perceived, it is understandable. That is, so long as one recognizes that an organist is playing spiritual music, the power of the music is felt and its effect accomplished. Many kinds of instruments were used in the time of the Old Testament (which, incidentally, is not to be explained away as mere allegory), and it is unrealistic to suppose that worshipers in the temple were always able to understand the words sung.

This line of argument found general acceptance among Lutheran writers of the early seventeenth century, a time when many churches were purchasing new organs and pastors were preaching organ sermons at the dedication of the organ. On such occasions the suggestion that they might be dispensable ornaments was inappropriate, and the distinction between praising God and praising Him with trumpets and organs was obscured. Instrumental music seemed to become an obligatory response to Old Testament exhortations to praise God. Johann Scarlach, for example, instructed the readers of his question-and-answer book on the Formula of Concord to respond to the Calvinist attack on organs with "the advice and command of the Holy Spirit" in Psalm 150 (191).

Meanwhile, among the devotional writers of the early seventeenth century, the metaphysical-mathematical tradition of musical theory was being combined with speculation on heavenly existence to produce a theology of music which also resembled Luther's only in part. The plagues of the late sixteenth and wars of the early seventeenth century drew the survivors' attention to death and eternal salvation. What they could read in the Bible about heaven indicated to them that the primary activity there was music-making—or, as some more carefully phrased it, praising God through music. Angels sang and played instruments in a manner far more beautiful than any known or imagined on earth. For some it seemed then to follow that the best preparation for heaven would be extensive musical training. Frequently cited was the following anecdote: "When Mr. Valentinus Trotzendorff, schoolmaster at Goldberg, wanted to admonish the young students to music, he said: 'Learn to sing, dear sons, learn to sing. Then when you come into heaven the holy angels will let you enter their choir'" (Herberger:481).

Such belief was combined with the revival of Pythagorean awareness of the natural basis of tonal relationships and a resulting belief in harmony as the fundamental principle of the universe./3/ Although little interest was shown in the hypothetical music of the spheres, the harmony of creation in all its parts served as analogy to the individual soul. For some thinkers, such as Johann Arndt, the importance of musical sound in this analogy was metaphorical. While not rejecting either instruments or singing in church, Arndt regarded the trumpets, psalteries, harps, and cymbals of the Old Testament as outward symbols of "our heart, spirit, soul, mind, and mouth" (547 [bk. 2, ch. 41]). Music as communicating God's Word was here replaced by a music which bore witness to God within. In a less profound mind such as that of Christoph Frick, whose *Musica Christiana* (1615)/4/ was prefaced with an endorsing letter by Arndt, the relation of music to the soul was treated on a literal level. Whereas devotion of the heart is essential, so is the music sung by the mouth. God cannot be pleased when either is lacking, for outward pursuit of music is evidence of inner harmony of soul, which in turn is the key to harmony with God, the creator of the harmonies and of the universe. Conversely, those who refuse to sing show themselves out of harmony with God and, if they continue to reject music, in danger of hell-fire. "It is certain that such people will be at the place where there will be nothing but howling and gnashing of teeth; with the hellish wolves and all the damned in eternity they will cry out dolefully. May God protect us graciously against this one and all" (1631:232).

Between Luther and Frick there is the common belief in the divine origin of music and its spiritual power. Those who abuse music by using it for carnal enjoyment offend God and show themselves unworthy, whereas the proper use of music confounds evil forces. The difference between the two rests primarily in the causal explanation. For Frick the devout person uses music to accomplish a good end. For Luther, God works through the combination of musician, text, and sound to accomplish His ends. This distinction becomes clearer through the oft-used example of Saul and David, which can well serve as a measure of a writer's music-theological position. As reported in I Samuel 16:23, "It came to pass, when the evil spirit from God was upon Saul, that David took an harp, and played with his hand: so Saul was refreshed, and was well, and the evil spirit departed from him."

A long tradition of biblical interpretation as well as music theory had given rise to several opinions on the nature of Saul's affliction or the cause of its abatement./5/ Both Luther and Frick treated it literally as possession by Satan rather than as melancholy and saw in music the power to drive him away. For Luther, however, the effectiveness of the music rested in its connection with the words of the Psalms. He reasons that David would not simply have played the harp but would have sung Psalms accompanied by the harp. The Psalter alone, because it sings and preaches of the Messiah, is "a sweet, comforting, delightful song, even if one reads forth or says the bare words without notes" (33). Music helps, however, "especially where the crowd sings along with proper seriousness" (34). Thus David's faith contributed to the effectiveness of the music, but the primary cause was the Word of God. "For it does not go well with the evil spirit when God's Word is sung or preached in correct faith" (34). Luther goes on to comment that David did not consider the Psalms his own but rather those of Israel in that they had been confirmed and recognized by the entire people: "For it depends on whether the masses of God, or God's people, accept a word or song and recognize it as correct; for the spirit of God, who wants to be and should be honored in his people, must be in such people" (34).

Frick, whose work was both less subtle and more devotional, omitted any reference to the congregation, though he agreed with Luther that the musical sound was not the force which drove the devil away. Rather, it was that "David struck a spiritual song from the bottom of his heart and sang on in fervent devotion to Christ" (1631:77). While the spirituality of the sung text remains important here, the devotion of the singer receives more weight than with Luther. That such was not an uncommon interpretation is apparent from Johannes Brenz in the previous century. "Many think," he wrote, "that the faith and prayers of David, which he played on the harp from faith, expelled Satan from Saul, in the same manner as the Apostles cast out demons from men in the name of Christ" (598). For Brenz, by contrast, the music was a purely natural phenomenon which had only the power to alleviate the suffering, not the ability to cure Saul's madness (which likewise was the result not of evil forces but of mental disturbance).

Such a naturalistic interpretation was not likely to be encountered among Lutherans of the seventeenth century, however. Much more common was the use of the incident to demonstrate the power and legitimacy of instrumental music. As Conrad Dieterich wrote in his oft-cited *Ulm Organ Sermon*: "Instrumental music drives away the restless, angry, melancholy spirit and brings in the open, happy, good spirit. When the evil spirit made Saul restless and David grasped his harp and opened forth, Saul was refreshed, he became better, and the evil spirit retreated from him" (18).

The two dominant strands of Lutheran music theology in the early seventeenth century, then, were (1) the devotional emphasis on the affinity of music to the individual soul and (2) the confessional affirmation of the spiritual value of artistic church music with choirs and instruments. Both of these, as well as the naturalistic, psychological approach, could be supported from the many elements combined in Luther's thought. One strand of Luther's thought which was left undeveloped, however, was the sense of corporate response to the gospel. Devotional writers saw themselves as part of the heavenly choir and, to that extent, of the body of Christian believers; but their focus on the individual soul's attainment of eternal salvation drew attention away from that soul's relationship to others still on earth. Confessional writers, on the other hand, went to great lengths to discuss past use of music among God's people on earth. The sense of continuity with a sacred tradition is strong, but not the sense of congregational participation in the present.

Already in Dieterich's organ sermon the reader senses a gap opening between musicians and congregation. Dieterich offers his listeners an arsenal of reasons why they should appreciate music in church and bemoans those who listen like bumps on a log. Further, he urges the musicians to play appropriate music and behave respectfully. His organ sermon is probably the most moderate and best informed of the time, yet it was not likely to ward off the battle against art music. Those who lack appreciation for any art form will hardly be won over when told in somewhat condescending terms that they ought to be grateful. "They regard church as church, organ as organ, and music as music even when the most eloquent preacher, the most famous organist, and the best musician are to be heard. But isn't that great blindness, great foolishness, great thanklessness?" (37).

If, as Dieterich reports, people avoided church music already in 1624, it is hardly surprising that the Italian-style music introduced in later decades alienated them even more. Nor, unfortunately, is it surprising that the lines of division among the different approaches became increasingly clearer. Only Johann Conrad Dannhauer, the Strasbourg professor under whom Philipp Jakob Spener studied, seemed to bring together all the strands of previous Lutheran interpretation, including that of congregational participation. He saw the psychological or humanistic value of sound and hence of instrumental music as preparation for devotion; but the actual spiritual effect, he felt, came from the words alone. The music of the angels, which for Dannhauer as for many devotional writers was the model for church music, was not textless but expressed the praise of God in words (1642:524). Dannhauer's interest in heavenly harmonies, however, served not as consolation for the suffering of this life and hope for eternal salvation but as a model for ecclesiological harmony. Just as beautiful music consists of several parts moving in consonance but with enough dissonance to maintain interest, so the church on earth brings together the many gifts of its members into a unity, though not uniformity. Human dissonances give rise to different practices, many of which can be tolerated under the rubric of adiaphora (1657:413–14)./6/ What is important is that music serve as a means of mutual edification, for just as one string may through sympathetic vibration cause another to sound, so one devout person may arouse devotion in another by singing of his faith. This may mean that a choir sings while the congregation listens; it is not necessary that all sing at all times. Nevertheless, singing of some sort, whether of congregation or choir, simple or artistic, is necessary as a proper expression of the praise of God (1642:521).

The center could not hold, however. Dannhauer's moderating synthesis was taken apart by both critics and defenders of art music. His concern for mutual edification among members of the congregation was carried to Rostock by his pupil Joachim Lütkemann./7/ His outbursts against the more ornamental artistry of his day are echoed by Theophilus Grossgebauer. His praise of angelic choirs, on the other hand, was cited by Hector Mithobius in his lengthy attack on Grossgebauer entitled *Psalmodia Christiana*. The battle lines, which had been drawn through such simplistic labels as "music hater" and "ear tickler," predisposed the participants to fight rather than negotiate.

Yet there were those who withdrew from the fray and turned inward instead. In a way similar to the devotional circle of Arndt and Frick, Heinrich Müller, a Rostock theologian who derived many of his ideas from Lütkemann, wrote for the individual soul in its search for union with God. Because of the exclusive attention to the individual, choirs and organs do not enter the discussion, even in analogy to the heavenly choir or cosmic harmonies. Müller's criteria for the worth of singing rest entirely in the singer. Not the Word but the Spirit validates music. Augustine had argued that music without words might result in mere sensual pleasure; Müller went a step further to argue that the poetry of the words might also appeal to the ear without penetrating to the heart (114). Music as preached Word entering through the ear is not part of Müller's discussion. Rather he writes in mystical terms of ridding the heart of the distractions of the senses: "In public places the eyes find much to see, the ears much to hear, or else they entice the heart out and scatter the thoughts into all the things which the eyes see and the ears hear. Therefore a devout Christian must either choose a secret little place or else close the senses in public gatherings, cover the eyes, turn away the ears, etc." (160–61).

Words are for Müller a means of kindling the heart but are unnecessary if the heart is already aflame. In fact they may even hinder devotion, for "the more the outward person rests, the more the inward person senses" (149). When the heart becomes full, however, it overflows and words are poured out. It is then that they are of greatest value, for the neighbor may also be inflamed and edified by this.

There is, then, some sense of mutual edification, but in contrast to Luther it occurs not through the psalms created and recognized by the entire people of God but from spirit to spirit. In Trinitarian terms, the second Person is bypassed in favor of the third. Christ as the Word of God does not encounter human beings through external means, but the Holy Spirit works from within. Significantly, when Müller writes of music as a means of driving away melancholy, he writes not of David singing to Saul but rather of David singing to counteract his own sadness. "For when a saddened person sings, the joyous spirit struggles, as it were, with the melancholy spirit and in the end maintains the victory" (84).

The devotional, nonpolemic tone of Müller's work and its focus on private singing prevented it from being drawn into the battle over liturgical music. Yet the subjective standards by which he judged music-making became the central theological issue of the ensuing debate. Significantly, beginning with Grossgebauer's book, the enemy is no longer Calvinism but popery. The legitimacy of choirs and organs is not in dispute; no writer finds them inadmissible in themselves. Rather the issues are those of pre-Reformation anticlericalism with musicians in the place of clerics: should those who are spiritually unworthy be allowed such an exalted role in the liturgy? Has not external ceremony replaced inward purity? Can the faithful believers benefit spiritually from ceremonies performed by the unfaithful? As in the pre-Reformation church, hardly anyone denied that there were abuses in church music. The question was whether the abuse invalidated the activity. Johann Muscovius, in his *Bestraffter Missbrauch der Kirchen-Music* (1694), applied the appropriate theological term to the issue when he exclaimed, "Ah! Let us lament to God that the *opus operatum* has inundated Christendom like a flood and that sly Satan has brought many thousands of souls into his net even from within the evangelical churches" (39).

Gottfried Vockerodt soon thereafter took the next logical step and demanded that those who provide music for worship also be regenerate. Just as the unworthy receipt of the sacrament can work towards damnation, so the unworthy practice of music can work spiritual harm. "For of what use is it to the musician if he reaches the highest level of musical knowledge and skill and thereby attains the favor of all great lords, the admiration of all professional colleagues, praise and honor in the whole world, and everything else his heart desires, and if in addition he has a secure and joyful heart, if he doesn't have the above-described living faith and its certainty which makes him happy, defiant, and cheerful in God, and if he is not reborn from God, if the old Adam is not killed in him, if his heart, mind, and spirit and all powers aren't changed, if he doesn't have the Holy Spirit. Would he not then with all his art, favor, and glory do harm to his soul?" (22).

Because singing or playing music should be an act of faith, it should not be done out of desire for either fame or financial gain. Vockeroth has only harsh words for those who view church music as a profession rather than an expression of faith: "Such evil and unfaithful musicians are all those who learn the art with false and fleshly intention, practice it with unholy mind, and exercise it for the Divine Being. These have seized upon the profession with the expectation of fulfilling their lusts thereby, having good days, and attaining riches, honor, and favor among men. Such persons love the world and what is in it" (29).

The implication that church music should be a voluntary activity was unlikely to meet with approbation among the musicians, who more and more were becoming a professional class. Accordingly they saw themselves as artists rather than as servants of the church. Their obligation, as composer and music theorist Andreas Werckmeister saw it, was to produce good music. Not all musicians, he admitted, were sufficiently skilled in their art, which was the explanation for the ridiculous or inappropriate sounds which were being criticized. Music, like oratory, is an art whereby the skilled artist brings about the intended result. To be sure, there are those who intend their own glory, which is an abuse. Had Werckmeister used the sacramental analogy, he might have said, in the best Roman Catholic tradition, that the outward form is valid in itself because orderly melodies and beautiful harmonies communicate the presence of God. Music is for him a mirror of divine creation and the wisdom of God, indeed God's image (11). Further, it is efficacious in the hearts of those who do not put an obstacle in its way. The efficacy is dependent only on the intention of the musician to perform spiritual music and on his care in accomplishing this. His spiritual worthiness or inward disposition has no bearing on the value of the music. Thus, in the case of David and Saul, it was neither David's faithfulness nor the power of the words but the skillfulness of his playing which brought the result: "If it was delightful, we must conclude that he also had to apply his art, for without art and knowledge no musician can bring forth loveliness" (15–16).

Werckmeister's work had preceded the writings of Muscovius and Vockerodt on the abuse of music. After a decade of controversy, the *opus operatum* theology was more explicitly developed by Georg Motz, cantor and school music director at Tilse. One must distinguish between the person and the deed, he writes. Music is good and necessary in the church as a condition of order and harmony. Artistic compositions are inspired by the Holy Ghost, whether or not the composer is a devout person: "One must neither blame nor scorn the artistic masters, the great artists, or the arts. Artistic compositions are no foolish fancies. They come from the Holy Spirit and not from a worldly spirit" (37). Musical knowledge is more important for a composer than is spirituality. Hitting at the weak point in the Muscovius-Vockerodt position, Motz argues that the spiritual faults of the congregation could eliminate the singing of chorales if those of the choir must eliminate the singing of figural music. Indeed only Müller's individualized purification could fully satisfy the criteria for purity; Motz, on the other hand, seems unduly eager to affirm impurity. Citing several Old Testament passages, he notes, "Indeed the prophets and priests themselves were not always adorned with faith and true godliness" (239).

The impurity, for Motz, resides in the people—not in ecclesiastical forms. Just as the Word of God is preached even though it may bring little fruit, so music is offered even if no one appreciates it. The musicians are no more blameworthy than are preachers when the Word falls on deaf ears. Just as the grace offered in the sacraments may meet an obstacle within the recipient, so the music may be scorned. Saul's reaction to David's music was not always positive, Motz notes; in an episode described in I Samuel 18:10–11, Saul's response was to throw his javelin at David: "And what can be said of the harp music of the crowned musical artist, David? Certainly his fantasies, psalms, and songs which he weds with his harp and by which he drove away the evil spirit from King Saul were no 'foolish fancies.' The recompense, however, which he earned and received for this was bad enough: for Saul wanted to pin him to the wall. Such is the recompense which the world gives for all faithfully executed services" (40–41).

Nothing could better symbolize the completion of the barrier between musician and congregation than this. A new elite had been spawned within the priesthood of all believers. The professional musician, supported by the unqualified affirmation of the sacred nature of music, offered his re-creation of the harmonious universe for those who were prepared to receive it. The primacy of the text was denied. A half century later this was explicitly confirmed by the Lübeck cantor Caspar Ruetz (or Rüetz), who drew many of his ideas from Motz: "But there is this dissimilarity between speech and music: namely, in speech one uses the sound of the voice for the sake of the words which are to be recognized and heard; but in music the words are for the sake of the sounds, because here one speaks more through sounds than words" (65). Given this development, it was virtually inevitable that sacred art music would begin to make its way out of the church and into the concert hall. It was a form of devotion unto itself, a means of experiencing the sacred as Beauty, not as Word.

Luther's ideal of a hymnody of the people was not entirely forgotten, however. Hymn writing flourished, and countless hymn books with new, old, and revised hymns were published to meet the growing demand. As hymnals grew to unmanageable lengths,/8/ Philipp Jakob Spener encouraged publication of a shorter hymnal specifically for church use. This should contain commonly used old hymns in their original forms for the sake of uniformity. Preference should be given to those composed in such a way that the congregation could sing them well (320ff.). Meanwhile, other writers, such as Johann Martin Schamelius, turned their attention to correcting errors which had crept into popular renditions of common hymns. Christian Gerber, pastor at Lockwitz, reported that he had taken time at the beginning of numerous services to explain the meaning of a hymn verse by verse (250–51). This, combined with the new custom of bringing a hymnal to church,/9/ must surely have improved the quality of congregational singing.

At the same time, however, private singing also flourished in the form of very subjective, emotion-laden devotional songs. Musically not dissimilar to the operatic church music which their proponents rejected, these pietistic songs had a very different theological justification. The criticism of solistic church music, after all, had not been directed against the expression of subjective feelings but against inappropriate expression. Whether inappropriate to the liturgical moment (as cheerful music during communion), inappropriate to the person (as an irreverent singer expressing piety), or inappropriate to the congregation (as a foreign or muddled text), art music in public worship seldom achieved a congruence of inner devotion and outer expression. In private worship such was by no means impossible.

Luther, after all, had also noted the inseparability of heart and mouth, which might seem to place him on the side of the devotionalists. But he had never made internal purity a prerequisite to the validity of outward forms. Just as his sacramental theology did not hinge primarily on the officiant, the recipient, or the physical action, but on the Word working through all, so his musical theology made the various elements inseparable. It is not surprising, however, given a natural human desire for clarity and simplicity, that such a scenario was difficult to enact. Some wanted to play David, others to play his harp, others to sing, and everyone looked with disdain on Saul. But few thought they needed a director.

NOTES

/1/   Because pietism is such a sensitive and divisive topic and is likely to evoke preconceptions in the mind of the reader, I have chosen to avoid use of the term and categorization of theologians into "orthodox" and "pietist." Until it becomes more generally recognized that both orthodoxy and pietism took on a variety of forms, it is preferable to derive classifications solely from the material at hand.

/2/   Organs were not generally used to accompany congregational singing in the sixteenth century but freqently introduced the chorale and alternated with the singing of the congregation. See Rietschel:46.

/3/   In addition to Söhngen's article preceding, see Dammann and Blankenburg.

/4/   The *Musica Christiana* reappeared with minor changes as part 1 of Frick's *Music-Büchlein* (1631).

/5/   For a survey from a medical history perspective, see Kümmel.

/6/   One should not mistake these comments as an indication of irenicism. Dannhauer was tolerant of deviations only in indifferent ceremonial matters. In doctrinal matters he was often strongly polemical. Even on the question of music he maintained a strong anti-Calvinist position. See his *Hodomoria Spiritus Calviniani*, 1239–42.

/7/   See his posthumously published *Apostolische Auffmunterung zum lebendigen Glauben*, 256.

/8/   The Lüneburg hymnbook of 1694 contained 2055 hymns, according to the calculations of Röbbelen, p. 18.

/9/   Gerber (256–57) tells an anecdote from 1697 or 1698 illustrating the resistance to congregational usage of hymnals. A farmer from the Merseburg area frequently took grain to Halle and went to church while there. In this urban setting he found that almost everybody present sang from a hymnal. Attracted to this custom, he bought himself a hymnbook and took it to church upon his return home. His elderly pastor was not pleased with this innovation, however, and forbade him to use it, saying that none but the schoolmaster should sing from a book. The farmer, though, appealed his case beyond the pastor, who was then overruled.

REFERENCES

Arndt, Johann
    1670   *Vier Bücher Vom Wahren Christenthumb*. Lüneberg.

Blankenburg, Walter
    1959   "Der Harmonie-Begriff in der lutherisch-barocken Musikan-
                    schauung." *Archiv für Musikwissenschaft* XVI:44–56.

Brenz, Johannes
    1576   "Homiliae in Cap. XVI, Lib. I Samuelis." *Opera* II. Tübingen.

Colloquium
    1587   *Colloquium Mompelgartense. Gespräch In gegenwart des
                    Durchleuchtigen Hochgebornen Fürsten unnd Herrn/Herrn
                    Friderichen/Graven zu Würtemberg und Mümpelgart.*
                    Tübingen.

Dammann, Rolf
    1967   *Der Musikbegriff im deutschen Barock*. Cologne.

Dannhauer, Johann Conrad
    1642   *Catechismusmilch, oder Der Erklärung dess Christlichen
                    Catechismi . . . Erster Theil.* Strasbourg.
    1654   *Hodomoria Spiritus Calviniani.* Strasbourg.
    1657   *Catechismusmilch . . . Sechster Theil.* Strasbourg.

Dieterich, Conrad
    1624   *Ulmische Orgel Predigt.* Ulm.

Erinnerungsschrifft
    1597   *Erinnerungsschrifft etlicher vom Adel und Städten, An den
                    Durchleuchtigen Hochgebornen Fürsten unnd Herrn, Herrn
                    Johann Georgen, Fürsten zu Anhalt, Graven zu Ascanien,
                    Herrn zu Zerbst und Bernburg.* Amberg.

Frick, Christoph (Friccius, Christophorus)
    1615   *Musica Christiana.* Leipzig.
    1631   *Music-Büchlein.* Lüneburg. Reprint Kassel, 1976.

Gerber, Christian
   1732   *Historie der Kirchen-Ceremonien in Sachsen.* Dresden and Leipzig.

Grossgebauer, Theophilus
   1661   *Wächterstimme Auss dem verwüsteten Zion.* Frankfurt am Main.

Herberger, Valerius
   1613   *Hertz Postilla.* Leipzig.

Kümmel, Werner
   1969   "Melancholie und die Macht der Musik: Die Krankheit König Sauls in der historischen Discussion." *Medizinhistorisches Journal* IV:189–209.

Lütkemann, Joachim
   1706   *Apostolische Auffmunterung zum lebendigen Glauben.* Hannover and Wolfenbüttel.

Luther, Martin
   1543   "Von den letzten Worten Davids." *Weimar Ausgabe* 54.

Mithobius, Hector
   1665   *Psalmodia Christiana . . . das ist gründliche Gewissens-Belehrung/Was von der Christen Musica, so wol Vocali als Instrumentali zu halten?* Jena.

Motz, Georg
   1703   *Die Vertheidigte Kirchen-Music.* N.p.

Müller, Heinrich
   1659   *Geistliche Seelen Musik Bestehend In zehen betrachtungen.* Rostock.

Muscovius, Johann
   1694   *Bestraffter Missbrauch der Kirchen-Music.* N.p.

Notwendige Antwort
   1597   *Notwendige Antwort Auff die im Fürstenthumb Anhalt Ohn langsten ausgesprengte hefftige Schrift.* Wittenberg. In Georg Dedeken, *Thesauri Conciliorum et Decisionum* I. Hamburg, 1623.

Rietschel, Georg
   1893   *Die Aufgabe der Orgel im Gottesdienste bis ins 18. Jahrhundert.* Leipzig.

Röbbelen, Ingeborg
   1957   *Theologie und Frömmigkeit im deutschen evangelisch-lutherischen Gesangbuch des 17. und frühen 18. Jahrhunderts.* Göttingen.

Rüetz, Caspar
   1752   *Widerlegte Vorurteile von der Beschaffenheit der heutigen Kirchenmusic und von der Lebens-Art einiger Musicorum.* Lübeck.

Scarlach, Johann
    1610   *Drey Nützliche Unterweisungen.* Wittenberg.

Schamelius, Johann Martin
    1712   *Vindiciae Cantionum S. Ecclesiae Evangelicae.* Leipzig.

Spener, Philipp Jakob
    1712   *Theologische Bedenken* I. Halle.

Vockerodt, Gottfried
    1697   *Missbrauch der freyen Künste, insonderheit Der Music.* Frankfurt.

Werckmeister, Andreas
    1691   *Der Edlen Music-Kunst Würde, Gebrauch und Missbrauch.* Frankfurt and Leipzig.

Rehearsal for Revival: Sacred Singing and the Great Awakening in America

Stephen A. Marini

The words, music, and theology of congregational singing in America's Evangelical Calvinist churches changed profoundly during the eighteenth century. Until the 1720s, Congregationalists, Baptists, and Presbyterians generally adhered to the tradition of singing psalms in unison as part of Christian worship. By the 1790s many of them were singing contemporary religious poetry in choral settings of multiple parts composed in a vigorous indigenous musical form. This development was arguably the most significant liturgical change in colonial American religion, one which occasioned fundamental debate not only about what ought to be sung and how, but also about the nature of worship, the interpretation of scripture, the constitution of the church, and the powers of regeneration.

Scholarly attention to this process has been largely confined to hymnologists and musicologists, whose concerns have focussed on questions of literary merit, musical style, and ecclesiastical transmission. Recent studies of eighteenth century hymnody, however, have underscored the complexity of the problem and its centrality to the religious culture of colonial America (Becker, Irwin, MacKay and Crawford). Such work suggests the need for a more comprehensive approach that explores the interconnections of music, language, church communities, and theology, especially during the largely unexamined period of the Great Awakening of 1734–1745 and its aftermath.

This essay will attempt to draw some of these trajectories. The inquiry can only be exploratory, asking what sorts of questions and perspectives emerge from placing the hymnody question in the context of the Awakening. But preliminary examination indicates a powerful and complex relationship between sacred singing and America's first great revival. In the 1720s the Regular Singing Controversy created theological, stylistic, social, and geographic divisions that would reappear in the Awakening. The revival itself restructured the American churches and produced different new combinations of text, music, and worship style in each major wing of the Evangelical communions. By the Revolution, the continuing consequences of the Awakening had broadened the spectrum of church song and synthesized an indigenous hymnody that dominated Evangelical praise for the next half-century.

I

In 1720 American Calvinists agreed on what they called the "matter" of Divine praise. The Psalms, along with other biblical texts like the Song of Deborah and the Magnificat, had been specified as the exclusive language of congregational praise in the Presbyterian Westminster Confession of 1643, the Congregationalist Savoy Declaration of 1658, and the Baptist London Confession of 1688 (Schaff:647, Walker:390, Philadelphia Baptist Association:80). John Cotton, in 1647, gave classic expression to the edifying and homiletic goals of Calvinist psalmody. "The end of singing," he taught, "is not only to instruct and admonish and comfort the upright, but also to instruct, convince, and reprove the wicked" (48).

The standard of canonical psalmody, however, did not obviate disagreement about which metrical version of the Psalms was to be used in worship. The Separatists of Plymouth sang Henry Ainsworth's *Book of Psalms: Englished* of 1612, while the Puritans brought Thomas Sternhold and John Hopkins's 1564 version of *The Whole Booke of Psalmes* with them to Massachusetts Bay. Baptists also used the "Old Version" of Sternhold and Hopkins, while Presbyterians adhered to Rous's Version recommended by the Westminster Assembly in 1650 (Foote:30). According to Cotton Mather, as early as 1635 the Puritans detected in Sternhold and Hopkins "so many Detractions from, Additions to, and Variations of, not only the Text, but the very sense of the Psalmist, that it was an offense unto them" (Mather, 1701:100). This concern for textual fidelity eventuated in the *Bay Psalm Book*, prepared by three Massachusetts divines in 1640, which served as New England's standard for the balance of the century. Mather knew of twenty-one versions, a fact which did not deter him from producing one more of his own, the *Psalterium Americanum* of 1718. Yet this variety did not violate the assumption that public praise existed within the biblical horizon. As Mather expressed the consensus: "such a version of the Psalms as keep most close to the original were most of all to be wished for" (1721:5).

It was not the "matter" but the "manner" of psalmody that first caused controversy over sacred singing. The Puritans were heirs of a tradition of psalm tunes drawn principally from Louis Bourgeois's *Genevan Psalter* of 1562 and melodies composed in the seventeenth century by Thomas Ravenscroft and Thomas Playford for the "Old Version" of Sternhold and Hopkins. After 1690 the *Bay Psalm Book* included a small collection of these tunes with bass accompaniment, a limited but sufficient repertory for the metrical demands of the New England version (Foote:51–54). By the early eighteenth century, however, the performance of these tunes in congregations sparked calls for reform by the Boston ministerium. In 1721 Thomas Walter of

Roxbury decried the prevailing conditions in rhetoric echoed by his colleagues in a fusillade of inflamatory sermons and discourses. "The tunes . . . are now miserably tortured and twisted and quavered in some churches into a horrid medley of confused and disorderly noises" (2).

The critics agreed that the principal cause of this declension was "usual" or "customary" singing by the method of "lining-out." Puritan psalm singing was led by a precentor who read or intoned—"lined-out"—each line for the community to follow. While lining-out assured that the text was clear to worshippers, it inhibited disciplined singing and fostered a diverse oral tradition. Among the most important alterations of tunes were slowing of tempo, lowering of pitch, and variation of intervals. These encouraged improvised part-singing, "falling-in" to other tunes or fragments, and embellishment with such "quaverings, turnings, and flourishes" that, to Thomas Walter's ears, Usual singing sounded "like five hundred different tunes roared out at the same time" (2–5). Small rural churches especially struggled to meet their obligation to praise God and edify themselves by psalmody lacking tunebooks, trained precentors, and capable singers.

Usual singing, however, should not simply be dismissed as without musical virtue. Musicologists have proposed a "folk-psalmody hypothesis" according to which the very qualities that the Boston clergy rejected conveyed a powerful folk tradition that treated tunes as an "ideal melody, or melodic idea, which is responsive to the momentary dictates of feeling or verbal necessity" (Bronson:101). The appropriateness of such a style for congregational singing may well be questioned, as it was by Walter and others, but not its capacity to express the religious devotion of the individual singer.

To meet the liabilities, real or imagined, of Usual singing, the reformers advocated "Regular" singing, the discipline of musical literacy, part-singing, and cultivated performance. In 1721 two systems of Regular singing were published in Boston, Walter's *Grounds and Rules of Musick* and John Tufts's *Introduction to the Singing of Psalm Tunes*. These manuals introduced tunes in three-part settings and supplied instruction in the rudiments of theory, notation, and performance. Just as important, the reformers called for the organization of "singing schools" in towns and parishes conducted by trained precentors using the new tunebooks as texts for their students. With ministers of prestigious Boston congregations leading the way, Regular singing quickly took root in and around the city, typically through the agency of the new singing schools (Buechner).

The reformers provided a wide range of theoretical and theological arguments for their new measures. Joyce Irwin has identified several different strands in their position. One, represented by Thomas Walter and Thomas Symmes, established the legitimacy of art as an aid to worship on the ground of its inherent rationality. This view buttressed "a natural theology of music" based on "the Baroque musical doctrine of the affections, according to which the music was to give expression to, and produce in, the

listener the 'affections' (mental or emotional states) described in the text"
(181–85).

The other major line of theological defense, advanced by Cotton Mather,
also drew on the doctrine of affections to explain that holy emotions were
requisite to spiritually efficacious singing. In his 1721 treatise, *The Accomplished Singer*, Mather summarized his view in verse: "'Tis not the voice, but
the desire; / Not noise, but hearty love; / Not loud cries, but a soul on
fire; / That God's ear will approve" (1721:11). Mather was clear that his
stress on affections in worship did not remove the primacy of scripture,
though it did reorient the role of the text away from John Cotton's "teaching, admonition, and praise" to sustaining the religious emotions through
what he termed the "porismatic method": "That is, to fetch lessons out of
every verse, and then turn them into prayers; to form a note and a wish
upon every clause before us: for which the time of dilatation [breathing]
which we take in our singing affords usually sufficient opportunity. While
we do by the action of singing, put our minds into a due posture for it. We
should first hear what the Glorious God speaks to us, and then with fit echo's
of devotion give our consent and answer unto it" (1721:14–15). Mather's
"accomplished singing" seems to have included lining-out, during which the
singer was to sustain meditative focus on the text while preparing breath to
sing the line just heard.

Though the reformers agreed on the program for improving congregational song, their arguments were essentially improvised and they existed in
uneasy tension. Their very diversity illustrated the instability of New England
theology in the 1720s and its ripeness for protracted controversy. Indeed the
reformers' thought expressed polarities that would expand into fundamental
differences under the pressure of revival. One example was the problematic
character of the doctrine of the affections. The human emotions naturally
aroused by music were not necessarily those induced by the Holy Spirit in the
regenerate. The two varieties required a further theological rationalization
that Mather's generation was unable to provide. Regular singing showed the
potential for a theology of the affections, but it also demonstrated the central
dilemma of such a theology, namely, adequately to explain how the Spirit acts
through human emotions. The task was finally essayed in 1746 by Jonathan
Edwards's *Treatise Concerning Religious Affections*, but in a real sense it was
occasioned by the singing controversy twenty-five years earlier.

Another major issue concerned the relationship of music to text.
Symmes and Walter argued for the autonomy of music and its development
through human art into a medium of praise. Mather insisted on the primacy
of the biblical text as the divine source of valid worship. If either claim were
pressed too vigorously, it could encounter objections from the other. The
rationalism and humanism of Symmes and Walter and the pietism of
Mather in this sense prefigured precisely the Arminian and Evangelical lines
along which New England theology would fracture in the Great Awakening.

Human reason and ability would shortly be pitted against divine initiative and inspiration; the varied arguments for Regular singing showed not only the growing sophistication of late Puritan thought, but the ominous dangers of its increasing reach.

The manifestos of the Boston reformers did not simply reveal latent intellectual tensions, they provoked serious conflict in New England parishes between reformist ministers and traditional congregations. Laura Becker has recently interpreted the controversy as part of the clergy's effort "to preserve their elite standing and to enhance their profession" through the "perceived benefits for spiritual and cultural life" and "new opportunities for ministerial leadership" provided by Regular singing (90). The aggressive, even abusive, tone of their jeremiads against the declension of psalmody and the numerous church councils convened to resolve singing disputes supports this interpretation. But the evidence also indicates that congregations, and especially Usual singers in them, were hardly passive in the controversy. As the author of *A Pacificatory Letter About Psalmody* observed in 1724, "what is called the new or regular way of singing, has been introduc'd in some places peaceably and quietly. In other places essays to bring it in have been withstood and opposed; and great heats, animosities, contentions, have been occasion'd among Christians hereby" (2). In the mid–1720s New England congregations experienced conflict over Regular singing in much the same ways that churches a decade later divided, to the point of schism, over the competing claims of the revivalists and their opponents.

The causes of division were perhaps best revealed in *An Essay, by several ministers of the Gospel: For the Satisfaction of their pious and consciencious Brethren, as to sundry questions and cases of Conscience concerning the singing of Psalms*, a document drafted for one of the numerous church councils called to resolve the dispute. *Cases of Conscience*, prepared by three ministerial advocates of Regular singing, Peter Thacher of Boston's New North Church, John Danforth of Roxbury, and his cousin Samuel Danforth of Taunton, replied to seventeen questions propounded on the nature, practice, and implementation of Regular singing. On aesthetic and theological questions the authors followed the positions of the reformers, but they also addressed crucial issues in the sociology of singing reform: whether it was "lawful and laudable to change the customary way of singing" and how to deal with the recalcitrant (6). An examination of both questions and answers provides insights into the controversy at the parish level.

Thacher and the Danforths were asked whether the reformers "are endeavoring to bring in . . . superstitious ceremonies." This query suggests that traditional singers had appealed to the plain style of Puritan worship, implying that the innovations smacked of deviation, Laudian superfluity, or worse, Popery. The authors discounted the accusation as a calumny on the piety and learning of pastors and people and in turn accused customary singers of "degeneration . . . from the Right and Established rules of musical singing" (7). The singing controversy involved disparate views of history and theology, each party accusing the other of declension and faulty ecclesiology.

Much of *Cases of Conscience* was devoted to generational conflicts. "The younger generation, being the majority for number, and having clearest and strongest organs of voice for singing," the ministers observed, "will prevail in carrying on the music in singing of psalms everywhere" (8). But in deferential eighteenth-century New England society, to vest innovation with the young required extreme care. The authors insisted that Regular singing did not involve favoritism or preference toward the young. They instructed youth to avoid "all self-admiration, self-exaltation, vain ostentation, and boasting," and to observe "modest and respectful carriage to their Fathers in age." They sought to mollify older traditionalists with positions that "a man who sings very meanly and with many irregularities, is accepted of God while he knows no better" and that it was "possible for Fathers of 40 years old and upward, to learn to sing by rule" (9, 12, 19). But the harsh reality of generational conflict brought on by an alliance between ministers and youth seems to have prevailed in many congregations debating Regular singing.

A closely related question was that of women's participation in singing. The Apostle Paul had forbidden leadership roles to women, and customary singers apparently resisted reform on the ground that it entailed "teaching and admonishing" of the congregation by women. To the query, "May persons of the female sex be admitted to sing in the church," Thacher and the Danforths answered "undoubtedly they may and ought." Citing scriptural accounts of women saints who joined "the primitive gospel church" in hymn-singing, they concluded that "singing therefore belonged to them." *Cases of Conscience* rejected the claim that the Pauline injunctions applied to singing and argued the opposite view: "When women are commanded to keep silence in the church, they are restrained from being authoritative teachers . . . but not from being melodious singers there; and how can they which have the pleasantest voices answer it to God, who gave them, if they don't improve them?" (15–16). Regular singing clearly democratized Congregationalist psalmody and brought women their first significant liturgical role, but not without strong objections from traditional singers.

A particularly thorny set of problems involved noncommunicant members, those admitted under the Halfway Covenant of 1662 to participate in the social and moral community of the parish but not the Lord's Supper or congregational decisions (Pope). Thacher and the Danforths took a strict construction, denying that Halfway members "have any power of privilege of voting about singing in the church." Singing had become politicized, subject to change by vote in congregations where Halfway members often constituted a majority. To endorse Halfway rights in the matter of singing would open reformers to the charge of revisionism they so assiduously sought to avoid. Yet barring Halfway members did not imply protection of

Usual singing. *Cases of Conscience* insisted that "our longsome, undulating, quavering, uncertain way of singing" should not be "a term of communion," perpetually protected by the covenant vows of full members (11).

Yet noncommunicants typically included youth and women constituents of Regular singing. Seeking a new legitimation for reform, the ministers urged that "noncommunicants, yea unconverted persons, old and young, and children also be allowed to sing psalms in our churches." To defend such openness against the charge of profanation of the Sabbath, they defined psalmody as "a converting ordinance," a public means of grace as efficacious as preaching or prayer (16). Here the reformers trod on dangerous ground, employing the same terminology and interpretation as Solomon Stoddard of Northampton had in his controversial practice of "open communion," the admission of Halfway members and even the profane to the Lord's Supper. Stoddard and the Boston reformers claimed that making restricted liturgical acts available to all would kindle piety and bring revival. But it could be asserted with equal cogency that to open the sacred ordinances to the reprobate would quench the Spirit. This question of "converting ordinances" was highly controverted and in the Great Awakening the Stoddardian position decisively rejected by prorevivalists, led by Stoddard's grandson and successor Jonathan Edwards, who rejected the Halfway Covenant and demanded evidence of the New Birth as a criterion for communion.

While ministerial aggressiveness surely accounts for some of these patterns of controversy over sacred singing, the foregoing account suggests that so powerful a reaction embodied multiple causes and entailed differences amounting to subdivision of New England's religious culture. Social and cultural historians have distinguished between cosmopolitan and traditional styles in colonial America reflecting the differentiation of coastal, commercial urban communities from rural, subsistence settlements in the interior (Henretta). The Great Awakening was most powerful in the latter area, its opposition concentrated in the former. The singing controversy was an early manifestation of this cultural differentiation.

The geography of Regular and Usual singing supports this view. Cotton Mather in 1723 provided contemporary evidence of the growing cultural rift: "Tho' in the more polite city of Boston," he wrote to Thomas Hollis, "this Design (of Regular Singing) mett with a General acceptance, in the Countrey, where they have more of a Rustick, some numbers of Elder and Angry people bore zealous Testimonies against these wicked innovations, and this bringing in of Popery" (Foote:109). Laura Becker lists thirty-one ministers who supported Regular singing, the overwhelming majority of them from cosmopolitan towns of coastal Massachusetts. And in a review of two hundred town and parish histories, Alan C. Buechner has found twenty-six churches that adopted Regular singing before 1744, virtually all of them in prosperous communities on or near the coast or in the Connecticut Valley (118–19). This evidence describes a distributive pattern of Regular and Customary singing unmistakably aligned with cosmopolitan and traditional cultures, indicative of deep stylistic differences that would explode into society-wide religious upheaval in the Great Awakening.

The intensity of the singing controversy spread beyond Congregationalism on the eve of the Awakening, reopening a long-standing debate on the issue among New England Baptists. English Baptists had been divided between General or Six-Principle Baptists who rejected the use of text- or tunebooks, adhering to the principle that all singing proceed directly from the Spirit, and Particular or Calvinist Baptists who began to use original hymns in the 1670s. The issue remained unresolved in England and America when in 1725 Valentine Wightman, a Particular Baptist minister at Groton, Rhode Island, endorsed "singing together by rule," with "a plea for a long neglected Ordinance, to wit, that of singing Psalms, Hymns, and Spiritual Songs" in *A Letter to the Elders and Brethren of the Baptised Churches in Rhode-Island, Narrhagansit, Providence, and Swansy; and Branches Dependent in Places Adjacent.* Wightman rested his case on the moral obligation of human beings to give praise to God as a "universal or perpetual rule to all that are capable of it." He argued that singing was a duty for all people, not only for Christians. "All men are under some law to God," he wrote, and therefore even "swearers, liars, drunkards, and whoremongers" bear responsibility to give praise in response to the First Commandment (4-6).

The thrust of Wightman's *Letter* was to preempt the General and Six-Principle Baptist interpretation of Colossians 3:16 that true praise was "singing mentally in their hearts, without their voices." But his efforts appear rather to have stimulated a reaction from these traditionalists, who found a champion on the eve of the Great Awakening in John Hammett of Warwick, Rhode Island. In his 1739 tract, *Promiscuous Singing No Divine Institution,* Hammett rejected Regular singing as a "lifeless custom" and condemned the mixing of men with women and saints with sinners in song. He taught that "the confused bawling noise of rash and inconsiderate mixed multitude" (iii) was "not according to David's musical institution, nor acceptable worship to God" (i). He argued against mixed-gender singing on the ground that in Regular singing "the women are all teachers and admonishers of the men" and hence violate St. Paul's "principle, that women ought not to teach in the church" (28). In his peroration, Hammett drew an inspirational criterion for church song and denounced human art as altogether without validity as worship of Almighty God. Here Hammett completely reversed the logic of Mather and Wightman, urging Christians to

> impartially examine themselves, whether they really feel and sensibly
> experience the living inspeaking word of Christ, and the grace of God,
> to dwell in their hearts, to qualify, excite, and direct them to sing; and
> that they are not exhorted by the Apostle to make a melodious or
> harmonious noise, to please the ears, or gratify the carnal humour of
> men, but solemnly, religiously, and devoutly to sing to the King of

Kings, and Lord of Lords, the dread of nations, who minds not, nor is pleased with the musical melodiousness or harmoniousness of the voice, . . . nor Fiddlers tunes. (28–29)

As the Great Awakening began in the mid-1730s, New England's churches had been riven by more than fifteen years of endemic conflict over the manner of sacred singing. It had divided the Congregationalist and Baptist communions, setting generations and genders, pastors and people against each other. It had raised serious constitutional questions that revealed weaknesses in the governance of the Halfway Covenant and exacerbated the rift over the right definition and employment of church ordinances. The controversy had produced more than a dozen published polemics in which deep theological tensions between human and divine agency, reason and affection, and biblical and ecclesiastical authority had emerged. And the dispute had cast into religious terms the growing polarization of New England society into cosmopolitan and traditional subcultures. It was in these many ways a rehearsal for the permanent fracture of New England religion effected by the Awakening itself.

II

The Great Awakening swept the American colonies from 1734 to 1745, bringing highly charged experiences of "the New Birth" and bitter internecine conflict to Congregationalist, Baptist, and Presbyterian churches from Maine to Georgia. The distinctive features of the revival included itinerant preaching, mass meetings, protracted services, charismatic manifestations, and spiritually heightened singing. This powerful religious movement permanently changed "the matter and manner of sacred singing" among these communions. The itinerants, led by George Whitefield, Gilbert Tennent, and James Davenport, were singing evangelists. And through their catalytic influence Evangelicals exchanged their tradition of singing psalms for the performance of new poetic genres of "human composure" through a diversity of musical styles.

The evangelists instilled the habit of singing hymns and spiritual songs in converts as a liturgical expression of their religious experience. And the texts they supplied were preponderantly those of Isaac Watts (1674–1748), the English Congregationalist minister whose poetry, educational and devotional writings, and advocacy of revival rank him among the most important Anglo-American religious leaders of the eighteenth century. In 1707 Watts published *Hymns and Spiritual Songs*, the first systematic collection of original hymns in English, containing among its three hundred sixty-four poems some of the most popular and enduring religious lyrics in the language: "When I Survey the Wondrous Cross," "Alas! And Did My Saviour Bleed?" and "When I Can Read My Title Clear." Twelve years later he capped his poetic career with *The*

Psalms of David Imitated in the Language of the New Testament, which included such notable poems as "Jesus Shall Reign Where'er the Sun (Psalm 72)" and "Joy to the World (Psalm 98)" (Benson:108–22).

Watts's sacred poetry did not gain immediate acceptance—even Cotton Mather resisted its employment in public worship (1721:6)—but in the Awakening itinerants found that singing Watts's hymns was a highly effective means to stimulate receptivity to the operations of the Holy Spirit. George Whitefield, the greatest of the itinerants, introduced Watts to revived churches and ministers throughout America in his immensely popular revivals from 1738 to 1770. At Northampton, Massachusetts, for example, Jonathan Edwards—at Whitefield's urging—began using Watts in his services during 1741; within a year he reported that his people "sang nothing else, and neglected the Psalms wholly" (Foote:147–49). In this manner the introduction of Watts to America followed the course of revival, aided by Whitefield's *Hymns for Social Worship* of 1753, in which "the hymns of Watts predominated" (Benson:319). Whitefield's fellow itinerants joined him in spreading the popularity of Watts to the revived Evangelical constituencies: Edwards to New Light Congregationalists and James Davenport to Separate Congregationalists in New England, Shubael Stearns and Daniel Marshall to Separate Baptists, and Gilbert Tennent and Samuel Davies to New Side Presbyterians in Pennsylvania, Virginia, and the Carolinas, and John Gano to Particular and Regular Baptists from Providence to Charleston.

The textual transformation was usually not as swift as at Northampton: the irregular pace of change was governed at the congregational level by local liturgical circumstance and incidence of revival. But by the Revolution the prorevival majority of the American Calvinist churches had embraced Watts, and by 1800 his psalms, hymns, and spiritual songs had become the canon of Evangelical praise. Such was Watts's popularity that he was the most widely-published and read writer in eighteenth-century America. Before 1800, *The Psalms of David Imitated* had appeared in seventy-four American editions—the most for any work in the century—*Hymns and Spiritual Songs* in thirty-four, and his children's hymnal *Divine Songs Attempted in Easy Language* in fifty-two (Heard:103–88). Also to be included in any assessment of Watts's American popularity is the circulation of British hymnals like Whitefield's which was reprinted thirty-six times in England between 1753 and 1796 (Benson:319).

Watts was a powerful advocate of revival whose poetry reflected a new experiential theology of praise that broke the biblical constraints of Puritan song. He traced the indifference of church singing to "the Matter and Words" of the Psalms "to which we confine our songs." He took the position that "the first and chief intent" of praise was "to speak our own experience of divine things" and in this claim he reversed the relationship of text to religious affections held by Cotton Mather (15). Whereas Mather had insisted that the psalm text be recited to form the worshipper's emotions, Watts argued that regenerate affectional responses themselves should constitute hymnic language. *Hymns and Spiritual Songs*, each lyric a homiletic meditation on a scripture passage or doctrinal subject, embodied Watts's program. The Psalms presented the more difficult problem of how Old Testament texts should be modified in accordance with current manifestations of the Spirit. His answer was to "imitate" them "in such a manner as we have reason to believe David would have composed them had he lived in our day" (13). To achieve his "renovation of psalmody" Watts developed a poetic style based on clear meanings, regular meters, and simple rhyme. "The metaphors are generally sunk to the level of vulgar capacities," he explained, "I have aimed at ease of numbers (meter), and smoothness of sound, and endeavored to make the sense plain and obvious" (128–29). The vast popularity of his lyrics during and after the Awakening attested the success of his execution. For thousands of revived Congregationalists, Baptists, and Presbyterians in America, Watts had given voice to the New Birth and the piety that flowed so powerfully from it.

Resistance to Watts came from the most traditional constituencies in each communion: ethnic Scots Presbyterians in Pennsylvania, Rhode Island's General and Six-Principle Baptists, and Strict and Separate Congregationalists in rural eastern Connecticut. Opposition took two very different forms, however, reflecting the extreme impact of the revival in rustic areas. Antirevival Baptists and Presbyterians attacked both Watts's poetry and his theology, insisting with Associate Presbyterian leader William Marshall of Philadelphia that biblical texts "which the Holy Ghost had indited, and not human composures, should alone be the subject of our praises" (23). Six-Principle Baptist John Hammett demanded the spontaneous inspiration of the Spirit for true "singing in the heart" and concluded that by such standards "the far greatest part" of worshippers "would not find themselves to be thus qualified and excited to sing" (29). As for the new poetry, "singing rhymes before and after sermon," he fumed, "it seems to be the height of dead formality and superstitious imitation" (27).

From the other end of the Evangelical spectrum, James Davenport's Separate Congregationalists, radical schismatics from New England's established church, claimed precisely the gift that Hammett had required: poetic inspiration of the Spirit obtained through the experience of the New Birth. In rural congregations where Davenport's movement was most powerful, traditional Puritan psalmody and its legitimation of original "occasional songs" had been best preserved before the Awakening. And as Davenport's preaching brought dramatic conversions, the awakened saints exercised their charisma in new and often spontaneous hymns and songs of praise. Davenport's own "Song of Praise for Peace of Conscience" (1742) initiated the publication of original American Evangelical hymn lyrics. Davenport was familiar with Watts and imitated the British Independent's style in voicing the revived spirituality of praise: "Where God doth dwell, sure heaven is there. / And singing there must be: / Since Lord, thy presence makes my heaven, / Whom shall I sing but thee?" (5). The habit of using original and locally-composed hymn texts was transmitted from the Separates to their successors the Separate Baptists, who by 1766 had published the first American Baptist hymnal at Newport and whose farmer-preacher missionaries had spread their rich mixture of original "spiritual songs" and Watts south and west as far as the Shenandoah Valley and the Carolina Piedmont. A succession of American Evangelical hymnists soon appeared including Baptists Anna Beaman and John Leland, Congregationalists Joel Barlow and Timothy Dwight, and Nova Scotian Separatist Henry Alline. These writers and their British Evangelical counterparts, including Anne Steele, Samuel Stennett, Phillip Doddridge, John Newton, and Charles Wesley, created a large corpus of hymns and spiritual songs that by 1790 had been anthologized and often bound together with standard editions of Watts (Benson:161–204). Watts had provided the new religious language needed to give the Great Awakening adequate liturgical expression in song. His followers developed his literary models and style into an ongoing tradition of poetic expression that has given continuous voice to the Evangelical experience in America since the Revolution.

As the Great Awakening transformed the language of church song, so it generated new music and performance styles across the range of American Calvinism. Again the Separates made the widest departure from traditional practice. The Separates were most numerous precisely in those "rustick" areas of central New England where Customary singing had remained most firmly entrenched and Regular singing most stiffly resisted (Goen). James Davenport's powerful evangelism and personal example loosed the gift of charismatic song among his converts. Davenport led processions of singing followers through the streets of eastern Connecticut towns on their way to his meetings. He was repeatedly arrested for this act of public disorder, which caused "shock and surprise on persons' minds," according to Jonathan Edwards. Edwards himself, though given to moderation on liturgical matters, gave careful approval to street-singing: "If a considerable part of a congregation have occasion to go in company in singing praises to God, as they go," he wrote, "I confess that after long consideration and endeavoring to view the thing every way . . . I cannot find any valid objection against it" (1971:491).

At Davenport's protracted meetings he harangued followers, demanding charismatic manifestations including spontaneous singing as signs of the New Birth. Antirevival Old Lights, led by Charles Chauncy of Boston, condemned the charismatic style as "enthusiasm": "The disorder of Exhorting, and Praying, and Singing, and Laughing in the same house of worship," Chauncy complained, "whatever the persons, guilty of such gross irregularity may imagine, and however they may plead their being under the influence of the Spirit, . . . 'tis evidently a breach upon common order and decency; yea, a direct violation of the commandment of God" (1742:14). Regardless of theological evaluation, it is clear that Separate meetings were indeed spontaneous and "disorderly," and that their songs were improvised musical expressions combining inspirational lyrics with popular and folk tunes. At a Durham, New Hampshire meeting, for example, "one Hannah Huckins . . . broke out into exclamation, Blessed be the Lord, who has redeemed me, Glory, glory, glory, etc. fell to dancing around the room, singing some dancing tunes, jiggs, minuets, & kept the time exactly with her feet. Presently two or three more fell in with her" (Pichierri:52–53).

From such evidence musicologists have concluded that while the Awakening "was not consistent with the performance requirements of carefully measured, precisely harmonized psalm tunes . . . it was in keeping with the common way of singing" (Buechner:335). Such a claim overgeneralizes on two counts. First, though indeed the Separates do not seem to have been Regular singers, the charismatic song of their meetings was not simply customary: the revival was a potent stimulus to include popular and folk tunes, with faster tempos and dance rhythms, into the rather staid repertory of traditional psalmody. Second, the Separates were not the only revived constituency in New England. The Awakening created a tripartite division among Congregationalists in which Separates and Old Lights occupied the extremes while moderate prorevival New Lights, led by Jonathan Edwards, were the largest faction. And in New Light parishes, like Edwards's at Northampton, Massachusetts, revival appears to have enhanced singing without bringing aesthetic disorder. "It has been observable," he wrote, "that there has scarcely been any part of Divine worship, wherein good men amongst us have had grace so drawn forth, and their hearts so uplifted in the ways of God, as in singing his praises. Our congregation excelled all that I ever knew in the external part of the duty before, generally carrying regularly and well, three parts of music, and the women a part by themselves. But now they were evidently wont to sing with unusual elevation of heart and voice" (1972:405–6). Regular singing had preceded the revival in cosmopolitan towns of the Connecticut Valley and in cases like Northampton, "abounding so much in singing" had reinforced both musical skills and the spirituality of song.

In rural New Light churches, too, this combination of spiritual and aesthetic quickening seems to have enhanced rather than retarded the cause of Regular singing. One example of this pattern appeared at Kingston, New Hampshire, where Joseph Seccombe, a young Congregationalist moderate, wrote *An Essay to excite a Further Inquiry into the Ancient Matter and Manner of Sacred Singing* in 1741. Responding positively to the early stages of the revival, Seccombe exhorted his readers to "cherish and give in to the divine rapture, to which the Spirit induceth" in their praise of God. Echoing Mather and Edwards on the compatability of religious affections and musical art, he taught that "the greater variety we have of tunes sung in a serious and regular, sweet and solemn manner, the more is the devout soul raised in rapturous joy, or melted into ingenuous grief, or otherwise moved agreeable to the manner of the Psalm" (2, 11).

Meanwhile in coastal Massachusetts and Connecticut, where Old Lights rejected the revival but accepted Wattsian poetics, Regular singing and singing schools continued to flourish and expand. Buechner lists seven towns that established Regular singing between 1739 and 1747, one-fourth of the total number to the latter date (118–19). Among Baptists, the forces of revival swept Particulars in New England and the Middle Colonies and Regulars in the South, again to the advancement of congregational singing. In 1742 the Philadelphia Baptist Association adopted a new confessional article that largely endorsed the position of Valentine Wightman fifteen years earlier: "We believe that singing the praises of God, is a holy ordinance of Christ, and not a part of natural religion, or a moral duty only; . . . and that the whole church in their Publick Assemblies . . . ought to sing God's praises according to the best light they have received" (83). After 1745 Separate Congregationalists in New England merged with Particular Baptists to create the Separate Baptist movement, which quickly spread its enriched folk-psalmody to the Middle and Southern colonies. And prorevival New Side Presbyterians matched their embrace of Watts with an increased concern for Regular singing. A clear instance of this interest was the publication in 1762 of James Lyon's *Urania, or a choice Collection of Psalm-Tunes, Anthems and Hymns*, "the most elaborate book of church music" to appear in America before 1770. Lyon was a New Side minister and his subscribers included "prominent Presbyterian clergy and laymen in Philadelphia and elsewhere" (Benson:18).

The Great Awakening stimulated new textual, musical and stylistic diversity of singing among Evangelical Calvinists in America. This transformation might best be conceived as the replacement of two sharply divided alternatives—Regular and Usual singing—with a new spectrum of texts and musical styles. On one end of this spectrum, Regular singing in cosmopolitan congregations was enhanced by the greater singability and expressiveness of Watts's hymnody. On the opposite end, antirevival Presbyterians and Baptists clung to their traditional Psalter texts and tunes. Between these two poles, which roughly corresponded to Regular and Usual singing, lay the great majority of Evangelical song in the Awakening.

New Light Congregationalists and New Side Presbyterians quickly embraced Watts, and, more important, the notion that singing could serve as a legitimate stimulus and manifestation of the New Birth. In cosmopolitan areas like the Connecticut and Delaware Valleys, these churches found that the techniques of Regular singing and the gifts of the Spirit in worship were mutually reinforcing. In rural New Light parishes the self-validating effects of cosmopolitan churches and revitalized singing removed traditional resistance to part-singing and musical art. This crucial change among the rural majority of the Evangelical movement was most visible among Separates and Separate Baptists, who had been the most tenacious in their embrace of Customary singing. The revival produced charismatic song among them, sweeping away the reserve of traditional singing and admitting new inspirational texts and popular tunes. Any given congregation in revival fused new texts, tunes, and musical styles in a pattern specific to its own religious traditions and cultural context. But out of this complex process the form, content, and indeed the very concept of praise in America had been transformed by the eve of the Revolution.

In addition to the pivotal role of the itinerants, three further structural dimensions of this complex process should be noted. First, women and youth remained the prime social constituency of renewed singing in the revival as they had been in the Regular singing controversy. Charles Chauncy observed that in the worship of Separates "'tis among children, young people, and women" that charismatic singing and dancing "chiefly prevail" (1743:105). Edwards and Hammett also noted the importance of these groups in the religious quickening and its musical consequences. The openness and participatory character of congregational singing seems to have made it the most accessible public dimension through which these restive constituencies could legitimate their spiritual equality as their patriarchal communities underwent revival.

Second, the diachronic and synchronic patterning of change in sacred singing was complex and irregular. The acceptance of Watts, for example, was slower among Presbyterians and Baptists than Congregationalists; the abandonment of Usual singing occurred at different rates among New Lights, New Sides, and Separate Baptists, and such rural congregations could remain in a transitional state of folk-psalmody for several generations. In 1771, for example, Zabdiel Adams was still defending Regular singing against traditional objections of Customary singers in the Congregationalist parishes of Lancaster, Massachusetts, only fifty miles west of Boston (29–37). And the numerous Separate Baptist converts gathered by the Shakers in the 1770s and 1780s in rural New England may have transmitted their style of charismatic singing to the new sect (Marini:88–95).

A critical element in this differential appropriation of Regular singing among Evangelicals was the fact that while the Awakening provided a new textual consensus with Watts's hymnody, it did not generate a correspondingly comprehensive musical style. This need was not supplied until William Billings, Oliver Holden, Daniel Read, and other New England composers began to produce powerful choral settings of hymns in a distinctive native musical idiom after 1770. Not surprisingly, Watts was the favorite poet of these and later compilers and composers whose tunebooks, beginning with Billings's *The New England Psalm-Singer* of 1770, and whose singing schools completed the triumph of Regular singing in Evangelical churches by the early nineteenth century.

Finally, the renewal of sacred singing in the Awakening fostered theological redefinition of church song. The latent tensions within the Boston
reformers' positions in the 1720s gradually differentiated into rival schools of
theological interpretation by the 1770s. In and around Boston, antirevival
Old Light ministers drew increasingly on the rational, moral. and natural
grounds of sung praise, echoing the arguments of Symmes and Walter in the
Regular singing controversy. Jonas Clarke of Lexington found "the Use and
Excellency of Vocal Music in worship" to be "clearly deduceable, by the
light of reason" (7). Zabdiel Adams carried aestheticism so far as to interpret
St. Paul's "singing with grace in our hearts" to mean "that we should sing
gracefully, and in a manner acceptable to others; and secondly, that we
should sing with grateful minds" (19). Oliver Noble of Newbury interpreted
church music through the characteristic Old Light theme of God's goodness
to humanity in creation: "that the blessed God, the author of nature . . .
should be worshipped . . . by all intelligences, is founded in the moral and
unchangeable fitness of things, and belongs to the religion or law of nature; and
will remain binding upon all moral beings, as long as the relation of Creator
and creature subsists" (3).

Evangelicals, by contrast, understood sacred song through the theology
of religious affections expounded by Watts, Mather, and Edwards. The task
of formulating an affectional theory of praise fell to one of the leading
New Side Presbyterian inheritors of this intellectual legacy, Samuel Blair of
Neshaminy, Pennsylvania. In his 1789 *Discourse on Singing*, Blair described
"an intimate connection between sounds . . . and the sentiments of the heart,"
through which "the foundation is laid in our nature for the moral operation of
external harmony" (11–12). Sacred music, according to Blair, "forms us into
the same kind of inward frame . . . into which we should have been brought
by moral affection itself," and thereby "that feeling which, in its first
appearance, was merely the result of musical impulses, hath now become a
real, effective, and profitable sentiment" (12).

Sound alone, however cannot provide "the real perception" of "moral
and religious objects." This comes to the reborn soul through the words of
the text, which "address the heart and the understanding . . . to create in the
mind a heavenly sweetness and ardor, and rekindle the spirit of duty and
devotion" (19–20). It is in the union of these religious affections—the
"inward sentiments or knowledge of the heart"—and the musical affections
generated by the "moral operation of external harmony" that the divine
beauty of true worship becomes manifest "in a kind of celestial rapture"
(20). In this analysis Blair applied Edwards's complex explanation of regenerate emotions in his 1746 *Treatise Concerning Religious Affections*
directly to the problem of sacred singing and concluded that it was the
audible sign of the Spirit's presence in the reborn soul.

Sacred singing was a central liturgical feature of colonial America's
Calvinistic churches that manifested important aspects of religious change

before, during, and after the Great Awakening. The Regular singing controversy of the 1720s revealed deep theological, sociological, and cultural tensions in the Congregationalist and Baptist communions that in the revival would become permanent lines of fracture in New England. The dispute between Regular and Customary singers announced the cultural disintegration of Puritanism. The Awakening included spiritually heightened singing as a distinguishing mark of regeneration and thereby fostered the development of new musical styles. Radical Separates claimed charismatic operations of the Spirit to incorporate popular, folk and dance tunes into their improvised inspirational song, while more moderate New Lights and New Sides practiced Regular singing with renewed "elevation of heart and voice" (Edwards, 1972:151).

Cutting across all musical styles of nascent Evangelicalism, Isaac Watts's new "language of the soul" eventually replaced traditional versions of the Psalter even among conservative congregations. Watts's "human composures" also kindled a lasting Evangelical tradition of original hymns and spiritual songs that supplemented and sometimes eclipsed the Wattsian canon. After 1770 these texts acquired an indigenous musical style provided first by New England composers and later by cosmopolitan and rural singing-masters to the south and west. Multiple settings of the new texts in vigorous four-part harmony lent the stability of fixed musical form to the burgeoning tradition of Evangelical hymnody. Accompanying the synthesis of music and text, the new hymnody obtained theological interpretations which reflected the Evangelical and Liberal positions that shaped Protestant thought in the new nation. Sacred singing was neither an unimportant nor indifferent aspect of eighteenth-century American religion. Quite to the contrary, its universality and publicity made it perhaps the most sensitive of all religious media to the complex changes wrought by the Great Awakening in America.

REFERENCES

Adams, Zabdiel
1771   *The Nature, Pleasure and Advantages of Church Musick.* Boston: Richard Draper. Evans 11955.

Anonymous
1724   *A Pacificatory Letter About Psalmody.* Boston: J. Franklin for Benjamin Eliot. Evans 2457.

Baptist Church
1766   *Hymns and Spiritual Songs, collected from the works of several authors.* Newport: Samuel Hall. Evans 10233.

Becker, Laura L.
1982   "Ministers vs. Laymen: The Singing Controversy in Puritan New England, 1720–1740." *New England Quarterly* 55:79–96.

Benson, Louis F.
1962   *The English Hymn: Its Development and Use in Worship.*
                2nd ed. Richmond: John Knox Press.

Blair, Samuel
1789   *A Discourse on Psalmody.* Philadelphia: John M'Culloch.
                Evans 21695.

Bronson, Bertrand
1973   "The Interdependence of Ballad Tunes and Texts." In *The
                Critics and The Ballad,* edited by MacEdward Leach and Tris-
                tram P. Coffin. Carbondale: Southern Illinois University Press.

Buechner, Alan
unpub.   "Yankee Singing Schools and the Golden Age of Choral Music
                in New England, 1760–1800." Unpublished Ph.D. dissertation,
                Harvard University, 1960.

Chase, Gilbert
1966   *America's Music.* 2nd ed. New York: McGraw-Hill.

Chauncy, Charles
1742   *Enthusiasm Describ'd and Cautioned Against.* Boston:
                J. Draper. Evans 4912.
1743   *Seasonable Thoughts on the State of Religion in New En-
                gland.* Boston: Rogers and Fowle. Evans 5151.

Clarke, Jonas
1770   *The Use and Excellency of Vocal Music in Public Worship.*
                Boston: Nicholas Bowes. Evans 11601.

Cotton, John
1647   *The Singing of Psalmes a Gospel Ordinance.* London.

Davenport, James
1742   *A Song of Praise.* Boston: Rogers and Fowle. Evans 4929.

Davie, Donald
1978   *A Gathered Church: The Literature of the Dissenting Inter-
                est.* New York: Oxford University Press.
1982   *Dissentient Voice.* New York: Oxford University Press.

Davies, Horton
1961   *Worship and Theology in England from Watts to Maurice,
                1690–1850.* Princeton: Princeton University Press.

Delattre, Roland
1968   *Beauty and Sensibility in the Thought of Jonathan Edwards.*
                New Haven: Yale University Press.

Dwight, Josiah
1725   *An Essay to Silence the Outcry That has been made in some
                Places against Regular Singing.* Boston: John Eliot. Evans 2627.

Edwards, Jonathan
1948   *Images or Shadows of Divine Things.* Edited by Perry Miller.
                New Haven: Yale University Press.

1959   *Religious Affections.* Edited by John E. Smith. New Haven:
                Yale University Press.
1971   *Treatise on Grace and Other Posthumously Published Writ-
                ings.* Edited by Paul Helm. Cambridge, England: James Clark.
1972   *The Great Awakening.* Edited by C. C. Goen. New Haven:
                Yale University Press.

Escott, Harry
1962   *Isaac Watts, Hymnographer: A Study of the Beginnings,
                Development, and Philosophy of the English Hymn.* London:
                Independent Press.

Fairchild, Hoxie Neal
1939   *Religious Trends in English Poetry.* Volume I: *1700–1740,
                Protestantism and the Cult of Sentiment.* New York: Colum-
                bia University Press.

Foote, Henry Wilder
1961   *Three Centuries of American Hymnody.* Hamden: The Shoe
                String Press.

Goen, Clarence C.
1962   *Revivalism and Separatism in New England: 1740–1800.* New
                Haven: Yale University Press.

Hammett, John
1739   *Promiscuous Singing No Divine Institution.* Boston? Evans
                4366.

Harazsti, Zoltan
1956   *The Enigma of the Bay Psalm Book.* Chicago: University of
                Chicago Press.

Heard, Priscilla S.
1975   *American Music, 1698–1800: An Annotated Bibliography.*
                Waco: Baylor University Press.

Henretta, James
1973   *The Evolution of American Society, 1750–1815: An Interdis-
                ciplinary Analysis.* Lexington, Mass.: D.C. Heath.

Irwin, Joyce
1978   "The Theology of 'Regular Singing.'" *New England Quarterly*
                51:176–92.

Jackson, George Pullen
1933   *White Spirituals in the Southern Uplands.* Chapel Hill: Uni-
                versity of North Carolina Press.

Lowens, Irving
1964   *Music and Musicians in Early America.* New York: W. W.
                Norton.

MacKay, David, and Crawford, Richard
1975   *William Billings of Boston.* Princeton: Princeton University
                Press.

MacDougal, Hamilton C.
1940   *Early New England Psalmody.* Brattleboro: Stephen Daye Press.

Marini, Stephen A.
1982   *Radical Sects of Revolutionary New England.* Cambridge: Harvard University Press.

Marshall, William
1774   *The Propriety of Singing the Psalms of David in New Testament Worship.* Philadelphia: R. Aitken. Evans 13395.

Mather, Cotton
1701   *Magnalia Christi Americana.* London.
1718   *Psalterium Americanum.* Boston: S. Kneeland. Evans 1946.
1721   *The Accomplished Singer.* Boston: B. Green. Evans 2241.

Moody, Carole
unpub.   "The Music of the Puritans to 1740." Unpublished B.A. thesis, Marlboro College, 1980.

Noble, Oliver
1774   *Regular and Skilful music in the worship of God founded in the Law of Nature.* Boston: Mills and Hicks. Evans 13503.

Philadelphia Baptist Association
1743   *A Confession of Faith put forth by the Elders and Brethren of many congregations of Christians.* 6th ed. Philadelphia: B. Franklin. Evans 5124.

Pichierri, Louis
1960   *Music in New Hampshire: 1623–1800.* New York: Columbia University Press.

Pope, Robert G.
1969   *The Halfway Covenant: Church Membership in Puritan New England.* Princeton: Princeton University Press.

Schaff, Philip
1877   *The Creeds of Christendom.* Volume 3. New York: Harper and Brothers.

Seccombe, Joseph
1741   *An Essay to excite a Further Inquiry into the Ancient Matter and Manner of Sacred Singing.* Boston: S. Kneeland. Evans 4798.

Thacher, Peter; Danforth, Samuel; and Danforth, John
1723   *An Essay, by several ministers of the Gospel: for the satisfaction of their pious and consciencious Brethren, as to sundry Questions and Cases of Conscience concerning the singing of Psalms.* Boston: S. Kneeland. Evans 2485.

Todd, John
1763   *An Humble Attempt Towards the Improvement of Psalmody.* Philadelphia: Andrew Stuart. Evans 9524.

Walker, Williston
1893
The Creeds and Platforms of Congregationalism. New York:
Charles Scribner's Sons.

Walter, Thomas
1721
The Grounds and Rules of Musick Explained. Boston: J. Franklin. Evans 2303.

Watts, Isaac
1813
The Works of The Rev. Isaac Watts, D.D. Volume 9. Leeds:
Edward Baines.

Wesley, John
1780
A Collection of Hymns for the Use of the People Called
Methodists. London: John Mason.

Whitefield, George
1753
A Collection of Hymns for Social Worship. London: William
Strahan.

Wightman, Valentine
1725
A Letter to the Elders and Brethren of the Baptised Churches
in Rhode-Island, Narrhangansit, Providence, and Swansy, and
Branches Dependent in Places Adjacent. Boston? Evans 2719.

The Early Chishti Approach to Sama^c

Bruce B. Lawrence

Sama^c, or the practice of listening to music, posed a major challenge to Sufi theorists because its external decorum was more readily describable (and more easily violated) than its internal reality. To defend *sama^c* was to justify the supremacy of the love relationship over all other religious obligations, while at the same time acknowledging that both music and love and, indeed, every aspect of life had to be experienced within an Islamic worldview upholding the Qur'an, the Traditions of the Prophet and the rudiments of Muslim law, i.e., the *shari^cah*.

Sama^c as a theoretical issue, therefore, related to a paradox larger than itself: the paradox of a reciprocal relationship between the Divine Beloved, who was also the supreme Creator, and the human lover, who was but a humble creature. The ambiguity of the Beloved/lover relationship inevitably determined the parameters for the debate over *sama^c*. On what basis could a continuing and mutually reinforcing relationship be posited between the divine and the human? Its fundamental precondition was separation. Separation was mandated, for without separation there could be no love relationship, and yet separation was also minimized, for union was the ultimate goal of every Sufi adept, just as proximity to the Beloved was the constant refrain of medieval Muslim poets. The problem of separation was elaborated by Sufi theorists into two seemingly opposite approaches to the divine: *wahdat al-wujud* (the unity of existence; all is the One; the One is all) and *wahdat al-shuhud* (the unity of witness; all is from the One but is *not* the One). As Izutsu has demonstrated (1971:69f.), the two viewpoints are not as opposite as they first appear to be. The ontological unity of *wahdat al-wujud* underlies the phenomenological dyad of *wahdat al-shuhud*. Neither is, by definition, preclusive of the other./1/

Sama^c may relate to the spiritual progress of a Muslim mystic or Sufi adept in one of three ways: (1) it may be totally excluded as inappropriate to Islamic teaching—mystical or nonmystical (as in the case of the Mughal Shaykh Ahmad Sirhindi [d. 1624] and his sub-order, the Mujaddidiya Naqshbandiya) or (2) it may be accepted as a penultimate stage on the mystical ladder leading to ontological unity, i.e., perfection, or (3) it may be viewed as the top rung on the ladder, itself the ultimate mystical experience when properly pursued.

Among early Sufi theorists who predated the introduction of mystical orders into the Asian subcontinent, the debate on *sama'* revolved around the second and third approaches. Which valuation of *sama'* was to be accepted and why? For proponents of the second approach, music was related to the epistemological or phenomenological rather than to the ontological or metaphysical core of Muslim mystical experience. Music was said to help the lover in attaining the ecstasy derived from imminent union with the Beloved, but it itself was not thought to be coextensive with ecstasy. For the genuine seeker, music was intended to optimize the dyadic relationship between a human lover and a Divine Beloved. Because of the subtlety of verse as well as the waywardness of human emotion, however, the dyad could be (and sometimes was) misconstrued as the love of two human beings for one another, whether that of a man for a woman or a man for a boy or occasionally a man for another man. It was on this account that proponents of the second approach argued that *sama'* should not be made available to beginners, for if they incorrectly perceived its intent, they might be led to experience sensual delight instead of spiritual catharsis.

Those who supported the third approach had no such reservations. For them music was both the ontological and the epistemological *sine qua non* of Islamic mysticism. It not only helped the lover to attain a state of ecstasy in the presence of the Beloved, but it itself was integral to the ecstatic moment. According to this view, *sama'*, in the early stages, presupposed the dyadic relationship, but after a certain point (which varied depending on the theorist) it absorbed the human listener into the place of music till there remained only the song./2/ Guidelines governing the conduct of listeners were advocated but the risk to potential listeners was downgraded since the benefits of *sama'* were viewed as at once limitless in scope and also unobtainable by other means.

The variant emphases between (2) and (3) were major enough to spark a debate within the fold of Sufism. The debate would not have had far-reaching historical repercussions for the Sufi brotherhoods (*tariqas/silsilahs*), however, had *sama'* been only a matter of personal preference, a diversion randomly elected by individual Sufi masters. *Sama'* became influential because it developed into a recurrent congregational expression of Sufi mystical devotion. Verses were chanted in a corporate setting, in the presence of a group of like-minded men, all of whom were presumed to share the same lofty motives for convening to listen to what is termed "the beautiful voice" (*al-sawt al-hasan*). Though there are instances of isolated encounters between individual adepts and an ecstasy-inducing voice (Hujwiri:409–10), the technical word for Islamic mystical music, *sama'*, applies mainly to corporate performances for the spiritual benefit of a gathered group of Sufis. Rather than as merely "hearing," it ought to be defined as "hearing chanted verse (with or without accompanying instruments) in the company of others also seeking to participate in the dynamic dialogue between a human lover and the Divine Beloved."

It seems probable that *samaᶜ*, like many aspects of Sufism, was known as an occasional experience before it came to be justified as a normative, legitimate activity. The experience, moreover, was so contextual, depending on where, when, how and by whom it was heard, that reaction to it was mixed, and Sufi authors from an early date verbalize the Muslim community's hesitancy to espouse *samaᶜ*. Most of the classical theorists, in fact, seem to deal with the topic marginally and then only because it reflects a prevalent practice that cannot be ignored. Many of their arguments both pro and con have been reviewed by Mole in the first part of his monograph, *La Danse extatique en Islam*. Yet Mole's analysis is rife with random selectivity: he offers thematic continuity but not a holistic perspective. He alludes, for instance, to the importance of *Adab al-muridin*, a Sufi manual written by Abu Najib Suhrawardi, *ᶜAwarif al-maᶜ arif*, a similar manual by Abu Najib's nephew, Abu Hafs 'Umar Suhrawardi and *Misbah al-hidaya*, a summary Persian translation of *ᶜAwarif* by *ᶜIzz ad-din Mahmud Kashani (Mole: 184); yet he gives no quotations from these sources nor does he compare their contents with those of the works he does cite.

The implicit assumption of Mole's essay and also of most scholarship on Sufism is that the mystical trends established in the Nile-to-Oxus region, especially in the urban centers of *ᶜajam* or non-Arab Islam, persisted with greater or lesser influence in the outlying areas of the Islamicate tradition, including South Asia. Four Indian writers are cited by Mole as important theorists of *samaᶜ*: *ᶜAli Hujwiri, Gesu Daraz, *ᶜAli Hamadani, and Muhammad Nurullah. The last is a nineteenth-century Chishti author, whose work (*Naghma-ye *ᶜUshshaq*) I have never seen previously mentioned in any connection. While the other three are all important, by no means do they exhaust the list of early Indian Sufi authors who speculated about *samaᶜ*, some from an original perspective that marked a theoretical contribution different in tone as well as in content from their non-Indian Muslim predecessors.

It is the counterthesis of this essay that in the Indian environment from the period of the Delhi Sultanate through the Mughal era (1206–1857) *samaᶜ* assumed a unique significance as the integrating modus operandi of the Chishti order. The Chishti were the largest and most important mystical order or *silsilah/tariqa* among South Asian Muslims in the early Sultanate period, i.e., the thirteenth and fourteenth centuries. They forged the first authentic specimen of South Asian or Indian Islam, and it was they who adopted a distinctive attitude to *samaᶜ*: far from being an embarrassment to the Chishtis, as the literature sometimes suggests, *samaᶜ* was aggressively defended as an essential component of the spiritual discipline or ascesis incumbent on all Sufis. The Chishti espousal of *samaᶜ* also served a valuable practical function: it separated the Chishti saints from the Suhrawardiya, their major mystical rivals in the Sultanate era of Indian Islam, and also opposed them to the *ᶜulama*, those too comfortable spokesmen for official, i.e., government sanctioned, Islam. *Samaᶜ* became, if not the monopoly of the Chishtiya, the preeminent symbol crystallizing their position vis-à-vis other Indo-Muslim leadership groups.

Sama' also became Indianized. We would like to know more about the precise process of Indianization; for instance, the contribution of the noted fourteenth-century poet-musician-lay Sufi, Amir Khusrau Dehlavi. Though it was undoubtedly a multileveled phenomenon, only one aspect of *sama'* can be critically examined in the earliest phase of Indo-Muslim history (1206–1526): the literary testament of those Sufi authors, especially from the Chishti order, who defended the practice of mystic music and elaborated its significance for their fellow worshipers. Unfortunately, the popular, nonelite, mass sentiment in favor of *sama'* fell outside the scope of their enquiry: popularization suggested vulgarization, and for the Chishti theorists, as for most of the Indo-Muslim elite, vulgarization of any mystical institution, including *sama'*, was firmly resisted. Hence, we find but a few, random references to the popular dissemination of *sama'*./3/

Yet the literary legacy on *sama'* from the Delhi Sultanate Sufis of the Chishti order is itself enormous, diverse and informative. It consists of three kinds of writings: (1) independent essays on *sama'*; (2) chapters on *sama'* that appear in biographical accounts of saints (*tazkirahs*) or books devoted to theological enquiry; and (3) anecdotal references to *sama'* in the *malfuzat* or recorded conversations of major saints. Each category has its special value. Collectively they present a unique profile of *sama'* as it first functioned in a predominantly non-Muslim region.

There are two extant treatises on *sama'*, one in Arabic by a disciple of the foremost Chishti saint of Delhi, Nizam ad-din Awliya (d. 1325), the other in Persian by Sufi Hamid ad-din Nagauri (d. 1274), a successor to the first Indian Chishti shaykh, Mu'in ad-din Sanjari Ajmeri (d. 1233). Both *Usul as-sama'* and *Risalah-e sama'* contrast with one another but even more with the sole extant treatise from an early non-Indian devotee of *sama'*. *Bawariq al-ilma'* of Ahmad Ghazzali is a brilliant, independent work by one of the most influential Baghdadian Sufis who is just now beginning to receive the scholarly attention he deserves;/4/ it provides an important benchmark for assessing the contribution of Indian Sufi theorists to *sama'*.

Bawariq al-ilma' is an odd book: over one half of its pages are devoted to an elaborate apologetic of *sama'* that first examines, then refutes the arguments of its opponents (75–97), while the advantages and the distinctive features of *sama'* assemblies are assessed in comparatively less detail (98–118). Two aspects of Ghazzali's treatise are especially noteworthy for the emphasis they convey: (1) he argues that *sama'* "is necessary for the people of knowledge, perfection, serenity and union" while it is to be assigned (as a duty) for disciples and allowable as a practice for aspiring lovers: (2) in condemning those who oppose *sama'*, he offers as his decisive argument the example of universally acclaimed saints of the past who practiced *sama'*. Citing the *hadith* "He who is hostile to a saint of mine has come forth

against me in warfare," he points to Junayd, Shibli, Ma ͨ ruf Karkhi and
ͨ Abdallah b. Khafif as model Shaykhs who "went into ecstasies in audition
and danced to destroy from their hearts what was a part from Allah"
(A. Ghazzali:97–98). He concludes that one who opposes *sama ͨ* is hostile to
these saints and, therefore, to Allah, and such a person is *ipso facto* an
infidel!

In form, *Usul as-sama ͨ* of Zarradi and *Risalah-e sama ͨ* of Nagauri are
unlike the *Bawariq* of Ghazzali. *Usul as-sama ͨ* is defensive but rarely
polemical. It consists of an introduction and ten sections, each enunciating a
particular aspect of *sama ͨ*. The introduction separates the religious leadership of thirteenth-century Islam into three groups: legalists, traditionists, and
Sufis. Of the three, the Sufis are unabashedly declared to be the best and
their superiority is extolled with reference to a cryptic *hadith* (Zarradi:8–
10)./5/ Zarradi then sets forth a point by point consideration of *sama ͨ*: (1)
the reality of *sama ͨ* precludes a female vocal accompaniment (*al-qhina*) but
(2) depends on a beautiful male voice (*al-sawt al-hasan*) comparable to the
Prophet David's. Of musical instruments the reed pipe alone is forbidden by
the Prophet Muhammad's directive, while (3) the use of other instruments,
such as the drum and tambourine, is permitted by analogy to the Prophet's
example. (4) Since inspired verse comes from the Creator and heightens the
desire of the creature for the Creator, its use is not only permitted but
encouraged for Sufis of all stages. (5), (7), and (8) Numerous citations from
the Qur'an and the sound Traditions support both the beautiful voice and
recitation of verse but (6) it is necessary to establish the appropriate setting
in which *sama ͨ* is to be conducted. (9) Examples and quotations from early
saints, including Shaykh Nizam ad-din, in support of *sama ͨ* are not lacking,
and they indicate (10) that one of the chief effects desired in *sama ͨ* is
tawajud, which Zarradi defines as "graceful movement that voluntarily
emanates from the listener when he is overcome by *sama ͨ*." A detailed
discussion of *tawajud* ensues in section 10 of *Usul as-sama ͨ*. It elaborates the
saying from Nizam ad-din quoted in section 9. The great Shaykh had noted
that there were three kinds of listeners in *sama ͨ*: the *mutasammi ͨ*, the
mustami ͨ and the *sami ͨ* (all three of which mean "listener" in English but
have subtle differentiations of meaning in Arabic). The *mutasammi ͨ* hears
music due to the moment (*waqt*) of his spiritual awareness, the *mustami ͨ*
hears music due to the state (*hal*) of his spiritual progress, while the *sami ͨ*
hears music due to (the direct agency of) God (*al-Haqq*). Hence, concludes
Nizam ad-din, the characteristic of the *mutasammi ͨ* is *tawajud*, that of the
mustami ͨ wajd, and that of the *sami ͨ wujud* (Zarradi:52–53).

The homologies are suggestive though hardly novel either to Nizam
ad-din or to the Chishti order. The effect of their presentation in Zarradi's
treatise, however, is to link the experience of *sama ͨ* inextricably with *tawajud*,
wajd and *wujud* in the normative outlook of the Chishtiya. Zarradi also
systematizes the approach to *sama ͨ* hinted at by his Chishti predecessor

Hamid ad-din Suwall in *Risalah-e sama'*. The latter offers less an explanation of *sama'* than a meditation on its benefits. He begins by declaring that he hopes his treatise will prove to "be of use to the seekers of Truth, and enhance the ecstasy of the lovers of God, at the same time that it brings grief to the souls of disbelievers."/6/ Hamid ad-din then sets forth his own series of homologies: *sama'* and *wajd* are "wings of the spirit by which it takes flight till it reaches the Divine Presence." *Sama'* is the power of the heart of dervishes, the centrifugal force of those who are distraught, the focal point of those who witness to the Divine Decree. Or, again, it is an oceanic bird transporting lovers to the treasures which they seek. At the end of his brief essay, Hamid ad-din offers samplings of his own verse, repeatedly implying the interconnectedness of *sama'* and *wajd*. One couplet, for instance, reads:

> *Har wajd Ke az sama' hasil ayad.*
> *Zawqe ast Ke az Wahmi asayad.*
>
> Every ecstasy (*wajd*) that is derived from *sama'*
> Is a taste which relieves the soul of anxiety.

Zarradi gives no poetic citations, and his treatise has less charm than the lyrical *risalah* of the attractive farmer/saint from Nagaur. Yet Zarradi makes a novel and monumental contribution to *sama'* theory. He integrates the theme of *tawajud* with the experience of *sama'* in a manner that is distinctly Indian. He constructs a system out of the terse sayings of his *pir*, Nizam ad-din, and that system influenced numerous later Chishti theorists, including Mas'ud Bakk and Ashraf Jahangir Simnani.

Antecedent non-Indian theorists had also dealt with the categories of *tawajud, wajd*, and *wujud* and occasionally applied them to *sama'*, but in a tentative, often deliberately ambiguous manner. Only Ahmad Ghazzali had been an enthusiastic advocate of *sama'*. Abu Nasr Sarraj, Hujwiri, Qushayri, and Makki—all non-Indian except Hujwiri—concurred that *sama'* might be more dangerous than useful to a novice or beginner.

The issue is deeper than what the classical authors state on this or any other particular point relative to *sama'*. The major Sufi theorists have been honored and their works remembered long after their own time precisely because they were able to summarize numerous perspectives rather than to advocate only one view (their own) and suggest 'that it was binding on all Sufis. Yet the tone and arrangement of their several writings does reveal the true sentiments of the theorists themselves on the subject of *sama'*. Hujwiri, for instance, is often seen to be Indian because he died and was buried in Lahore. Yet he lived prior to the Sultanate period and his reflections on *sama'* are closer to the non-Indian than to the Indian, especially the Chishti, attitude. Hujwiri ably summarizes the several conflicting views toward *sama'* which were voiced by contemporary and earlier Sufis, but he severely criticizes sensual gratification through *tawajud* (Hujwiri:398). Moreover, when a contemporary Traditionist reports to Hujwiri that he had written a book on the permissibility of *sama'*, the Lahori shaykh replies: "It is a great calamity to religion that the Imam should have made lawful an amusement which is the root of all immorality." Still, he goes on to admit that he himself practices *sama'* (Hujwiri:402)! To the extent that he affirms *tawajud* Hujwiri is constrained by the well attested *hadith* of the Prophet, "When you recite the Qur'an, you should weep, and if you cannot weep, then you should try to weep" (Hujwiri:415–16). Elsewhere, however, he quotes approvingly the rebuke which he once received from a venerable Shaykh who indulged Hujwiri's desire for *sama'* and then told him: "A time will come when this music will be no more to you than the croaking of a raven. The influence of music only lasts so long as there is no contemplation, and as soon as contemplation is attained music has no power. Take care not to accustom yourself to this, lest it grow (to be) part of your nature and keep you back from higher things" (171). It is perhaps with the Shaykh's reprimand in mind that Hujwiri closes his section on *sama'* and concludes *Kashf al-mahjub* with a petitionary prayer requesting divine forgiveness for his sins of the past in *sama'* (420).

Almost despite himself, Hujwiri gives some of the claims made on behalf of *sama'* and for the first time links the topic of *sama'* to the discussion of *tawajud, wajd, wujud* "empathetic ecstasy," "ecstasy," and "finding (oneself in God)." It is the linkage of *sama'* to *tawajud* that made possible the later and distinctive Chishti contribution to *sama'* theory. A preliminary examination of the non-Indian theorists, Qushayri, Abu Nasr Sarraj, and the Suhrawardis, will highlight the speculative advances of the foremost Indian exponents of *sama'*, all of them belonging to the Chishti brotherhood.

Qushayri treats *tawajud, wajd,* and *wujud* independent of *sama'* in the section of his treatise concerned with technical terms; and while he does refer to *sama'* in the latter section, he fails to make mention of *tawajud, wajd,* and *wujud* in the section on *sama'*, except for the solitary cryptic aphorism: "*sama'* is the invitation, *wajd* the intention" (Qushayri:154). Qushayri also quotes some remarks that are openly critical of *sama'*.

Abu Nasr Sarraj, like Qushayri, is inherently hostile to *sama'* or at least dubious of its effects on beginners. He identifies all three groups of listeners; the first are the sons of truth (*abna' al-haqa'iq*), the second, the people of invocation(s) (*ahl al-munajat*), the third the isolated *fuqara'*, who, for him as for Qushayri, are "the nearest to God in peace" (Sarraj:288). One would expect that here, as in most triadic sequences of Sufi inspiration, the first is the least and the last is best. Both Sarraj and Qushayri do state that the last is, in fact, the best, but how are the *fuqara'* rated above the groups which precede them, especially since the first group are said to be 'Sons of truth' in direct contact with the Truth?

A later generation of Sufi theorists, including Abu Najib Suhrawardi, author of *Adab al-muridin*, and Abu Hafs Suhrawardi, compiler of *'Awarif*

al-ma'arif (which was later summarized by Mu'izz Kashani in *Misbah al-
hidayah*)/7/—all borrowed from Sarraj or Qushayri this same three-part
categorization of listeners. The Suhrawardis, despite their inclusive, synthe-
sizing minds, felt constrained—perhaps by their own experience, perhaps by
the dictates of community consensus—to suggest that *sama'* was a limited
and potentially dangerous experience. Their outlook is the more surprising
because, unlike Hujwiri, who was the disciple of a Shaykh disinclined to
sama', both Suhrawardis were direct spiritual descendants of Ahmad
Ghazzali. In *Adab al-muridin* Abu Najib gives the following description of
the three classes of listeners (Suhrawardi, 1975:63–64): "First there are those
who refer, when they are listening, to what is communicated to them from
the Real One (*al-haqq*). Then there are those who refer, when they are
listening, to what is communicated to them by means of their states, stations,
and moments of experience. The third class are the poor (*fuqara'*) who have
entirely detached themselves from worldly things; *sama'* is suitable for
them." Immediately he adds: "It is said that only one whose state is weak
needs the *sama'* (to arouse his spirit), but the vigorous one does not need it.
One of the Sufis said: 'How low is the state of a person who needs someone
to stir him! Upon my life, a bereaved mother does not need a mourner!'"

The implication of Abu Najib's juxtaposition of citations is that one of
the three groups of listeners is weak, or perhaps that all three are weak. In
either case, he offers less than whole-hearted support for the practice of
sama'.

His nephew, Abu Hafs, provides a novel twist to the same citation of
three groups of listeners. He quotes it in its entirety from Sarraj and adds
the qualifying phrase that the isolated *fuqara'* are not only the nearest of
people to peace but they are the best preserved from iniquity (*fitnah*) since
every heart which is contaminated with love of the world listens to *sama'*
(only) at the level of sensuality and affection (Suhrawardi, 1966:184–85).

In general, Abu Hafs' disinclination from *sama'* is milder than his uncle's.
He follows Qushayri in separating the explanation of *wajd* and *wujud* as
technical terms from the treatment of *sama'* as a Sufi endeavor. Yet he does
integrate the categories of *wajd* and *wujud* with his presentation of *sama'*, at
least to the extent that he can distinguish between spiritual states with rare
dexterity, as in the following passage (Suhrawardi, 1966:196–97): "Though
ecstasy (*wajd*) is the culmination of the spiritual state (*hal*) of the beginners, it
is a defect in the perfected ones because it signifies that they have reverted to a
state of *shuhud* ('witnessing') after they had already passed beyond it into the
state of *wujud* ('finding [God]'). In *sama'* the one who experiences ecstasy
wants to lose it because loss of the state of *shuhud* signifies the appearance of
the qualities of *wujud*."

Despite his sensitivity to the dynamic tension between *wajd* and *wujud*,
Abu Hafs is almost silent on the point of *tawajud*. Mu'izz Kashani, however, in summarizing this section of the *'Awarif*, takes the liberty to expand

its slim references to *tawajud*. He adds that *tawajud* may be a proper pre-
lude to *wajd*, since the Prophet had noted that those who cannot weep over
a recitation of the Qur'an should still try to weep (Kashani:135). Later he
states that *tawajud* is permissible for beginners though inappropriate to the
spiritual state of Shaykhs (Kashani:197). Kashani's assessment of *tawajud* is
more adequate than that of any other non-Indian classical theorist of Sufism,
but it is still brief, especially in comparison to his treatment of *wajd* and
wujud.

Ironically, *tawajud* becomes the pivotal technical term in distinguishing
between non-Indian and Indian theorists' approach to *sama'*. Unlike Qushayri,
Abu Nasr Sarraj, the Suhrawardis, and also Hujwiri (who, though Indian, lived
in the eleventh century), the Chishti authors of the Sultanate period (1206–
1526) to whose works we will now turn our attention, maintain that *tawajud* is
indispensable to the entire experience of *sama'* and ought to be emphasized as
much as *wajd* and *wujud*, even though the latter are technically "higher"
spiritual states.

How strange that the inspiration or justification for this new approach to
sama' comes from one of the most ambivalent advocates of musical assemblies, Qushayri! The saying which Zarradi attributed to Nizam ad-din concerning the three types of listeners (not to be confused with the three classes
of listeners just discussed) was a direct quotation from Qushayri, who in turn
had been quoting Abu 'Ali Daqqaq: "There are three types of people who
participate in *sama'*; the *mutasammi'*, the *mustami'*, and the *sami'*, etc."
(Qushayri:157–58). Elsewhere Qushayri discusses *tawajud* as the beginning
(of mystical experience), *wujud* as the culmination, and *wajd* as the inter-
mediary state (Qusharyi:34). What Nizam ad-din does is to conflate the two
texts, pairing each listener with an appropriate level of experience: the characteristic of the *mutasammi'* becomes *tawajud*, that of the *mustami'* *wajd*,
and that of the *sami'* *wujud*.

How do these extended definitions affect the Chishti theory of *sama'*?
Initially, it adds a new dimension to *tawajud*, as we saw in the outline of
Zarradi's tenth section of *Usul as-sama'*. But the fuller implications of
Nizam ad-din's gloss were worked out only after his death in other Chishti
writings, the principal focus of which was not *sama'* but either the speculative enquiry into several theoretical aspects of *tasawwuf* or the biographical
recapitulation of a particular saint's life and teaching. We will briefly examine
the chapter on *sama'* that appears in a representative work from each category: *Mir'at al-'arifin* of Mas'ud Bakk, written ca. 1378 A.D., and *Lata'if-e
Ashrafi*, compiled by Nizam Gharib Yamani at about the same time.

The former is one of the most brilliant and seldom recognized theological
essays from the hand of a fourteenth-century Indo-Muslim saint. Mas'ud Bakk
was a Delhi recluse of the Chishti fold who produced few successors but many
poems, together with some essays, before his execution by order of the regnant
Tughluq monarch ca. A.D. 1380. One of his essays is *Mir'at al-'arifin*. It

consists of 14 chapters covering all the major topics of Sufi speculative thought and corporate discipline. The thirteenth chapter treats *sama*ᶜ, with special reference to *tawajud, wajd*, and *wujud*. Though many medieval biographical writers laud the fourteenth and final chapter because of its subtle exposition of *ruh* (spirit), the thirteenth chapter of *Mir'at al-ᶜarifin* also marks an advance over any previous Indian essay on the topic of *sama*ᶜ.

Bakk begins by providing his own list of Qur'anic verses and Prophetic traditions that support the practice of *sama*ᶜ. Some of them overlap with scriptural references given elsewhere. Others are original to him. Like Hujwiri, he proceeds from a general description of hearing and its role in Islamic revelation to a particular exposition of the Sufi practice of *sama*ᶜ. His tone, however, is much more decisive than Hujwiri's: concerning the prophets, for instance, he argues that since none of them was ever deaf, they all, by their reception of revelation, attest to the legitimacy of *sama*ᶜ ("hearing") (160)! Nor does he hesitate to invoke the authority of past saints: in a manner reminiscent of Ahmad Ghazzali, he declares that many of the ancient Sufis participated in *sama*ᶜ and none of them ever denied its efficacy (162). He then goes on to elaborate the parallelism between melodies and the heavenly spheres, and declares that after one's musical sensitivities have risen to the orbit of Venus (the third of the seven planets in an ascending scale), there is no longer an experience of self: instead, through the remaining four orbits one "hears the word of God through God without letters or voice" (163).

In the central portion of his essay, Bakk tries to distinguish the different levels at which *sama*ᶜ is experienced. He condemns no group of listeners; he evaluates all of them according to their capacities, and he uses as his classical proof text in the Arabic language *al-Risalah al-Qushayriyah*. No less than six citations from both sections of Qushayri's handbook are set forth in Masᶜud Bakk's defense of *sama*ᶜ./8/ However, the tone is one that Qushayri would hardly have recognized or approved, and it is perhaps appropriate that Bakk, who is much better than most medieval authors in citing his sources, never once mentions Qushayri by name.

As with Zarradi, the critical aspect of Bakk's essay is the attention he accords *tawajud* as a threshold experience integral to *sama*ᶜ. Bakk links both *sama*ᶜ and *tawajud* to a third term, *hizzat*, which means for him both the physical shaking or agitation of the body and the spiritual state of ecstasy. He begins the final section of his chapter on *sama*ᶜ by stating that "whoever does not experience *hizzat* in *sama*ᶜ will never have the pleasure of seeing the face (of God)" (167). He then enumerates the three stages of *hizzat: tawajud, wajd*, and *wujud*. To legitimate his accent on *hizzat*, he quotes a *hadith* in which the Prophet Muhammad declares to his personal attendant: "O Muᶜawiya, no one experiences my kindness who is not agitated at hearing mention of the Beloved." The Prophetic tradition is reinforced by a saying from Shaykh Nizam ad-din, to the effect that every disciple in *sama*ᶜ should experience *hizzat* at the mention of his Beloved and if he does not, then his heart is certainly dead and his soul frozen.

Yet the levels of *hizzat* vary, as do the stations of mystical progress: that which appears in the body, according to Bakk, is *tawajud*, in the heart *wajd*, in the spirit *wujud*. The distinction cannot be pressed, though, since each of the three anticipates and/or is anticipated by the other two. After quoting the isolated dictum of Qushayri (*sama'* is the invitation, *wajd* the intention) (Bakk:168; Qushayri:154) to prove that *tawajud* invites *wajd*, even as *wajd* is intent on *wujud-e mahbub* (the existence of the Beloved), Bakk cites still another supporting passage from Qushayri: "*tawajud* is an uprooting, *wajd* a submersion and *wujud* a destruction of the self of the seeker. It is as if some one sees the ocean, then rides upon it and finally is drowned in it" (Bakk:169; Qushayri:34). In summation, he explains the successive stages of resolving, entering, witnessing, finding, and being extinguished (*qusud, wurud, shuhud, wujud,* and *khumud*), also from Qushayri, by deducing that finding lordship (*wujud-e rububiya*) causes the extinction of humanity (*khumud-e bashariya*). It is a dazzling display of mystical logic which ends, as do all of Bakk's chapters and most of his subchapters in *Mir'at al-'arifin*, with a verse (in this case, a quatrain) of his own composition appropriate to the theme under discussion (169):

> *Anku be-sama' dar tawajud ayad*
> *Wajdash ze-khoda ruye be-dil benamayad.*
> *Pas wajd su-ye wujud-e mahbub Kashad*
> *Anja chu rasad namord ba khud ayad.*

> Whoever in *sama'* anticipates ecstasy
> Ecstasy appears in his heart from God.
> Ecstasy draws him toward the realm of the Beloved,
> He arrives there but does not die; he enters himself.

The second Indian work to be considered is *Lata'if-e Ashrafi*. It is an enormous biography, which partly consists of the collected sayings, of the major Chishti saint of Eastern Uttar Pradesh in the late fourteenth and early fifteenth centuries, Sayyid Ashraf Jahangir Simnani (d. 1428). He was a man of diverse talents, who dabbled in magic as well as mysticism. He is remembered as a well traveled, highly esteemed saint who sought out the company of wise and famous and powerful men, from the local rulers of Jawnpur to the lyricist of Shiraz, Hafiz. He is even reputed to have once met the Mongol warlord Timur. His literary monuments are several. Two of them have survived: both *Miktubat-e Ashrafi* and *Lata'if-e Ashrafi* are frequently cited in medieval as well as modern works on Indo-Muslim mysticism. It is in the twentieth chapter of the *Lata'if* that his biographer, Nizam Gharib Yamani, collates the numerous observations of the saint on the practice of *sama'* (Yamani:45–69). The chapter is far more anecdotal and wide ranging than the corresponding chapter from Mas'ud Bakk's *Mir'at al-'arifin*. Yet both authors emphasize the beneficial aspects of *sama'*, including *tawajud*, and they boldly elaborate the Indian antecedents for participation in musical assemblies. The chapter in *Lata'if-e Ashrafi* is divided into three parts: (1) the explanation of proofs for the permissibility of *sama'*, derived from Qur'anic verses and Prophetic traditions as well as from the decisions of jurists and the deeds of "masters of guidance," i.e., early Muslim leaders; (2) the statements of Sufi theorists regarding the practice of *sama'* and the example of ancient Shaykhs (referred to as *al-kubara al-kamilin*); (3) guidelines for the conduct of *sama'*, including observations about the concurrence of "time, place, and brethren" as well as grounds for permitting the use of musical instruments.

The first and second parts of this chapter in the *Lata'if* are the most intriguing. The Sayyid begins by defining *sama'* as itself *tawajud*. The definition is not his own but one attributed to an anonymous saint: "*sama'* is the attempt (*tawajud*) of Sufis to understand the meaning which arises from different voices." Like all his predecessors, the Sayyid stresses that there are variant levels of understanding which correspond to the variant capacities (and intentions) of the listeners. He proceeds to give a three-part classification of listeners, but *not* on the model of Zarradi or Bakk; instead, he follows (with slight modification and without acknowledgment) the three categories of seekers first set forth by the thirteenth-century Chishti saint, Jamal ad-din Hansawi: (1) those who forsake this world and seek the next; (2) those who forsake the next world and seek this; and (3) those who forsake both worlds and seek only God (Yamani:45–46; also Hansawi:8–10). The last are obviously the preferred group, and it is to them alone that all the subtleties of *sama'* are revealed, but neither of the other two is to be excluded from musical assemblies according to the Sayyid. In considering the legality or illegality of *sama'*, he quotes a famous dictum of Shaykh Nizam ad-din, according to which the great Shaykh of Delhi states that *sama'* is neither absolutely forbidden nor absolutely permitted but dependent on what is heard and who is hearing (Yamani:46). Numerous quotations from both the Qur'an and traditions are then adduced to indicate that both the beautiful voice and the sung verse are a bona fide element of the Islamic tradition. Simnani's treatment is fuller and more systematic than Zarradi's: he even looks at Qur'anic verses which seem to prohibit *sama'* and "correctly" interprets them (Yamani:49). In addition, he cites the opinions of notable Traditionists, e.g., Muslim and Ahmad b. Hanbal, and the decisions of Hanafi jurists with reference to *sama'*. The latter are especially notable because they support the permissibility of not only *sama'* but *tawajud* for those who otherwise discharge their mandated Islamic duties (Yamani:50–53).

Having established the legal basis for musical assemblies, Simnani next reviews the statements of Sufi theorists concerning *sama'*. He makes brief reference to Makki, Imam Ghazzali, Abu Hafs Suhrawardi and Nizam ad-din before discussing at length the question also raised by Imam Ghazzali:

Why are Qur'anic passages inappropriate for chanting in *sama ͨ* (M. Ghaz-zali:132–48)? The principal point of the second part of Simnani's synopsis, however, concerns the authority for *sama ͨ* which has been established by the example of past saints. He mentions some of the same ancient Shaykhs extolled by Ahmad Ghazzali in the *Bawariq* (e.g., Shibli and Ma'ruf Karkhi) and even quotes the same *hadith*: "He who is hostile to a saint of mine has come forth against me in warfare." But Simnani adds three elements to his advocacy of *sama ͨ* that are not present in the *Bawariq*: (1) he extends the list of bygone saints who favored music to include Indian Shaykhs, viz., Qutb ad-din, Qazi Hamid ad-din, Farid ad-din and, of course, Nizam ad-din; (2) he describes these saints not merely as advocates of *sama ͨ* but as those who "experienced *tawajud* and danced" (Yamani:53–69); and (3) he recreates the condition and lauds the example of saints who died in *sama ͨ*, from Zu'l-Nun Misri and Shibli to Qutb ad-din Bakhtiyar Oushi and Ruzbihan Baqli Shirazi. It is an impassioned, protracted exposition of *sama ͨ*, with abundant references to classical authorities and frequent poetical citations, that we find set forth in the twentieth chapter of *Lata'if-e Ashrafi*.

One could undoubtedly explore the Chishti attitude to *sama ͨ* in further detail with documentation from other chapters of major authentic writings by Indo-Muslim saints and/or their followers. The foremost medieval Chishti *pir* of the Deccan, Gesu Daraz, has written extensively on *sama ͨ*; and, fortunately, his numerous statements have now been analyzed in a section of S.S.K. Hussaini's recent master's thesis at McGill University (140–219). Other writings still await the attention that is due them. For instance, the ninth chapter of *Siyar al-awliya*, the biography of Nizam ad-din, is replete with information that relates to every phase of the great Shaykh's attitude toward *sama ͨ*. It repeats arguments already set forth in Zarradi's *Usul as-sama ͨ*, but it adds biographical, often anecdotal, data that are early, presumably authentic, oral as well as literary, and conveys the flavor of Nizam ad-din's attractive spiritual outlook. It is also a lengthy essay, delving into nearly every aspect of *sama ͨ* that concerned the fourteenth-century Indo-Persian elite of Delhi.

Chishti approaches to music are exhaustively surveyed in the seventeenth chapter of a doctrinal handbook (or, better, encyclopaedia) written in the Deccan by a disciple of Burhan ad-din Gharib, himself a disciple of Nizam ad-din. Rukn ad-din's *Shama'il-e atiqiya* culls references from over twenty literary documents, Indian as well as non-Indian, some of them no longer extant, to describe "the meaning of chanting, the benefit of the beautiful voice, and the permissibility of poetry and ghazals, in accordance with the example of the Prophet and his companions." The *Shama'il* also discusses procedures for organizing musical assemblies and cites variant opinions about what is proper and improper conduct in such gatherings (R. Kashani:221–39). Less systematic but still valuable is the information about the *sama ͨ* experiences of both Suhrawardi and Chishti saints which can be culled from the vast *malfuzat* literature (Khurd:491–534).

The broadest canvas of the extant manuscript and lithograph works would probably confirm the major points already broached in this essay:

1. The theoretical approach to *sama*ʿ among Indian Sufis is related to non-Indian antecedents. At the most general level, it follows the Sufi penchant for triadic progressions and often distinguishes between classes of listeners with reference to commonly accepted authorities who cite the same classes. Both Indian and non-Indian theorists share a sensitivity to the differentiation of human capacities for participating in *sama*ʿ. Because they assume that gradation is a universally mandated religious phenomenon, the adequacy of their approach ought to be assessed in theoretical studies on mystical experience and the truth claims of mystics.

2. Not all non-Indian writers are sympathetic to musical assemblies, and even those who present evidence in favor of *sama*ʿ often express their personal antipathy to the self-indulgence (rather than divine *elan*) to which they feel immature listeners are prone. Among non-Indian classical Sufi authors Ahmad Ghazzali stands out as an unqualifiedly enthusiastic proponent of *sama*ʿ.

3. The essayists of the Chishti fold are more directly the heirs of Ahmad Ghazzali on the issue of *sama*ʿ than their Sultanate rivals, the Suhrawardiya, even though the latter were Ahmad Ghazzali's avowed spiritual successors. Nagauri, Zarradi, Bakk, and Simnani all champion the experience of mystic music for perfected Sufis as well as for beginners. Their advocacy of *sama*ʿ, moreover, is less defensive than that of Ahmad Ghazzali: instead of destroying the arguments of their opponents, as he had done, they delineate the benefits which, in their opinion, accrue to sincere participants in *majalis-e sama*ʿ (musical gatherings).

4. At the theoretical level, the sole but significant innovation of Indian essayists is the stress on *tawajud* as a normative, essential aspect of *sama*ʿ: for the Chishtis, every seeker on the path of *tasawwuf* was obliged to experience *tawajud* prior to attaining *wajd* and ultimately *wujud*. The intellectual possibility of integrating *tawajud* into *sama*ʿ was already present in *al-Risalah al-Qushayriyah*. Emotively, the two were associated with one another in Ghazzali's *Bawariq*. But it remained for Nizam ad-din and his successors to explicate the subtlety of *tawajud* as the threshold experience incumbent on all Sufi aspirants. The subsequent doctrinal development was not uniform: Bakk, e.g., subsumed *tawajud* (as well as *wajd* and *wujud*) under a new category, *hizzat* "agitation," while Simnani linked it to *raqs* "dancing." However, both positions as well as others not elaborated in this paper were consistent with the Chishti advocacy of *sama*ʿ as the pride or adornment of their devotion to inner—and sometimes also outer—poverty.

5. The legacy of the Chishtis was cumulative. Each generation built on the experience, and referred to the statements, of past generations of renowned saints. Ahmad Ghazzali had cited the examples of ancient Shaykhs as the unimpeachable, personal authority for his own participation in, and support of, *sama*ʿ. The Chishti essayists adopted a similar authority and extended it to

include their own saints, especially those who were martyred to love because of their attraction to verse chanted in musical assemblies.

The Indianization of *sama'* began with the Chishtis. Its tone, direction, and persistence were secured by the many talented Delhi saints who formed the inner circle of Nizam ad-din's entourage. Their writings mirrored the influence that the early Chishti attitudes were to have not only on their own devotees but also on Indo-Muslim Society as a whole, including the contemporary Suhrawardiya and later orders such as the Qadiriya and Firdausiya./9/ It is a signpost of the Chishtis' success that among Indian Muslims the wholesale rejection of *sama'* was not voiced—either as a theoretical desideratum or a practical requirement—till the advent of the Mujaddidiya Naqshbandiya in the late sixteenth and early seventeenth centuries.

NOTES

/1/   Using a more linguistically fixated approach than Izutsu, Mole (1965:59–62) has made the same point. See also the discussion in Schimmel (1975:267).

/2/   Mas'ud Bakk, discussed elsewhere, refers to an experiential state cosmologically linked to Venus in which the Sufi adept "hears the word of God through God without letters or voice," i.e., he hears but does not hear; there is a song but no singer (Bakk:162).

/3/   Most literary evidence for the role of *sama'* in disseminating Sufi beliefs through the Asian subcontinent derives from the Mughal period and later. See Eaton, 1974:117–27 and 1978:157–64.

/4/   H. Ritter, for example, edited the *Sawanih* from Istanbul in 1942, and N. Pourjavady of Tehran is hoping to complete an English translation, with commentary, of the recent Iranian edition prepared by Jawad Nurbakhsh (Tehran 1352 Sh.).

/5/   The reference is to *ihtiyar al-mazhab al-mu'ayyan*, i.e., opting for the fixed or rote doctrine, which Zarradi interprets as an approach disparaged by Muhammad, even though it was subsequently enthroned by traditionists and legalists, the Sufis alone having adhered to the spirit of the Prophetic mandate.

/6/   Nagauri, n.d., has been quoted in preference to Nagauri, 1963, because the former text seems to be the more plausible of the two.

/7/   Two important translations of both works have recently appeared. See Abu Najib Suhrawardi, 1975, and Abu Hafs Suhrawardi, 1978.

/8/   The pattern of citation is consistent without being either redundant or imitative: Bakk:164/Qushayri:155; Bakk:166/Qushayri:154, 158; Bakk:168/Qushayri:154; Bakk:169/Qushayri:34^2. The last two citations are especially significant since they reflect the innovative reinterpretation of *tawajud* advanced by the Chishti theorists on *sama'*.

/9/   See Lawrence, *passim*, but a continuation of the equivocal posture of Hujwiri and Qushayri vis-à-vis *sama'* may be found in Maneri:382–93.

REFERENCES

Bakk, Mas'ud
    1310/1891   *Mir'at al-'arifin*. Hyderabad: Mafid-i Dakan.

Dehlawi, 'Abd al-Haqq Muhaddith
    1283/1866   *Akhbar al-akhyar*. Delhi: Matba'-i Muhammad Mirza Khan.

Eaton, Richard M.
    1974   "Sufi Folk Literature and the Expansion of Indian Islam," *History of Religions* 14/2:117–27.
    1978   *The Sufis of Bijapur*. Princeton: Princeton University Press.

Ghazzali, Ahmad
    1938   *Bawariq al-ilma'*. Trans. by J. Robson, *Tracts on Listening to Music*, Oriental Translation Fund, N. Series XXXIV:63–184. London: The Royal Asiatic Society.

Ghazzali, Imam Muhammad
    1901   *Ihya 'ulum ad-din* (section on music). Trans. by J. B. Macdonald, "Emotional Religion in Islam as Affected by Music and Singing," *Journal of the Royal Asiatic Society*:732–48.

Hansawi, Jamal ad-din
    1306/1888   *Mulhamat*. Alwar: Matba'-i Yusuf.

Hujwiri, 'Ali
    1976   *Kashf al-mahjub*. Trans. by R. A. Nicholson. E. J. W. Gibb Memorial Series, XVII. Repr. London: Luzac & Co.

Hussaini, S. S. Khusro
    1976   "Sayyid Muhammad al-Husayni-i Gisudaraz (721/1321–825/1422) on Sufism," ch. III: Audition of Music (*Sama'*):140–219. McGill University M.A. thesis.

Izutzu, Toshihiko
    1971   "The Basic Structure of Metaphysical Thinking in Islam." In M. Mohaghegh & H. Lamdolt, eds., *Collected Papers on Islamic Philosophy and Mysticism* (Wisdom of Persia Series, No. 4), 40–72. Tehran: Tehran University Press.

Kashani, 'Izz ad-din
    n.d.   *Misbah al-hidaya wa miftah al-kifaya*. Ed. Jalal Humai. Tehran: Kitab Khana-i Sana'.

Kashani, Rukn ad-din ibn 'Imad
    n.d.   *Shama'il-i anqiya o-dala'il-i atqiya*. Persian ms., Maulana Azad Library, Aligarh Muslim University.

Khurd, Amir
    1302/1885   *Siyar al-awliya*. Delhi: Chirangi Lal Malik.

Lawrence, Bruce B.
  1978   *Notes from a Distant Flute: The Extant Literature of pre-Mughal Indian Sufism*. Tehran: Imperial Iranian Academy of Philosophy.

Maneri, Sharafuddin
  1980   *The Hundred Letters*. Trans. by. P. Jackson. New York: Paulist Press.

Mole, Marijan
  1963   *La Danse extatique en Islam*. Sources Orientales 6:147–228. Paris: Presses Universitaires de France.
  1965   *Les Mystiques musulmans*. Paris: Presses Universitaires de France.

Nagauri, Hamid ad-din
  n.d.   *Surur as-sudur*. Persian ms., Maulana Azad Library, Aligarh Muslim University, f. 33–37.
  1963   Trans. by Ihsan al-Haqq Faruqi in *Sultan at-tarikin*, 261–80. Karachi: Da'ira-i Muͨ in al-maͨ arif.

Qushayri, Abu'l-Qasim
  n.d.   *Risalat fi ͨ ilm at-tasawwuf*. Beirut: Dar al-kitab al-ͨ arabiya.

Sarraj. Abu Nasr
  1914   *Kitab al-lumaͨ fi't-tasawwuf*. Ed. by R. A. Nicholson. E. J. W. Gibb Memorial Series, XXII. Leiden: E. J. Brill, and London: Luzac & Co.

Schimmel, Annemarie
  1975   *Mystical Dimensions of Islam*. Chapel Hill: University of North Carolina Press.

Suhrawardi, ͨ Abd al-Qadir (Abu Hafs)
  1966   *ͨ Awarif al-maͨ arif*. Beirut: Dar al-kitab al-ͨ arabiya.
  1978   Trans. R. Gramlich. *Die Gaben der Erkenntnisse/ͨ Awarif al-maͨ arif*. Freiburger Islam-Studien 6. Wiesbaden: Otto Harrassowitz.

Suhrawardi, Abu Najib
  1975   Trans. by M. Milson. *A Sufi Rule for Novices: Kitab Adab al-Muridin*. Harvard Middle Eastern Studies 17. Cambridge: Harvard University Press.

Yamani, Nizamgharib
  1295/1878   *Lata'if-i Ashrati*. Delhi: Matba'-i Muhammad Khan.

Zarradi, Fakhr ad-din
  1311/1894   *Risalat Usul as-samaͨ *. Jhajjar: Mathaͨ -i Ahmad.

The Role of Song
in a Ga Ritual

Barbara L. Hampton

Among the Ga/1/ of southeastern Ghana song is the principal musical element associated with ritual. In fact, song is one of the criterial attributes of public ritual ceremonies; without it, such activities would not be valid instances of the class. For rituals there are two types of singing, analytically distinguished according to the membership of performers in particular social categories, their primary roles in performance contexts, the kinds of ritual events for which they perform, and the content of their songs. The first type of singing is entrusted to cult figures (mediums, priests and other cult officials) who are acting primarily as ritual specialists; the second type of singing is entrusted to noncult figures who are acting solely as musicians. Ritual specialists sing for periodic or calendrical rites (i.e., at regular and prescribed times) and for occasional rites in response to specific crises (e.g., natural disasters such as floods and earthquakes). Musicians sing for rites of passage. The content of the songs in both cases generally refers to the place of humans in relation to other beings in the universe; however, ritual specialists tend to emphasize relations between gods and humans while musicians emphasize relations among humans. The purpose of the ceremonies in which ritual specialists sing is either redressive or system-maintaining and serves as supplication to the gods (Kilson, 1971:21–24); the purpose of the ceremonies in which musicians sing is to mark the passage of humans through the various stages of life. This accounts, at least in part, for the difference in emphasis.

The funeral in Ga society is one kind of ritual in which musicians (Adowafoi), through the performance of the song corpus known as "Adowa," are responsible for "displaying communicative competence to an audience, are susceptible to evaluation by that audience and are available for the enhancement of experience" (Bauman, 1978:5, 11). Like other West African music-making activities, communication through Adowa performances is multichanneled (Nketia, 1974:206–17); meaning is conveyed through audio-acoustic and kinesthetic-visual channels (cf. Stone and Stone, 1981:216). Specifically, within the Adowa performance domain, marked, segregated aesthetic genres—music, literature, dance and costume—are tied together forming a unified whole. I have discussed the component genres and the issue of ritual symbolism elsewhere (Hampton, 1982). In their evaluative statements about Adowa songs, however, the Ga say that the most important element is the words./2/ Their evaluation has directed my attention to the song texts, the unit of analysis for this study. Central questions that I attempt to address are: How is the ritual socially situated? How is Adowa defined through performance as an interpretive context or communicative resource? What are the meanings that undergird these songs, what do they say about the Ga belief system, and what do they say about the Ga as people? Why and how do the songs contribute to the goals of this ritual? The primary analytical value of Adowa song texts lies in the fact that Adowa is the one song corpus used by all Ga people for the same rite of passage./3/

The Act Sequence

When a death occurs the elder matrikinsmen and patrikinsmen of the deceased send a kinsman between twenty and thirty-four years of age to various houses within the community and its environs to notify people whose presence is desired at the ceremony. (People who are not informed in this manner are not socially obligated to attend.) This kinsman is sent with a gift of drinks to negotiate with a representative of the musicians; when the musicians accept the invitation to perform at the funeral, their representative—in the case of the Adowafoi, the eldest member of the ensemble—accepts a gift of money on behalf of the ensemble. The gift is, in turn, shared with all the Adowafoi. If the deceased is an Adowa musician or member of an Adowa musician's kinsgroup, the ensemble will not accept monetary payment for the performance.

On the eve before the actual funeral ceremony (yarafɛɛmɔ) there is a wake which continues throughout the night. The participants disperse at dawn. Other musical ensembles may be present, but they perform because they were associated with the deceased during his lifetime or with members of the surviving family and not because the music that they perform is itself specially designated for wakes and funerals. Because the activities of individuals vary, these musical ensembles will also vary from one to another wake and funeral. Additional musical variety derives from the several ensembles that are paid to perform, being neither affiliated with the deceased nor members of his kinsgroup. (Each ensemble usually performs a particular corpus of songs.) They perform simultaneously in the courtyards of the family house of the deceased, or the street nearby may be closed to traffic and used for this purpose. This same setting is used for the funeral ceremony which begins in the late morning or early afternoon on the day following the wake.

The same musical ensembles gather once more and perform simultaneously for the funeral. By this time, the sun is at its zenith and a sailcloth may be hung on bamboo poles to shield participants from its direct glare.

Musicians are given chairs or benches on which to sit. Adowafoi bring out their instruments, select them (in the case of rattles and bamboo stamping tubes) and prepare themselves for the occasion. Then they begin the performance during which conversation and laughter can be heard. Libations are poured and prayers said. Participants give money or drinks to the musicians and dancers and make monetary contributions to the family to assist with expenses. The audience responds openly with dancing, gestures, and even spoken words to show that they evaluate the performance positively and that the musicians are rendering a valuable service to the community.

Before dusk, an elder male of the surviving family indicates that the corpse should be removed from the bedstead in the family house where it was placed for viewing. It is put into a coffin and the processional to the grave begins. Two young males carry the coffin, one at each end, and are said to be possessed by the spirit of the deceased during the processional. For this reason, they seldom take a direct route to the gravesite. The spirit of the deceased may first guide their steps to certain houses in order to bid farewell to the residents or they may be led to the house of a person who is responsible for the death in order to identify him to others. Afterwards, the processional continues to the gravesite, all the while to the accompaniment of Adowa songs. At the gravesite a few words are said, more songs are sung, and the body is interred. The interment marks the end of the ceremony.

The Performers

An Adowa musical ensemble is constituted by about 20–35 elder women who live in the same town or quarter of town (*akutso*) and who have the responsibility to perform at the funerals of all residents of the town or *akutso* and for nonresidents with family houses in the town or *akutso*. The identification of an Adowa ensemble with the town or *akutso* in which it is based is manifest in the name of each ensemble, for the town or *akutso* name precedes the designation Adowafoi.

Ensembles use either a drum or a set of three bamboo tubes, a set of 8–16 rattles and a bell to support the voices. The drummer or the master bamboo stamping tube player (*pamploshilo*) is required to improvise rhythmic patterns, the structure of which is determined by the mood of the occasion at any given moment, the dancers' steps and general abilities, the meaning of the song text and the overall mood of the song. Other instrumentalists perform unvarying rhythmic patterns that either outline or fill in the time span or basic temporal unit. The pattern of the bell, the instrument with the highest carrying power, serves as the reference point by which the other instrumentalists order their patterns; it is also the identifying element for all Ga Adowa music.

There are two vocal parts: solo and chorus (i.e., members of the chorus sing as part of one undifferentiated whole, mostly in unison or with occasional two-part harmony). The soloist must improvise texts commenting on

micro-events observed during the performance, for example, the arrival of
the king or certain other dignitaries, and on notable social events that
occurred prior to the ritual, including special deeds done by the deceased
during life. She provides mnemonics for the chorus, which responds with an
unvarying phrase or set of phrases for a given song. Moreover, she shapes
the emergent quality of the performance by introducing songs that comment on the relationships among the participants in the ceremony and songs
that educe action from the participants.

Adowa Songs

Within the framework of the overall ceremony, specific acts of the
performers situate the ritual socially. This is achieved through the musical
metadimension which (a) contextualizes the song corpus by providing a
foundation for its perception and appreciation and (b) categorizes and comments on the event (Hymes, 1972). The first metacommunicative device
used by Adowafoi at the funeral is an *ŋkpai* or (spoken) prayer to the
Supreme Being, the lesser gods, and the ancestors. It serves to invoke Adowa
songs as an interpretive frame: "Supreme Being . . . all grandfathers and
grandmothers . . . we will play Adowa. . . ."/4/ The Adowafoi continue
with a request for a successful performance. And they ask that the
Adowafoi in the spirit world/5/ not obstruct the performance, but move
aside and allow mortal Adowafoi to sing the songs; they ask that spiritual
Adowafoi bless the occasion of performance. This *ŋkpai* represents an
appeal to tradition. It identifies the song corpus as a communicative
resource that has been used by the Ga since "ancient times"; it identifies
Adowa as songs performed by the elders, which gives it special authority;
and it identifies Adowa songs, the musicians and their audience with the
world of the supernatural, thus signaling that it is "insufficient to interpret
what we will communicate literally; interpret it also in a special sense"
(Bauman:9).

The second metadevice used by Adowafoi is a song, of which there are
several kinds. The first serves to mediate musical and other social relationships among the participants in the ritual, including that of Adowafoi-chief,
Adowafoi-audience, and Adowafoi and audience-chief. Adowa songs accomplish this largely through the use of pronomials or "purely relational units,"
which not only encode the relationship between singers and listeners, but
also enable a shift of attention back and forth between the singing and the
funeral as ritual event (Jakobson, 1960:353–58; Uspensky, 1973:139–40).
"Yɛara yɛnam" is an example of such a song; it is the first song performed at
the ritual.

Yɛara yɛnam oo. Yɛara yɛnam oo.	We are walking; we are walking.
Yɛkɔ m'agya fiee. Yɛnam oo.	We went to our father's house.

Yɛkɔ nana fiee. Yɛnam oo.
Akwamu Akoto Aduafo yɛkyi
amanko oo. Yɛnam oo ee.

Kwao ayɛ bi agya aa yɛwia.

Yɛkɔ ma agya akyi.
Yɛnam oo.

We are walking. We went to the chief's
house. We are walking.
Akoto of Akwamu's Adowafoi dislike
quarrels between nations. We are walking.
Kwao did something good and left it (for us).
We are finished.
We are going to say "Good morning"
to father. We are walking.

The song text communicates the special relationship between the musicians ("we") and the chief ("our father"). It, like the ŋkpai, appeals to tradition, citing the Akwamu origins of the Ga Adowa song corpus and referring to the social history shared by the Ga (Hampton, 1978b), thus identifying the Adowafoi with all other Ga.

A second song text communicates the special relationship set up between the musicians ("I," "Adowafoi") and their audience ("you") through song performance (Bateson, 1972:178) and further establishes an identification between them by citing the chief, the custodian of the culture and political head of the town or *akutso*. The chief is someone with whom both musicians and their audience share a special relationship.

ɛyɛ odikro na
m'aba wo fiee oo.
Krepong odikro na
m'aba wo fiee oo.
Aduafo refrɛ wo;
ɛyɛ odikro na
m'aba wo fiee oo.

It is the chief of the village, and
I have come to your house.
Chief of Krepong and
I have come to your house.
The Adowafoi are calling you;
It is the chief of the village, and
I have come to your house.

Another kind of Adowa song has the function of announcing the death and commenting on it from different perspectives. The Ga belief system incorporates a view of death (*gbele*) not as a process by which life ends, but as a process by which one's status changes from mortal being to that of spiritual being with supernatural powers. Upon death it is believed that one's spirit leaves the body to eventually inhabit a place (*gbohiadzeŋ*) separate from the world as humans know it; spirits only come into contact with humans when they initiate. This belief underlies the meaning of one Adowa song which says: "A message is not sent to the dead. If so, I would have sent a message." Analogy is used here, for in human life when one assumes residence in a distant community those of the home community exchange messages with him through travelers between the two points. This song laments the nature of the separation caused by death and the fact that it precludes such contact.

Several songs that announce and comment on death were composed at different times during Ga history and refer to particular events, institutions and individuals of the past. With the transformation of social structure over time there has been a transformation in meaning, for meaning does not "lie only in the fact that music is organized as part of the process of living together, but also in the fact that formal structures and context of use often interact . . . music occurs as an event in a context of situation" (Nketia, 1962:3). Current meanings of Adowa songs are, therefore, grounded in and emerge from the funeral ritual. They are created and experienced in terms of the concrete situation facing the participants at the performances.

One song expresses shock in figurative language ("Today a bird has spoken") and mourns the loss of someone who was the focal point of an important community activity ("The sun has stopped for us"). The first phrase eulogizes a former Adowa musician, Akɔle; it was on the occasion of her death that this song was composed.

'K ɔle mo oo! Ewia gyina yɛn.	Akole well done! The sun has stopped for us.
N'ewia gyina yɛn.	The sun has stopped for us.
ɛnnɛ anoma kasa!	Today a bird has spoken!
N'ewia gyina yɛn;	The sun has stopped for us;
m'ewia gyina yɛn.	the sun has stopped for us.

A second song refers to the high status of the deceased and bemoans the loss of one who made an inimitable contribution to the community. (The imagery stems from the fact that this song was used to encourage bravery when the Adowa company acted as an auxiliary to the warrior company.)

Wɔ na na ɔbɛma atuduro yɛnko?	Who is he that will give gunpowder
Otwa mmorɔdɔ . . .	so that we fight? He has fled.
ɔsafohene otwa mmorɔdɔ.	The leader of the army has fled.

Using similar imagery, recalling the history of Adowa, a third song expresses a view of death ("burning") as something which reduces the population of the *akutso.*

Anfrɛ rehyew oo!	Members of the Asafo are burning!
Boa me ee! ɔhene agoro bue, bue!	Help me! The chiefs play, help, help!
Yoo okogyetuo ee, yoo a yo ei!	Yoo, one who is invulnerable to bullets.
Hmm. Gyama, ɔhene Kwao akɔɔ man	Hmm. Perhaps Chief Kwao has gone
bi akɔko agye yɛn.	to the town to fight to save us.
Agyae nkrɔfo akye yɛn! ɛhɛɛ.	He left the people to capture us! Yes.
ɔhene Kwao akɔko agye yɛn ee.	Chief Kwao has gone to fight to save us.
Boa me ee!	Help me!
Yee, boa me ee! ɔhene agoro	Yea, help me! The chief's play,
bue, bue!	help, help!
Yoo okogyetuo ee,	Yoo, one who is invulnerable to bullets,
yoo a yo ei! Hmm.	yoo a yo ei! Hmm.

A fourth song emphasizes some special quality of the deceased, in this case fairness. (It bewails the death of Kwao, a member of the Council of Elders, who was responsible for adjudication.)

Kwao wowɔ mu a, eye po.	Kwao if you are in, it is especially good.
Ɛhɛɛ. Kwao ee, yɛkɔ agyina a,	Yes. Kwao, we go to make a decision,
yɛn lu oo.	but we can't.
Yɛkɔ nkongua a, yɛnfle (yɛnfrɛ) ee.	(When) we go to the stools, we call.
Ɛhɛɛ. Kwao wowɔ mu a, eye ee.	Yes. Kwao if you are in, it is good.

A fifth statement about death is that people do not fully recognize the value of a person during his mortal life. (This song also recalls the Akwamu conquest and the time when the Ga were Akwamu subjects with a resident emissary.)

ɛmo ɔman Nkranfo	You people of the Ga nation,
mose Gyaasehene nyɛ mpo.	you say that the Gyaasehene
ɛmo a mose Gyaasehene	is not good at all. You say that
nyɛ oo.	the Gyaasehene is not good.
ɔman Nkranfo mose	Ga nation, you say that the
Gyassehene nni hɔ.	Gyaasehene is not there.
Gyaasehene Kɔbla nyɛ oo.	Gyaasehene Kɔbla is not good.
Nkwaseafo besu no da bi oo.	Foolish people will weep for him someday.

While the elevated status and new powers of the deceased are honored, as seen in the festive aspects of the occasion, the Ga response to death is not merely the ideologically based jubilance that some authors have attributed to the celebrants at West African funerals. Death for the Ga is a matter of greater complexity. This second species of Adowa song, as we have interpreted it, shows that death brings temporary instability through a loss of persons who ensure the smooth operation of institutions; a reduction in the population of a society whose survival depends on labor-intensive agriculture; shock; and grief. To the Ga, death also has meaning on a personal, highly subjective level. This second species of Adowa song refers to both ideas and feelings; it is used to articulate both the concepts concerning the fate of the deceased according to the Ga belief system and the community's emotional responses to the death.

Yarafɛɛmɔ is an occasion not only for the deceased, but also for the community. Death happens not solely to significant others but also eventually to each member of the society. For this reason, death "posits the most terrifying threat to the taken-for-granted realities of everyday life. The integration of death within the paramount reality of social existence is, therefore, of the greatest importance for any institutional order" (Berger and Luckmann, 1967:101). Songs that comment on the death contribute to its integration into the fabric of social life. But a third species of Adowa song goes beyond this to apprehend the objectivated social reality and reproduce the world of meanings that undergird it, thus forming a shield against the terror of anomie kindled by death (101–2). These songs emphasize vital institutions in Ga society and the values upon which they are founded; they enable everyday life to resume.

Such songs depict the family and the *akutso* as symbols of personal identity/6/ which help to create a sense of belongingness. One shares rules of guidance, a perspective on everyday life realities and a history with the people of one's *akutso*, and, by extension, with one's town and other Ga. An Adowa song expresses this and describes the situation of a stranger (cf. Schutz, 1964:104–5).

Mebaa ha akyɛ oo.	I have been here for a long time.
Mɛkɔ agya kurow mu oo.	I am going to my father's town.
ɔmanfrani yɛ aboa.	The stranger to a nation is a beast.
Kuro bi kyiri ɔhɔ ho. Me nnim . . .	A certain town dislikes a stranger. I don't know . . .
Nimo nimo yɛbɔ. Mebaa ha a'ɛy oo.	They gossip about you. I have been here for a long time.

The family can operate as an instrument of social pressure on behalf of its members. It is a social welfare institution upon which one can rely for assistance in times of crisis, for sustenance in time of need and during old age. Its influence can ensure fairness in cases of adjudication. One song comments on this in an oblique manner. (Tawia is the name of anyone, male or female, who is born after twins. To mention the name in this song is to say that one is not alone, that one has siblings, a family. The phrase "I have gathered mushrooms to show to the people of Osu," a town, is a gesture of peace used in the song to demonstrate that the singer is without bitterness over the decision. Her song is simply an observation of the way things are.)

Woyi de m'agyae oo.	As for this, I have stopped.
Adedenkuma owia 'manfa,	Uninhabited place, poor lonely person.
ɔbaakofo mɔblo.	Lonely person, I have entered into a case;
ɔbaako asɛm m'adi m'adi fɔ.	I am guilty.
Eyi de m'agyae oo.	So I have stopped.
Metu mlɛ (mmre) mekyerɛ Osu,	I have gathered mushrooms to show to Osu.
na ɔbaakofoɔ, m'agyae	And poor person, I have stopped.
ɔbaako asɛm m'adi m'adi fɔ.	Lonely person, I have entered into a case; I am guilty.
Otwea ɔklabilifɔ (ɔkrabirifoɔ),	Foolish, hopeless person,
m'agyae.	I have stopped.
M'agyae akyinnye (nkyirimma)	I have stopped arguments.
Yoo, otwea, kontomponi m'agyae.	Foolish liar, I have stopped.
M'agyae akyinnye. ɔba nyansafo,	I have stopped arguments. Modern people,
bɛbua Tawia, bɛbua Afoama,	you give judgment to Tawia,
Tawia na ne nua.	you give judgment to Afoama, Tawia and
Na ɔbaakofo, m'agyae.	his brother, and lonely person, I have stopped.
ɔbaako asɛm m'adi m'adi fɔ.	Lonely person, I have entered into a case; I am guilty.

Both natal and conjugal families are considered important and thus there are songs which portray marriage as the natural state for adult life, like a crocodile in water. (For emphasis, the song relates the dread of removal.) Children are viewed as sources of marital cohesion and embody the union of two different families; couples are, therefore, urged to have children. The principle of male superordination, so significant among the Ga (Kilson, 1971:12), is stressed in the song about children.

W'ayi me nsuo mu oo!	You removed me from water.
Menyε dεn?	What should I do?
ɔdεnkyεm ee, w'ayi me nsuo mu!	Crocodile, you removed me from water.
Obi mbra (mmra) mεgye me asetena.	Somebody should come to save my situation.
Na w'ayi me kwan nnε.	Today, you will see me off.
Menyε dεn ee?	What should I do?
Agyanka, w'ayi me nsuo mu oo!	An orphan, you removed me from water!
. . .ɔdasani ee, w'ayi me nsuo mu!	A human being, you removed me from water!
Onipa a ɔwɔ din na wɔbɔ ne din	The person who has a name is the one
'baa Adzua.	whose name is called, woman Adzua.
Onipa ɔwo mmanin so gyina yie.	The person who gives birth to men also stands well.
ɔwo mmanin ee; ɔwo mmanin ee!	She gives birth to men; she gives birth to men.
'nipa ɔwo mmanin so gyina yie.	The person who gives birth to men also stands well.

These Adowa songs about the family, marriage and childbearing suggest that the world is patterned and ordered. However, Ga cosmological conceptions include a definition of humans as rational beings who largely determine their lot through the exercise of choice. Other songs of this species, then, furnish the other dimension and suggest that everyday life to the Ga is only partially patterned and ordered and partially unpatterned and disordered. Together these songs present a world in which the nature of human experience is both contingent and free. Members of a family can quarrel (the fox and the hawk); marriage can be terminated willfully; a woman can be scorned if she has only daughters (feeling cold in the sun).

Mεkɔka mabomu oo.	I am going to join them.
Mεkɔka mabomu ee.	I am going to join them.
A mawie mekɔka mabomu.	I have finished. I am going to join them.
Me ne ɔsɔ ahyia oo.	I have met a fox.
Osansa refa me.	A hawk is taking me.
Asεm a ɔnnyε no na yεnndi ekyiri.	The case that we are following is not good.
Oo yεnndi ekyiri bi ara.	We should not follow (it) again.
Aware bone sεe ɔbaa pa.	A marriage that is bad will spoil a good
sane Adzua.	woman. It affects Adzua.
Aware bone, yεnndi ekyiri oo.	A bad marriage, we should not follow (it).
Metu mlε (mmire) mekyerε Osu,	I gather mushrooms to show to the people
sane Adzua.	of Osu. It affects Adzua.
Asεm bone, yεnndi ekyiri oo.	A bad case, we should not follow (it).
Aware bone sεe ɔbaa pa.	A bad marriage will spoil a good woman.
Yεnndi ekyiri oo.	We should not follow (it).

Kasa bone, awerɛho nkonkonko.	Bad speech is full of sadness.
Yɛnndi ekyiri oo.	We should not follow (it).
Nam ewia, na aw⁷ de me oo;	Walking in the sun, but I'm feeling cold.
Manwo mmanin ee.	I did not give birth to men.
Nam ewia oo, na aw⁷ de me oo.	Walking in the sun, but I'm feeling cold.
Mawo mmesia; manwo mmanin.	I have given birth to women; I have not given birth to men.

Groups comprise individuals and qualities that individuals possess are also valued. A fourth species of Adowa song calls attention to the importance of reciprocity, generosity, hope, patience, persistence, and self-control, especially in resisting the temptation to gossip, lie and meddle or otherwise disturb relations among humans.

Woma me bi ee; woma me bi ee.	You give me something; you give me something.
Me menya a me de mɛma wo oo.	When I get mine, I will give to you.
Woma me bi me nni;	Give me something to eat;
menya me de mɛma.	When I get mine, I will give to you.
Ee kɔtu bra oo, kɔtu bra oo,	Oh! Remove it and bring it, bring it, bring it.
Ayee, kɔtu bra oo.	Ayee! Remove it and bring it.
Onibi ndaama bɛyɛɛ ade.	One who has nothing will do well in the future.
Ayee, kɔtu bra oo.	Ayee! Remove it and bring it.
Nam nyaa; mɛkɔ Dunkwa.	Walking slowly, I am going to Dunkwa.
Nam nyaa; mɛkɔ Nkran.	Walking slowly, I am going to Accra.
Nam nyaa; mɛkɔ Dunkwa.	Walking slowly, I am going to Dunkwa.
Mentumi nante. Mekura poma.	I can't walk. I hold a walking stick.
Nam nyaa; ɔkra Akua, nam nyaa,	Walking slowly, my soul Akua, walking slowly,
mbɛko Dunkwa.	I will come to Dunkwa./7/
Mesu apem yoo. M'ano oo.	I am carrying thousands. My mouth.
Eyi nti menkasa m'ano.	Because of this, I do not talk.
Mesu apem yoo.	I am carrying thousands./8/
ɛkɛ enadzi ntslɔʃi ee!	She with her legs dips ee!
Aʃimaʃi ee! Okɛ onadzii ntslɔʃi ee!	So and so ee! You with your legs dip ee!
Mimon, miiyɛ nsadzi ee,	Myself, I have my own case.
nohewɔ owɔ nyɔŋnyɔŋ yɛhe.	That is the reason you don't sleep at midnight.
Asɛmpɛ basiaba,	One who likes to meddle,
ɛkɛ enadzii ntslɔʃi ee!	with her legs dips.
Apasafɔ bediakɔ,	One who tells lies,
ɛkɛ enadzii ŋhlumi ee!	with legs deceiving me./9/

A fifth species of Adowa song consists of texts which comment on micro-events within the ceremony. They are intended to evoke certain responses from the audience or themselves are responses to specific acts performed by members of the audience. They are metacommunicative in that they shift attention from the ceremony itself to the relationships among the participants.

One song solicits monetary donations from the audience, "helpers of the people." In their efforts to persuade, the Adowafoi refer to any potential contributor as Queen Mother ("Yaa Ahenewa"), Chief ("ɔhene"), "loved one," and "beloved wife of the chief." Although pronomials ("we," "you") appear in this song to establish the relationship, fewer pronomials and more appellations are used in this song of solicitation than in others of this species.

Manyɛfoɔ, manyɛ ayie oo.	Helpers of the people. You should contribute in this funeral.
Ɛhɛɛ. Yaa Ahenɛwa dɔfoɔ,	Yes. Yaa Ahenewa, loved one;
ɔhene dɔf ɔ.	ɔhene, loved one.
ɔhene, ne yere dɔfoɔ yi wo ayɛ.	ɔhene, beloved wife of the chief, (we) give you praise.

The meaning of this song is rooted in the belief that the new status of the deceased as ancestral shade,/10/ just beneath the Supreme Being and lesser gods in the Ga hierarchy of beings, should be honored with an elaborate ceremony. This calls for an abundance of food and drink, ritual objects of the finest quality, and as many different musical ensembles as possible. *Yarafɛɛmɔ*, therefore, entails considerable financial expenditure at short notice. Because members of the community share this belief, families are financially assisted by those who attend the ritual. Sometimes a table is set up near the site where a kinsman of the deceased is stationed with a book and pen to record the contributions. Since the family must pay some of the musicians and provide all of them with drinks, donors often give money and also drink directly to the musicians.

Adowafoi immediately perform a song of gratitude to donors, whether the contribution is made to the family or directly to them. The soloist will sing the phrase "one who does good" and "one who gives drinks" in the first song. She will further embellish these phrases or substitute more appropriate ones according to the situation; the chorus responds with the subsequent phrases. In the third song of this species the word "afterwards" is used to express the depth of the gratitude, for being thankful in the future is more than momentary gratitude; the gift or deed has been pondered. Customarily, one will go to the donor's residence to give thanks at a time in the future, but when one cannot, something is said to indicate future gratitude.

Eee me da ase Ahenewa oo.	I thank you, Ahenewa.
Me da ase.	I thank you.
Oyade, me da ase Ahenewa.	One who does good, I thank you, Ahenewa.
Me da ase.	I thank you.
Onimpa ɔkyɛ nsa, me da ase, Ahenewa.	One who gives drinks, I thank you, Ahenewa.
Me da ase.	I thank you.
Wɔma yɛnda ase oo,	Let us thank him (for)
blibi (biribi) wayɛ yɛn oo.	something good he has done (for us).

W ɔma yɛnda ase nya.	Let us give thanks, nya.
Akyiri, yɛkɔ nana, blibi	Afterwards, when we have gone, (we thank you)
woyɛ yɛkyɛ yɛade	Nana for something you have done./11/

Finally, attention must be given to the manner in which Adowa singing emerges in the context of the yarafɛɛmɔ, that is, within the boundaries of the ŋkpai (initial) and the interment (terminal). There is no prescribed sequence for individual items within the song corpus. The order of the songs is not programmed a priori. A single rendition of a song involves several repetitions of the versions given above with variations supplied by the soloist. There may be more than one performance of a given song during the ceremony, but these repetitions do not occur at predetermined points. Except for times when all the musicians may pause to rest, the instrumental parts continue uninterrupted. Adowa songs are connected during performance in such a way that there is no pause between them. When a soloist determines that a song should end, instead of following the ending choral passage with the opening phrase of the same song, she substitutes the opening phrase of another song. The chorus then follows with the appropriate choral passage.

It is possible, however, to identify a set of variables which determine the choices of the performers and ultimately shape the performance. The repertoire and memory of the soloist determine how many songs can be sung and repeated. Since there may be two musicians with somewhat different repertoires acting as soloist, the number of soloists may be a factor. The character of the extramusical act sequence, particular items and their ordering, determines when and how often certain songs that comment on the ritual will be repeated. For example, when the frequency of the contributions begins to wane, songs soliciting donations will be sung several times until the situation changes; when unsolicited contributions are frequent and regular, the songs of thanks will be sung more often than those of solicitation; and the frequency with which songs of solicitation and thanks are performed affects the frequency with which the others are performed. The character of a dancer's movements will determine whether the soloist repeats a song or introduces another that more closely corresponds to the movements. A dancer's relationship with the soloist, although more so with the drummer, is an interactive one (cf. p. 113). Overall, the emergent quality of any Adowa performance hinges on the aggregate of these conditions and is unique to that particular occasion of performance.

Coda

Adowa is the principal song corpus designated for performance at funerals of the Ga people. By citing, through the ŋkpai and through song, the principal actors in the ceremony and their relationships, the Adowafoi begin by situating the ritual socially. Principal actors include various social categories of spiritual and mortal beings who share social values, who are connected to the deceased and who sustain and are comprised by the Ga cosmos. The participants are, thus, joined together to affirm the death and the importance of the deceased in this cosmos. Performances of the *nkpai* and the opening songs further establish Adowa as an interpretive context in which song "messages"/12/ must be understood in a special way (Wheelock, 1982:66).

Adowafoi then proceed to define institutionalized areas of conduct and particular kinds of situations subsumed by them. They describe roles to be played in the context of certain vital institutions—the family, marriage, and parenthood, inter alia. They abstract from the experience of interaction within Ga society and re-present a meaningful world in which honesty in individuals, as well as patience, hope, persistence, self-control and overall amity are the ideal. These models are conveyed through texts relating incidents in which the ideal was achieved and others in which it was violated; striving for the ideal is underscored. By extension, references to Ga social history are continually made, suggesting that out of the Ga experience emerges this framework for orienting human life and defining the universe, and highlighting the Ga worldview as a basis for unity among the celebrants.

Why should they sing about "what everyone knows"? The crisis precipitated by the death has engendered certain feelings. These are given expression in Adowa songs. Death has also shaken the foundations of everyday life realities. To counterbalance the instability of the human organism, the Adowafoi reconstruct the stable environment that the Ga have created for their conduct. Adowa songs bring back and thereby reinforce the paradigmatic realities shared by the participants. As a result of the performance "sensation, emotion and other areas of pre-reflective consciousness are brought into harmony with clear thought and culture" (Zuesse, 1975:519). The purpose of the Adowa performance and the goals of the funeral are thus accomplished.

NOTES

/1/   The Ga live in an area approximately 40 miles along the Gulf of Guinea between the Laloi lagoon and the Densu River with the Akwapim Scarp as the northern boundary. They number approximately 250,000 and speak a Niger-Congo language (Kwa group). The song corpus that serves as a basis for this study was borrowed from the Akwamu ca. late 17th century and the song texts are in various dialects of the Akan language, including Akwamu. Adowa musicians continue to compose songs in Akan and recently have begun to compose songs in the Ga language. Where the pronunciation is not true to the Akan, I have indicated the Akan pronunciation in parentheses immediately after the word. Of the six Ga towns and their dependent villages the examples discussed here were taken from two, Osu and Nungua. I believe them to be representative of Ga Adowa, generally. All examples discussed here can be heard on the album *Music of the Ga People of Ghana* (Hampton, 1978a).

/2/ This raises the question, Why melody or song? "The song gives it strength" or power, Ga musicians say. There are also "things that somebody can sing, but if he/she (*le*) says them it would arouse anger."

/3/ For each of the other rites of passage, the songs will be different from one Ga town to another and even, in some cases, from one *akutso* to another. This is explicable by the fact that the various groups who, through confederation, became the Ga had different origins and migration histories. It is expected that the songs used by all Ga will reveal much about the people as a whole.

/4/ See Hampton, 1978b:3 for a discussion and complete translation of the *ŋkpai*.

/5/ Each social group, including the Adowafoi, consists of both mortal and spiritual members. In the case of the Adowafoi, the spiritual members are musicians who performed Adowa as mortals.

/6/ In Ga society individuals are also named according to two (i.e., for alternating generations) sets of patronyms which are distinct for each sex, each family, and each *akutso*.

/7/ Ga exegetes use a proverb to explain the meaning of this song: "Little by little a fowl drinks water, but he satisfies his thirst." They say that patience is represented by the cane in this song. Akua is the name for a female born on Wednesday. *ɔkra* is an expression of understanding. Accra is the largest Ga town and the capital of the Republic of Ghana; Dunkwa is a smaller town to the west.

/8/ A proverb is also used to explicate this text. "If I am carrying a firearm, I should not smoke a pipe." The singer knows many secrets; she chooses to remain quiet. One who wishes to protect her reputation must not risk spoiling that of others. Mano is elliptical. If completed, the statement would be "my mouth is closed."

/9/ This is one of the few songs in the Ga language (with the exception of the terms "Asɛmpɛ basiaba" and "Apasafo bediakɔ," translated as "one who likes to meddle" and "one who tells lies," respectively). Ga exegetes say that a person whose legs dip is one who cannot face others in a straightforward manner because of antisocial conduct. One of the most serious social offenses is to create conflict among people, especially by deceitful means. The singer says that one who carefully attends his own matters will sleep peacefully at night. The technique of sharply criticizing a nameless person for bad conduct is often used in Adowa songs to admonish and to encourage good behavior.

/10/ Ancestral shade is the status that the deceased ultimately attains. After death the soul remains with the body for 3 days. It then leaves the body to wander until about one year after *yarafɛɛmɔ* when *faafo*, a rite at which the deceased "crosses the river" (*faa-fo*), is performed. The deceased officially assumes the status of ancestral shade at that time.

/11/ *Nya* is an appellation. *Nana* is another title for a chief.

/12/ "Message" is used here in the same sense that Wheelock defines it: "as less an idea to be taught and more a reality to be repeatedly experienced."

REFERENCES

Bateson, Gregory
1972   *Steps to an Ecology of Mind*. New York: Ballantine Books/
                Chandler Publishing Company.

Bauman, Richard
1978   *Verbal Art as Performance*. Rowley, Mass.: Newbury House
                Publishers, Inc.

Berger, Peter L., and Luckmann, Thomas
1967   *The Social Construction of Reality: A Treatise in the Sociol-
                ogy of Knowledge*. Garden City: Anchor Books/Doubleday
                and Company, Inc.

Hampton, Barbara L.
1978a   *Music of the Ga People of Ghana*. Vol. 1: *Adowa*. New York:
                Folkways Records and Service Corporation, Inc. FE 4291.
1978b   "The Contiquity Factor in Ga Music," *The Black Perspective
                in Music* 6(2):33–48.
1982   "Music and Ritual Symbolism at the Ga Funeral," *Yearbook
                for Traditional Music* 14: 75–105.

Hymes, Dell
1972   "Models of the Interaction of Language and Social Life," in
                Directions in Sociolinguistics, ed. John J. Gumperz and Dell
                Hymes. New York: Holt, Rinehart and Winston.

Jakobson, Roman
1960   "Linguistics and Poetics" in *Style in Language*, ed. Thomas A.
                Sebeok. Cambridge, Mass: Massachusetts Institute of Technol-
                ogy Press.

Kilson, Marion
1971   *Kpele lala: Ga Religious Songs and Symbols*. Cambridge,
                Mass.: Harvard University Press.

Nketia, J. H. Kwabena
1962   "The Problem of Meaning in African Music," *Ethnomusi-
                cology* 6(1):1–7.
1974   *The Music of Africa*. New York: W. W. Norton and Company.

Schutz, Alfred
1964   "The Stranger: An Essay in Social Psychology," *Collected
                Papers II: Studies in Social Theory*. The Hague: Martinus
                Nijhoff, pp. 91–105.

Stone, Ruth M., and Stone, Vernon L.
    1981   "Event, Feedback, and Analysis: Research Media in the Study of Music Events," *Ethnomusicology* 25(2):215–25.

Uspensky, Boris
    1973   *A Poetics of Composition: The Structure of the Artistic Text and Typology of a Compositional Form.* Berkeley and Los Angeles: University of California Press.

Wheelock, Wade T.
    1982   "The Problem of Ritual Language: From Information to Situation," *Journal of the American Academy of Religion* 50(1):49–71.

Zuesse, Evan M.
    1975   "Meditation on Ritual," *Journal of the American Academy of Religion* 43(3):517–30.

Music in the Theravāda Buddhist Heritage: In Chant, in Song, in Sri Lanka

John Ross Carter

In this chapter we will explore the legitimation of and foundations for religious music in the Theravāda Buddhist tradition and particularly in Sri Lanka today. Leaving aside technical ethnomusicological considerations for those more competent in these matters, holding for, perhaps, another time an attempt to trace a possible historical development, we will move from text to contemporary context to demonstrate two strands within the Theravāda cumulative heritage: an old admonition about restraint of the senses and an appreciation for, a legitimization of, religious music. These strands are current today in Sri Lanka. Although the former tends to be applied to the monastic form of life and the latter primarily to the laity, the two strands, on occasion separate and parallel on occasion plaited, tend to converge in a common feature of shifting attention from the self and in developing wholesome dispositions of mind that are conducive in leading one from where one finds oneself to the moment of the first vision of Nibbāna.

I

Among the precepts that provide the regulatory basis for persons in the Theravāda Buddhist monastic order (*sangha*) is the precept to refrain from seeing performances or shows of dancing or singing, or instrumental music./1/ Moreover, when a text relates how one might praise the moral virtue (*sīla*) of Gotama the Buddha, one finds that he kept aloof, as it were, from performances or shows, dances, singing, instrumental music, stylized lyrical recitations, and rhythmical hand-tapping on the beat, among other things (*D*:I,6). Singing and dancing are unbecoming to a monk; indeed, singing is called a lamentation in the context of the training of a noble disciple, and dancing, further, is considered as going out of one's mind (*A*:I,261).

Apart from the matter of attending performances or shows involving dancing, music in itself, both vocal and instrumental, has tended to be a matter requiring watchfulness on the part of persons in the Buddhist monastic orders.

This should not suggest that Buddhists have merely written off music as base, below one's dignity, a simpleton's enterprise. In an engaging aside, one reads a description given to Ānanda, one of the Buddha's closest disciples, of beautiful gold and silver bells, in a marvelous palace, which produce a sound like that produced by skilled musicians, a sound that is sweet, delightful, charming, and intoxicating (D:II,183). And one becomes alert to the beguiling quality of music, that quality which is a featured characteristic of Māra, the tempter, the one who misleads. It is recorded that Khemā, a nun (bhikkhunī) of note, was approached by Māra as a young man who beckons her to come, enjoying the sounds of music (Thig, 137, vs. 139)./2/ And much the same is recorded elsewhere regarding the experience of another nun, Vijaya (S:I,131).

Yet there apparently is no reluctance to compare the proper exertion or effort in purifying the mind or heart with the skillful tuning of a lute (vīṇā),/3/ neither overlax nor too taut; hence the example given by the Buddha in a discussion with Soṇa, who was skilled in playing the vīṇā when he was a youth at home prior to becoming a bhikkhu (A:III,375)./4/ And according to an account in the birth stories (Jātakas) about the previous lives of the Buddha, the then Buddha-to-be was on one occasion Guttila, a master musician, superbly skilled on the seven stringed vīṇā. (See Jā:II,248–257.)

Could it be the case that music must be kept in check because it is a hitherto not fully comprehended art of human communication with a heightened capacity to penetrate the psyche, to instill moods and motivations not engendered by conscious processes? Proficiency in music was an accomplishment shared by the monk Soṇa, as a boy, the Buddha, as a Buddha-to-be (bodhisatta) in a previous life, and Māra, the Bad One, the distorter, the tempter. Did the Buddha, Soṇa, Khemā, Vijayā, and no doubt others, somehow go beyond an engaging and potentially disorienting charm of music? Is Māra yet to make this move?

Music, of course, if it is communicative relies upon the activity of the senses, and Buddhists have left a record over two millennia old that one is to guard one's senses, the five strands of sensual delight and desire (pañca-kāma-guṇa).

> These five, O monks, are the strands of sensual delight. What five?
> [1] Material forms discerned by the eye, wanted, desired, captivating the mind, enticing, comprised of sensuality, alluring, [2] sounds discerned by the ear . . . [3] smells discerned by the nose . . . [4] tastes discerned by the tongue . . . [5] tangible objects discerned by the body. . . . (M:I, 85)

This is the given condition of the human constitution according to the Theravāda tradition. But also, according to this tradition, the human constitution is not limited by this condition.

And what, O monks, is the exit from sensuality? O monks, the driving out of delight and desire, the putting aside of delight and desire for sensual desires—this is the exit from sensuality. (*M*:I,87)

Dancing, singing, and instrumental music involve sight and sound and the engagement of the eyes and ears. In the context of meditational pursuits, desire and delight in modes of sense impression tend to present formidable obstacles. Discussing such a context, one passage relates how regular tendencies of greed, hatred, and confusion can continue in one's thinking when one has not come to know through immediate insight, as it has actually come about (*yathābhūtaṃ sammāppaññāya*), that sensual desires are of little satisfaction and of much misery; that one is to be aware of the danger or unfortunate consequences related to those sensual desires (*M*:I,91–92). And elsewhere in the texts one reads that "greed" is a synonym for these five strands of sensuality (*A*:III,312-14); that a "knife and chopping block" are likewise synonymous (*M*:I,144), so, too, is "fodder for fattening" (*M*:I,155), and a "whirlpool" (*Itv*, 114)./5/ Hardly have we here casual references to sense desires, minor asides indicating a lighthearted attitude toward sights and sounds, among other sensual impingements. "Watch out! Handle with care!—if at all," seems to be the thrust of the passages.

Some might say that the admonitions related to the perils of sense pleasures, including sounds—and in our concern here, singing and instrumental music—were designed for monastics and not primarily and necessarily for the Buddhist laity. And this observation is for the most part on the mark. However, the perils of sensuality are so often stressed in the tradition that the laity also, when given pause, is not uninformed about the matter.

If one were to arrive today in Sri Lanka and set about to attend as many Buddhist ceremonies as possible, one would hear the sound of drums and *horanā* and be told this is a form of worshipping or paying homage in sound (*śabdapūja*);/6/ one would hear rhythmic lyrical chanting performed according to carefully prescribed and learned patterns, by monks in their chanting of ancient texts (*pirit*);/7/ and over the radio, and elsewhere, on special religious holidays one would hear devotional songs. How does one explain the presence of devotional songs, formal chanting, the sound of drums, cymbals, and horns in this tradition that so clearly stresses the guarding of sense pleasures? Is the ritual activity and song merely a soteriologically irrelevant, parallel but dissociate concession made by the monks for the laity?

Let me suggest that the questions appear to have been answered long ago apparently without necessitating a debate or formal convocation. The bases for this suggestion appear to be rooted in what Westerners might call a mythological stratum of the text on the one hand and, on the other, what one might consider a disarmingly common-sense approach to a development within a cumulative tradition represented in the words of the Buddha.

II

We turn again to Māra; this time to Māra who meets the Buddha and attempts to lure the serene one from his meditative endeavors. "You, O lean one, are pale; you are nigh to death," Māra said. He continued, "Ah, life, sir, life is best!" (*Sn* [HOS], 100, vss. 426–27). Māra's point, in the full passage, is, in short, that one should enjoy the fullness of life, to draw it all in, including the performance of customary religious rituals in order to acquire merit. Struggles in meditative pursuits are tough, Māra suggests.

The major portion of this passage of verses in the *Sutta-nipāta* is comprised of the Buddha's reply to Māra. In describing the tenfold army of Māra, the Buddha mentions that sensuality, i.e., sensual desire, is the first army (*Sn* [HOS], 102, vs. 436). Seeing that the Buddha was resolute and totally unperturbed, Māra, disappointed, left. The Buddha provides the closing verse of the sequel:

> The lute (*vīṇā*) of that one overcome by grief
> Fell down from under his arm.
> Then that sad spirit,
> Vanished right then and there. (*Sn* [HOS], 104, vs. 449)/8/

The dropped lute (*vīṇā*)—what is one to make of it? In another text (S:I,122), Māra is depicted as carrying a yellow hued vilva wood lute—and there, too, he is said to have been dejected, and to have dropped it./9/ It appears that the lute (*vīṇā*) is symbolic of the entrancing charm of music and dalliance. Māra, having let fall his lute, has shown his despondency—gone is his power to beguile one into wanton amorous play, gone is his subtle snare of music and song.

But the lute is not grounded for long. The commentary on this *Sutta-nipāta* passage says that this yellow hued lute (*vīṇā*) of vilva wood (*beluva-paṇḍu-vīṇā*) which fell from under Māra's arm, this lute which, when plucked with the fingers, released sweet music lasting for four months, was picked up by the god Sakka and given to one Pañcasikha (*SnA*:II,393–94), a heavenly musician (*gandhabba*). Now the setting shifts with Pañcasikha in ways that are instructive for our considerations.

In the *Dīgha-nikāya*, one of the collections forming part of the received canon, there is an interesting episode involving Sakka, lord of the gods, Pañcasikha, a heavenly musician or *gandhabba* who attends the gods, the Buddha, and Bhaddā, daughter of the *gandhabba* Timbarū. Sakka and Pañcasikha, who was carrying his lute (*beluvapaṇḍu-vīṇā*), vanished from the celestial realm of the Tāvatiṃsa, and appeared on the Vediya mountain just north of a brahmin village called Ambasaṇḍā to the east of Rājagaha in Magadha. The mountain was said to have become resplendent with the presence of the celestials—even the village of Ambasaṇḍā is said to have become radiant. On that mountain, in a cave called Indasāla, the Buddha

(*Tathāgata*) was deep in meditation (*jhāna*). Sakka, wishing to ask questions of the Buddha, but sensing that such meditating ones are hard to approach by the lord of gods, asked, "But if you, Pañcasikha, would first cause the Blessed One (*Bhagavan*) to be calmly disposed, then I might approach to see the Lord, the Worthy One, Fully Enlightened One who first has been made calmly disposed by you" (*D*:II,265).

Being the dutiful attendant that he was, Pañcasikha took his lute and approached the Indasāla cave. Taking a position neither too close to nor too far from the Buddha, but at a distance just adequate for his song to be heard clearly without startling his hearer, he played his special lute and sang a song. Of what did he sing? He sang, the text tells us, of the Buddha, of salvific Truth (Dhamma), of worthy ones (*arahants*), of love (*kāma*) (*D*:II,265)./10/

The song itself is a love song, one in which the suitor praises the beloved's beauty, seeks to be caressed, and pleads to be embraced. The metaphors are rich and powerfully suggestive./11/ Love (*kāma*) is the theme—reference to the key doctrinal elements are by means of analogy. For example, one reads in the fourth line of the verses, "O radiant One, you are dear to me as is Truth (Dhamma) to worthy ones (*arahants*)" (*D*:II,265). And the celestial composer continues by noting how his love for his beloved achieves abundance like that achieved through gifts of honor given to the worthy ones (*arahants*); how, as the Silent Seer, i.e., the Buddha, desires to acquire the deathless (i.e., Nibbāna), he desires his beloved; how, as the Silent Seer would rejoice having attained incomparable full enlightenment, he would rejoice in attaining union with his beloved.

Two other important ideas are present in Pañcasikha's song: the notion of merit (*puñña*) and divine favor (*varam*). "O beautifully proportioned one," the heavenly bard sings, "being with you is the fruition of the merit done by me to such worthy ones (*arahants*)" (*D*:II,266). Indeed, such is considered the fruition of the bard's meritorious action throughout the entire world; so he sings in the immediately following verse. Later, Pañcasikha sings that if the god Sakka were to grant a divine favor to him, would that he grant to him his beloved.

The song then ends as it began, by praising the father of the beloved for his offspring. In the formal structure of the song, the poet-singer, with focal attention given to his beloved, speaks directly of his praise of his beloved's father, of his performance of meritorious action and the consequence, of his wish for a divine boon. References to the key doctrinal features by means of which the song is introduced are made by analogy.

The performance of religiously meritorious actions, ideally to be insepara-bly concomitant with an "interior transformative effect" (Palihawadana, 1979:136), and the practice of wishing for a divine favor or boon are customary features of lay Buddhist life today in Sri Lanka, as apparently they were in the case of the celestial musician Pañcasikha, recorded approximately two millennia ago. The technical term for this religious behavior is *lokiya*, denoting literally "worldly" but in the wider, and deeper, Buddhist frame of reference connoting something like religiously customary practices and orientations circumscribed by our own capacities of conceptualization.

When Pañcasikha completed his song, the Buddha complimented him, noting both the complementarity and balance of the music from the strings of his instrument and from his voice. Then the Buddha asked when Pañcasikha composed this song about the Buddha, Dhamma, Arahants, and love.

The reply by Pañcasikha introduces another story-frame within the larger frame. It seems that Pañcasikha was in love with Bhaddā, another *gandhabba*, who was in love with someone else. Not being successful in his attempts to catch her fancy in any other way, Pañcasikha took his special lute (*beluvapaṇḍu-viṇā*) and sang the song. When Bhaddā heard it, she said to Pañcasikha that although she had not met the Blessed One (*Bhagavan*), she had heard of him when dancing (*sic*) in the Sudhamma hall in the heavens of the thirty-three gods (Tāvatiṃsa). She suggests that since Pañcasikha praised the Blessed One, they arrange a meeting that very day. Pañcasikha brings the inner-story frame to a close by doffing his hat to propriety, as it were, and relating to the Buddha that he did not actually meet her on that day, but later. The main story line continues with Sakka telling Pañcasikha to salute the Buddha and to announce the coming of the lord of the gods. The questions of Sakka for the Buddha ensue.

Pañcasikha appears elsewhere in the cumulative accounts in the tradition. He is met again, descending with the Buddha, when the latter descended from the heaven of the thirty-three gods (Tāvatiṃsa), having there continued his teaching ministry. Pañcasikha, with his special lute, venerated (*pūja*) the Buddha (*DhpA*:III,225).

What might one conclude about this passage relating to Sakka, Pañcasikha, the Buddha, and Bhaddā? It is possible that one has, in this account, a continuation of a kind of old, "all-India" motif of a god beseeching a *gandhabba* to tempt a meditative ascetic whose psychic powers were beginning to rival those of the god or gods concerned. If this was the case originally, one is confronted with a reworking of the passage by a redactor or redactors. Pañcasikha, by his singing, brings the Buddha out of his deep meditation, but he does so by a song carefully introduced, in the prose portion of the text, as having to do with the Buddha, Dhamma, worthy ones, and love. The first three ideas, representing core concepts in the Buddhist heritage, have made legitimate the presence of this song at this place in the text. In the full passage, Pañcasikha gets his wish, his beloved's willingness to be with him, not as a result of his having tempted or tricked the Buddha and not as a result of receiving a divine favor. Although such notion of a divine favor (*varam*) would have been fitting in the cultural context, it might have led to ambiguity about Pañcasikha's motive and role. His wish is fulfilled as a consequence of his having revered (*pūja*) the Buddha in song.

Sensual desire (*kāma*) is a means by which Māra ensnares, while romantic love (*kāma*) is an emotion among humans and gods made legitimate.

According to the tradition, the lute, with which Māra sang of sensual desire (*kāma*) in attempting to seduce disciples and the Buddha, has fallen to the ground. Yet the lute has been lifted again and sounds again in a song of romantic love (*kāma*) which is now wholly accepted by the Buddha, because that emotion has been placed into the proper context. The expression of romantic love once considered beguiling, deceiving, ensnaring, now receives illustrative, explicative, additional force by means of analogy with fundamental religious orientations among Buddhists, orientations to the Buddha, Dhamma, and the Arahants./12/

Music that can pervert oneself or another, song that has the subtle capacity to turn one aside, can now be utilized in expressing the sentiment of romantic love, can now also be a part of manifesting reverent praise. Buddhists would agree with the adage of romance—"love makes the world go round." *Saṃsāra*, the whirl (*vaṭṭa*) of existence through many life cycles, is kept spinning, as it were, by sensuality, even the long acknowledged emotion of romantic love. This kind of love, Buddhists have attested, is applauded in its ideal expression but is inadequate in itself as a means for transcending *saṃsāra*, i.e., as a means of transcending itself. So, too, is reverent praise (*pūja*) of the Buddha, Dhamma, and Arahants or other noble disciples. For Buddhists there is more involved in the soteriological process. There is that dimension of human experience, that ineffable realization, which is not religiously customary (*lokiya*), not circumscribed by our own capacities of conceptualization, is higher (*uttara*) than all of this (*loka*), goes beyond this (*lokuttara*); that moment when the world-transcending path arises before one's mind and in one's consciousness and one gains one's first vision of Nibbāna.

Music and song, when placed into the proper context, are customarily considered to be religiously supportive. When songs contribute to the arising of wholesome (*kusala*) dispositions, the predominating bent of one's thoughts (*citta*), those songs are fitting.

III

Quite consonant with this strand of the cumulative tradition are the contemporary modes of expressing religiousness in music and in song in Sri Lanka. That the music and song be recognized as Buddhist, as religious, does not necessitate their incorporation into liturgy or ritual, but a recognition that they are anchored by themes fully consonant with the Buddhist religious heritage.

The songs that have made the register of the most popular, most appreciated, most meaningful, are those that point the hearer to the existential reality of a dimension of the teachings passed down in the tradition and to the efficacy of those teachings, when personally appropriated, to enable one to discern salvific Truth—the abiding reality of which provides the *raison d'être* of the teachings.

In communicating what Buddhist laity are doing religiously with music and song today in Sri Lanka, one can note three general modes, only the first and third of which will receive our attention in the body of this article: (1) sung chant either in Pāli or Sinhala, in a ritual setting or while on pilgrimage, usually corporate in nature; (2) *kavi* or sung Sinhala verse;/13/ and (3) contemporary Sinhala musical compositions. The themes are didactic, hortatory, and expressive of personal insights or wonder. In most cases, the songs engage the hearer in a commonality of shared experiences by repeating teachings sanctioned by tradition or by evoking mutually recognized moments of personal religious awareness.

To the first category belongs the *Jayamaṅgala Gāthā*, "Verses of Wonderful Victory," numbering approximately nine verses in the Pāli language, sung on auspicious occasions and regularly at weddings, often by young girls. Among the laity, perhaps there is no group of verses that carries a greater sense of invoking corporate supportiveness to mingle with one's wishes for good fortune. Each verse recounts a marvelous accomplishment of the Buddha and closes with a repeated refrain wishing one joyous or wonderful victory by the power of the Buddha's illustrious accomplishment./14/

One of the most popular Pāli verses in the Theravāda heritage, known by heart by laity and monks alike, has been put to music and sung by W. D. Amaradeva, one of the leading contemporary composer-singers in Sri Lanka. The verse, often heard over the radio on religious holidays, might be considered the core statement of the Buddhist tradition.

> Refraining from all that is detrimental,
> The attainment of what is wholesome,
> The purification of one's mind;
> This is the instruction of the Buddhas./15/

In a moving Sinhala rendition of an old theme, the threefold refuge, a group of men and women musicians have recorded a song, replete with instrumental accompaniment (chimes, *śruti*, flute and drums), long associated with pilgrimage to Śrī Pāda, or Adam's Peak. In a particular recording of only three verses in length, the opening verse, sung by women, indicates a totality of personal involvement.

> Bearing on my head the refuge that is the Buddha,
> Cleansing the mind, the refuge that is Dhamma,
> Donning the robes, the refuge that is the Sangha,
> I will live, having faith in the threefold refuge./16/

The second verse, sung by men, by mentioning the three times of day, dawn, midday, and evening, each being indicative of a dimension of the threefold refuge, suggests the totality of commitment in the process of human existence. The third verse is culminative in religious affirmation, although this might not be readily communicated here in English:

Refuge, refuge, Buddha is refuge.
Refuge, refuge, Dhamma is refuge.
Refuge, refuge, Sangha is refuge.
Refuge, refuge, these three are refuge./17/

An interesting rather recent development in ritual procedures performed at the temple on religious holidays is a form of corporate sung chanting in which both monks and laity chant melodiously together in Sinhala. Although the customary procedure is for the laity to listen attentively while the monks chant canonical passages in Pāli, and although one occasionally hears some criticism of this new form,/18/ those who participate in this new form in Sinhala speak very highly of it and will go to considerable inconvenience in travel to be present for it. Venerable Panadure Ariyadhamma has created the chanting patterns and has composed many verses in Sinhala for such purposes. The following, from a recording,/19/ provides an example:

May there be wholesome thoughts in every mind.
May they be bathed with loving kindness and compassion.
May concord, community, and loving kindness spread afar.
May all persons on earth attain well-being./20/

To the third category belong a variety of contemporary compositions that draw upon religious themes but are not particularly associated with religious holidays or corporate ritual settings. In a Sinhala motion picture, "Kiṇkiṇi Pādā" ("Anklets"), a song begins by quoting, in a sung chant mode, a Pāli canonical passage, with a repetition of the second phrase, thereby focusing sharply the religious context. An English translation of the Pāli is

Death destroys one's human form
It destroys not one's name and lineage./21/

The two singers, a man and woman, then move into Sinhala. Representative phrases are

Everything that is beautiful gives but brief satisfaction;
Sorrow is at the end of it,
Sorrow is at the end of it./22/
If with both eyes one can see, if one can smell,
If one's ears are not deaf;
There is the advantage of enjoyment—yet, misfortune is near.
What's the benefit of the fivefold sense desires?/23/

The last verse says,

While the lamp of Dhamma true is burning,
Why become immersed in the darkness of wrong?
Without Buddha-dhamma, there is no welfare;
Without Buddha-dhamma, there is no welfare.
That is the highest gain./24/

From the soundtrack of another movie, "Sat Samudura" ("Seven Seas"), one
hears W. D. Amaradeva sing,

> Unstable is the ocean of *saṃsāra*;
> No calmness there, so turbulent.
> Ten thousand times within
> One nudges death./25/

And the song continues,

> This filthy body is pithless; it does not last.
> Only the good that was done remains in this world.
> There is poverty, helplessness, sickness, and sorrow
> For us, us human beings.
> Why does one not think of this,
> In this unstable ocean of *saṃsāra*?/26/

Victor Ratnāyake, a leading contemporary composer-singer, in one of
the most famous, most appreciated performances, called "Sa" (the first note
of the musical scale), begins the evening of song with an introduction not
unlike an invocation,

> By the power of the Sambuddha and Dhamma true,
> With the peace of Viṣṇu and Śrī Skanda,
> With the blessing of Sarasvati, who sits on the lotus seat,
> For the purpose of your enjoyment
> In this beautiful night that gives birth to joy,
> May twenty-four thousand ears
> Be uplifted with delight,
> Be uplifted with delight./27/

In this same concert, Victor Ratnāyake sings "Devram Veherā" (Pāli:
Devārama Vihāra), a song representing one's longing to have been alive at the
time when the Buddha was residing at a monastic dwelling called Devārama.
But, apparently, since insufficient meritorious acts had been done, and
consequently one was not living then in the presence of the Buddha, one takes
one's place before a statue of the Buddha, there to meditate in hopes of being
reborn in the future in the presence of the next Buddha, Maitreya. With
subtlety of voice and insight, Ratnāyake sings,

> Among a thousand fires of lamentations and sorrows,
> In the darkness of fires burning in my heart and mind,
> O Lord, by simply seeing your statue,
> They become completely extinguished—what is the mystery?/28/

Addressing the complex of human emotions and cluster of ideas that are
present in one who stands reflectively before a statue of the Buddha,
W. D. Amaradeva sings of a famous statue in the ancient city of Anurādha-
pura, and concludes with the following:

Like a mighty flood that overflowing moves,
Like a cooling cascade flowing down,
That soothes the weariness of this desert of existence,
The majesty of Buddha's virtues that gives Nibbāna.
The Samādhi Buddha Statue in Mahāmevunā Park,
The Samādhi Buddha Statue.

Falling currents of loving kindness, gentleness, compassion,
Flowing from eyes half-closed,
Falling currents of loving kindness, gentleness, compassion,
Flowing from eyes half-closed./29/

We have already mentioned Śrī Pāda, or Adam's Peak, in relation to an old refrain sung by pilgrims and recently performed by musicians and singers for radio broadcast. W. D. Amaradeva sings a brief song, well known and often heard, about Śrī Pāda. Omitting refrains, the words are

At the blessed feet of the Sage
Where a world-transcending sound spreads afar,
There comes a breeze extinguishing fatigue,
Which gives a silver calm, which pacifies the heart./30/

Music whether in liturgical or non-liturgical settings has a place in the Theravāda Buddhist tradition. Although it has no formal place in long estab-lished ritual procedures, except for drums and *horanā* to inaugurate auspi-cious moments, its presence appears to have been long assured insofar as its legitimization derives from the religious themes on which it focuses. Music is accepted in this tradition as an authentic form of religious expression insofar as it points beyond itself as an art form.

IV

From the incipient phase of the Buddhist movement there has been a contrast between the regulated living patterns established for those in the monastic life and the guidelines proposed for the laity. What is not accept-able behavior for a monk is clearly enunciated in order to assist a monk in the movement through training and mental discipline nearer to a state of clarity and purity of mind, and so to be poised for an arising of the first vision of Nibbāna. "Beware of what might detract and distract from this movement," the monastic regulations exhort.

Recommendations about guarding the senses, about putting at a dis-tance the adhesive weight of sensuality, including attachment to sound, are part of the monastic regimen of disciplined reflection. The ancient text which provides the major guidelines for monastic living includes an admoni-tion by the Buddha against singing in the ordinary manner:

O monks there are five disadvantages for one singing the teaching in
an extended sung intonation. [1] He is attached to himself regarding
that sound, [2] and others are attached to that sound, [3] and even
householders are irritated, [4] there is a dissolution of concentration
on the part of one straining to lock in on the sound, and [5] people
who follow after [this procedure] undergo an adherence to opinions.
(*Vin*:II,108)/31/

The Buddha is here recorded as establishing a stylistic difference between
the chanting of the monks/32/ and the singing of the laity. Rather than chant,
he might tend to focus on the sound and not on the meaning of the teachings,
might think the sound of his voice to be beautiful—in vibrato or pitch or
tone—might think of himself as skilled, might think of himself. Also, others
might find their attention turning from the meaning of the teachings to the
sound of the singing. And the laity consider such singing as not proper for a
monk, as being undecorous. Such a singer loses his focused concentration since
the focal awareness shifts from meaning and purpose to notes and scales. And,
further, people would tend to endorse one mode over others, would begin to
become attached to their opinion about which mode is the most beautiful.
Straightforwardly, resolutely, the statement is that the meaning is in the
message, set apart in metrical chant from the commonplace, but otherwise
unadorned.

Institutionally, therefore, the distinction between monastic and lay modes
of conduct has tended to produce two different approaches to music. Ideally,
the mainstream position of the tradition avers, while a layman might compose
songs about the religious life, a monk is to meditate on the fundamentals of
religious truth and to compose his life as an expression of that truth. The laity
creates musical compositions; the monks enter into meditation and concentration. Not all laymen are composers, and, it is widely held in Sri Lanka, not all
monks excel in their exacting discipline.

What, for Buddhists in Sri Lanka, would constitute good religious music?/33/ The tradition has recorded that music that evokes passion is to be put
aside—Māra dropped his lute. Music that is discerned as heavenly is acceptable—Sakka picked up the lute and gave it to Pañcasikha, a heavenly *gandhabba*. Heavenly music, as the old texts say, which is beautifully rendered in
quality of instrument and of voice, in harmonious balance of instrument with
voice, and utilized in reverent praise of religious themes, symbolized in the
reference to the Buddha, Dhamma, and the Arahants and other noble ones, is
acceptable and is positively endorsed.

But is not there still a fundamental dichotomy, a fundamental cleavage
between creating, performing, sharing, hearing, and appreciating religious
music and the higher pursuits of meditation and quiet contemplation? Institutionally and behaviorally, yes (see Karunatillake:3–5 and Perera:79–100).
But existentially, as a dimension of human experience, the matter is much
too fluid and subtle for one to categorize in terms of dichotomy or cleavage.

Just as there are institutionally two dimensions, so the soteriological process within the Buddhist context of faith is spoken of as having two dimensions: *lokiya*, what is customary, that which is limited by agential conceptualization; and *lokuttara*, that which is not limited by what is humanly customary, that which transcends even what one might consider to be heavenly. We have touched on these two ideas above and return now to them to reinforce the point of the legitimation of music and song in the soteriological process in the contemporary setting.

It would misrepresent, by being stunningly inadequate, the subtlety of Buddhist religious insight to equate *lokiya* with the life of the laity and *lokuttara* with the monastic life. The latter form of living is considered more conducive to a quest or a realization of *lokuttara*-wisdom. But confusion occurs when one takes what is conducive to a pursuit, or the quest itself, as synonymous with the realization itself. Both modes of life, the lay and the monastic, are to be interpreted from the perspective of each particular person involved; and, as a fundamental religious aspiration of Theravāda Buddhists, it is wished that each person live well within the *lokiya* frame of reference in the hope that the *lokuttara* occurrence will arise.

The primary concern of this cumulative religious tradition is not to have everyone enter the monastic order, obviously. It is to contribute to a religiously meaningful orientation of one's life within the *lokiya* dimension of human existence by providing a context broader, deeper, higher (*uttara*) than that existence (*loka*), a context assured to be available to human awareness both because of the testimony of those noble ones (*sāvakasangha*) who have seen through to it, and because this availability is inherent in the order of reality (*dhammatā*).

Music of praise for the Buddha, Dhamma, and the Sangha (*sāvakasaṅgha*, the noble witnesses, and, symbolically, the *bhikkhusaṅgha*, the order of monks), is *lokiya*, but it is properly and consistently oriented when it turns one away from self-focus and when it enhances, by a *lokiya* medium, a message that the *lokiya* is not all there is to human life. All human effort, creations of the human mind, exertions of the will, even compositions of religious music, must fall away at a moment of mind's "creative passivity"/34/ when the first vision of Nibbāna occurs.

The monastic regimen (*vinaya*), by making more restricted the day-to-day processes of life, keeps sharply highlighted an awareness of a broader, more meaningful context of human living. And in this regimen (*vinaya*) religious music plays no part. Persons of the laity, who are met with day-to-day contingencies and uncertainty, might not keenly discern the stability of an awareness of a broader, more meaningful context of human living. And in this setting of lay life, religious music plays a substantial role. For monks well along the way of contemplative discipline, religious music might be a distraction. For other monks and for the laity, it might provide direction.

The soteriological process, although fused in customary interpretations in Sri Lanka with the act of entering the monastic order, is not to be confused with it, as being synonymous with this shift in institutional status./35/ The monastic discipline (*vinaya*) and the religious utilization of the lute (*vīṇā*) are *lokiya*, limited. Both can be means for one who seeks a further goal; both can be obstacles for one who clings to them.

Like everything else that is *lokiya*, limited to the whirl of life that is *saṃsāra*, religious music is also, finally, unstable, fleeting. At the dawning of world-transcending (*lokuttara*) salvific insight (*paññā*), even the strings of the lute fall silent, for it is in mental quietude that the mind becomes poised with a spontaneously alert receptivity to the arising of the first vision of Nibbāna. Those who have realized this moment are neither tempted by religious music, nor are they disturbed by it. Music, for them, has lost its delight:

> For such a one there is no delight
> In music's fivefold sound
> Like that for one discerning Truth fully,
> Who has one-pointedness of mind. (*Thag*:43, vs. 348)

> Some delight in *mutiṅga*-drums,
> In lutes (*vīṇās*) and *paṇa*-drums.
> But I at the base of a tree
> Delight in the instruction of the Buddha. (*Thag*:49, vs. 467)

In commenting on a phrase "Delight in Dhamma prevails over all delights," occurring in verse 354 of the *Dhammapada*, the commentary on that text says: "The delight in sons and daughters, in wealth, in women and the numerous [other] kinds of delight, such as that for dance, song, music, etc., are [ultimately] causes for suffering alone, causing [one, as they do,] to fall into the whirl of *saṃsāra*. But this joy that arises within one who either speaks out *dhamma* or hears *dhamma* produces a sense of elation, causes tears to fall and makes [one's] hairs to stand on end. It puts an end to the whirl of *saṃsāra*; it is [a state] having [its] end in the Fruit of Arahantship. Hence of all delights this kind of delight in *dhamma* is the best."/36/

V

The Theravāda Buddhist tradition takes a position that music which might contribute to the arousal of sensuality, even music which might call attention to itself as a noteworthy human creation, must be put aside. In its place is to be religious music that is put into the service of communicating Dhamma, an old and historically successful Buddhist enterprise, and our references to the contemporary setting in Sri Lanka have demonstrated the continuing response through faith of Buddhists in placing their musical talents into this service. Even when put into this service, religious music still might draw attention to itself, pull focal awareness from the message to the medium. However, religious music among Buddhists in Sri Lanka is considered at its best when it tends to efface itself in the presence of the message. In this way, religious music becomes fully consonant with the religious activity of renouncing the cosmic centrality of the self, a mode of renunciation with which Buddhists are familiarly conversant, even to the extent of renouncing the self completely in the presence of salvific Truth to which the message points.

In conclusion, and speaking metaphorically, the lute of ordinary music and song is to be dropped, and then to be picked up again to be played in praise, and finally to be put aside, appreciatively, when one hears that sound not produced by human creativity or, as the point is more frequently put in English, realizes that vision which arises uncaused by human agency.

The institutional dichotomy of *vinaya* vs. *viṇā* formally remains. Practically, meditative concentration on psychic processes is difficult when in a musical concert. Hence, *viṇā* yields to *vinaya*; but both at their best are not in themselves conclusive, but are conducive to a more noble event, not at all synonymous with entering the monastic order.

Of the arising of the path on which one can walk through this world (*lokiya*) in a process of transcending this world (*lokuttara*), a contemporary Buddhist has written: "Thus the *magga* [path] event, swiftly arising after a moment of the mind's creative passiveness, regenerates and makes a new person of the pilgrim and gives him his first vision of Nibbāna. It is the true blessed event of the religious life of the Theravada Buddhist. What is infused into mind at that moment is *lokuttara paññā*: 'world-transcending insight'" (Palihawadana, 1978:191).

NOTES

/1/   *Naccagītavāditavisūkadassanā veramaṅī* (Vin:I,83). This precept also occurs in a section dealing with moral virtue at *D*:I,5. The practice of seeing performances or shows involving dancing, singing, and instrumental music is considered a *dukkaṭa* offense for monks (Vin:II,107–8). A *dukkaṭa* offense is a light offense. This practice is considered a *pāccitiya* offense for nuns (Vin:IV,267). A *paccitiya* offense is more serious in that it puts a person in a state requiring expiation or rectification before the person is again considered of proper disposition.

/2/   Mrs. Rhys Davids translates this verse: "Thou art fair, and life is young, beauteous Khemā! / I am young, even I, too—Come, O fairest lady! / While in our ear fivefold harmonies murmur melodious. / Seek we our pleasure" (*Psm S*, 83).

/3/   It is not yet established to what degree the *viṇā*, in the strata of texts consulted, was similar to what has evolved into the classical *viṇā* of South India.

/4/   E. M. Hare, in a note to his translation of the passage, refers to a commentarial observation: "*Satta sarā, tayo gāmā, mucchanā ekavīsati, / Thānā ekūnapaññāsaṃ, icc' ete sara-maṇḍalaṃ* (Seven notes, three scales and one and twenty tones, / Forty-nine stops,—such is the scope of music" (*BGS*:III, 267, n. 1). The Commentary concludes, "So he [Soṇa] was thoroughly well-versed in the art of the [heavenly] *gandhabbas*." (See *AA*:III, 390.)

/5/   The references to synonyms (*adhivacana*) are listed in *PTSD*, esp. 205b, *sv.* *kāma.*

/6/   For a brief interpretive excursus of a few Buddhist rituals in Sri Lanka, see Carter, 1979a, esp. 181–87.

/7/   There are noteworthy differences in chanting techniques among the three monastic communities (*nikāyas*) in Sri Lanka: the Siyam-nikāya, the Ramañña-nikāya, and particularly in the case of the Amarapura-nikāya. A careful study and documentation of these differences has yet to be undertaken.

/8/   This same verse occurs also in S:I,122. In that passage, Māra asks the Buddha whence has the rebirth-linking-consciousness of one Godhika gone. On receiving a reply from the Buddha that such consciousness can no longer be found, Māra dropped his lute (*vīṇā*) and vanished. Of interest in this account is the notation that Māra, when he approached, was carrying a yellow hued wood lute (*vīṇā*). The passage reads: "*Atha kho Māro pāpimā beluva-paṇḍuvīṇam ādāya yena Bhagavā tenupasaṅkami.*"

/9/   This lute (*vīṇā*) has been described in the commentarial literature. For references, see under *Beluvapaṇḍuvīṇa* in *DDPN*:II,314.

/10/   *Gāthā abhāsi Buddhūpasaṃhitā dhammūpasaṃhitā arahantūpasaṃhitā kāmūpasaṃhitā.*

/11/   For a fine, but slightly guarded, English translation of the song, see *Dialogues*:II,301–2, 303–4.

/12/   On the standard threefold formula of the Buddha, that which he taught (Dhamma), about that of which he taught (Dhamma), and the noble disciples (*Sāvaka-saṅgha*—including but not limited to Arahants), see Carter, ed., 1982.

/13/   A representative collection of examples of *kavi* was done by Hugh Nevill. The Sinhala *kavi* are by no means limited to themes derived from the Pāli canonical and commentarial strata. The religious heritage reflected in the *kavi* is cumulative and complex. For *kavi* examples dealing with the threefold refuge (*tunsaraṇa*), see I,48; II,122,149; Śri Pāda or Adam's Peak, see I,47,234.
      An old *goyam kavi*, "verse of the farmers," is often sung while working in the paddy fields and communicates an attitude of longing for the presence of the Buddha. The verse in my recording is considered old; the title is unknown; the author is anonymous, and the style is traditional. "Is it not with an eye on the seasons that you do your plowing? / Is it not when the blossoms have gone that the paddy matures? / Is it not Saturn who withholds the mass of rain? / O, when will I see the world-transcending Buddha?" The Sinhala is: "*kal balā noveda govi tän karannē āṅgāṅgā / malvara noveda kiriväda päsennē āṅgāṅgā / senasurā noveda väyipala nodunnē āṅgāṅgā / lovuturā budun kavada dakinnē āṅgāṅgā.*" Another example of a *kavi*, in sung chant, based on a rhythmical meter of upcountry (Kandy area) dance

patterns, tells of the coming of the sacred tooth relic of the Buddha to Sri Lanka. The verses begin with an invitation of the gods Brahmā, Ganes̄, S̄iva, Skanda, Sumanā, and Viṣṇu (*sat at vat at tisulat harihara sumanā ēranyagarbha*), and a host of other deities, that the Buddha descend to India, there to become enlightened. The verses continue: "Having come from the heavens of the thirty [three] / He entered the womb of famous Māyā and later was born. / Having sat at twenty-four auspicious seats [of previous Buddhas], / Having fulfilled twenty-four innumerable perfections, / Having caused twenty-four thousand to attain Nibbāna, / The King of Sages, who had become the Buddha, passed away." The Sinhala is: "*āvit pasiñdu māyā kusa väsa bihi veminā tidāsa pura / suvisi maṅdapayaka vāḍa siṭalā / suvisi asaṅkaya peruman puralā / suvisi dahasak nivanaṭa häralā / vädiyayi muniraja budu vī ekalā.*" On occasion dancers, while in procession, will chant these verses, and some might chant them before the tooth relic at Daladā Maligawa, the temple of the tooth relic, in Kandy. The procession of the tooth relic, *daladā perahära*, has provided a context for dance and a subject for song. "The Golden Chimes," a contemporary "pop-group," have recorded a song with rhythmical patterns derived from the Portuguese. The song is youthful, popular, rather descriptive, but not without insight. Two verses are: "The clinking sound of those selling beetle, / Like the sound of dancers' anklets, / The cracking sound of whips / Tell us the *perahära* is coming nigh / And it spreads afar the majesty of the venerable tooth relic," and: "Faintly hearing from their moving lips *kavi*-verses sung with *horanā̄* / Upcountry dancers come, / Moving feet to the rhythm of *gäṭa*-drum, / Bringing auspiciousness to the *daladā perahära*." The Sinhala is: "*kiṅkini nadadena sārabulatviṭa vikuṇana ayagē / kasa haṇḍa pupuraṇa apahaṭa perahära / laṅga ena bava pavasayi / daladā samiṅdugē teda paturayi / horanā nadeṭa kiyamin kavipada tolpeti maturannā /gäṭabera tāleṭa tabamin pā deka uḍa raṭa naṭu ennā / daladā perahära siri ganvā.*"

/14/ An English translation of the *Jayamaṅgala Gāthā* is provided by the Venerables Nārada Mahā Thera and Kassapa Thera in *The Mirror of the Dhamma* (Colombo: Ceylon Daily News, June, 1961), pp. 45–48. A recording of these verses, beautifully sung by a male voice, accompanied by only a *thambura*, followed by a Sinhala translation in prose, finely articulated and softly spoken by a male announcer, was broadcast by the Sri Lanka Broadcasting Corporation—Sinhala Service, on Vesak, 1980.

/15/ "*Sabba pāpassa akaranaṃ / kusalassa upasampadā / sacittapariyodapanaṃ /etam buddhāna sāsanaṃ*" (*Dhp*: vs. 183).

/16/ "*Buddaṃ saraṇē sirasa darāgena / dammaṃ saraṇē sita pahadāgena / sangaṃ saraṇē sivuru darāgena / iññayi tun saraṇē adahāgena.*" This verse, and the second sung by the group, but with very slight modification, can be found in *Purāṇa Tun Saraṇaya*, author(s) unknown, but probably at least two centuries old (my copy; Mātara, Sri Lanka: Kānti Veḷando, n.d.), vss. 16–17, p. 3.

/17/ From my recording, the Sinhala reads: "*Saraṇayi saraṇayi buddaṃ saraṇayi / saraṇayi saraṇayi dammaṃ saraṇayi / saraṇayi saraṇayi sangaṃ saraṇayi / saraṇayi saraṇayi mē tun saraṇayi.*" When an idea occurs twelve times in one verse so positioned, one can hardly fail to note the significance of this idea, namely, refuge, in the Theravāda heritage. On the idea of "refuge," see Carter, 1979c:41–52, reprinted with slight revision in Carter, 1982.

/18/   The occasional critical comments or reticence to approve this new ritual form might reflect a reluctance to break with tradition. It might also reflect a sense that monks do well to refrain from composing verses for the laity. So *D*:I,11, regarding *kavi*, and the *Daṁbadeṇi Katikāvata* (13th century), paragraph 49 in *Kk*:55, regarding *ślokas*.

/19/   My recorded copy was taken from a recording made by Dr. B. Sirisena, who worked with me in July, 1981, as we both searched for relevant data by listening to our tape holdings.

/20/   The Sinhala of the verse: "*häma sitkama pin situvili vēvā / metta karunā diyaren näha vēvā / samagiya sāmaya met pätirēvā / siyaludenā lova suvapat vēvā.*"

/21/   *S*:I,43: "*Rūpaṁ jīrati maccānam nāmagottaṁ na jīrati.*"

/22/   "*lassana säma dē mohotaka suva dē / ehi kelavara duka vē / ehi kelavara duka vē.*" Compare *Dhp*:vss. 186–87.

/23/   "*deneta penēnaṁ suvaṅda dänēnaṁ / savana bihiri näti nam /säpata vāsi vī vipataṭa vī / kimada säpeka paskam.*"

/24/   "*dälvena atarē sadaham dīpē / maṅda gilennē aṅdurē pāpē /bududahamin tora säpak näte / bududahamin tora säpak näte / parama suvaya ēkayi.*"

/25/   "*ataraturē nomäri märe / dasa dahas varē / nisala nätē sasala vetē /notira sasara sāgarē.*"

/26/   "*kuṇu kaya nisaruy näta pavatinnē / kala hoṅda pamaṇayi melova räṅdennē / näti bärikama leda duk äti vannē / apaṭayi minisunē / äyi meya nositannē /notira sasara sāgarē.*" (Cf. *Dhp*:vss. 6, 146–48.)

/27/   "*sambuddha saddharma anuhasin / gōvinda śrī skanda śāntiyen / kamalāsanārūdha sarasvati āsirvādayen / rasika oba milanayen / ānanda janakavū soṅduru rātri yāmayē / suvahasak savan yuga / prītiyen udam vēvā / prītiyen udam vēvā.*"

/28/   "*sahasak domnas duk gini atarē / dävena mahada situvili gini andurē / samiṅda obe piḷiruva duṭu pamaṇin / nivī nivī yayī arumaya kimadō.*"

/29/   "*pirī tirī yana maha vaturak sē / galā hälena sihiläl gaṅgulak sē /giman nivālana mē bava katarē / nivan sadālana budu guṇa mahimē / maha mevuna uyanē / samādhi budu piḷimē / samādhi budu piḷimē // aḍavan vū denetin galanā / met muditā karuṇā dhārā / aḍavan vū denetin galanā / met muditā karuṇā dhāra.*" The English translation appearing in the text was jointly made with Professor M. Palihawadana in Kandy, Sri Lanka, in 1971.

/30/   Omitting the refrains, the Sinhala is: "*muni siripā piyumē lovuturu haṅda pävarē / pavan hamā ē giman nivālana / ridī pahan dī laya sänahē.*"

/31/   These five disadvantages are also given in *A*:III,251. However, there, the irritation of the householders is explained with reference to the third disadvantage in the sequence of five by the observation, "these recluse Sakya-sons sing just like we sing."

/32/   In fact the Pāli term that stands behind the usual English rendering of "council" is *sangīti*, a word meaning a "song" or "chorus," and was used to refer to the early convocations because the texts were chanted and through this means of comparing memories an established memorized canon took shape.

/33/   There is some discussion in Sri Lanka, not yet widely conducted or available in published form, about whether *bhakti-gī*, devotional music/singing, is indigenous to the Theravāda heritage. A frequently met opinion is that this genre of religious music in the tradition is a recently reconstructed borrowing or response to religious music of Western and Christian origin. Such appears to be the case especially at Vesak, the festive occasion of celebrating the birth, enlightenment, and the complete, final Nibbāna/Nirvāna of the Buddha, on a parallel with Christmas carols and hymns of Christmastide. But the degree to which this opinion represents a comprehensive statement of the case remains to a considerable degree based on an argument from silence: there has not been a tradition of preserving in written documents a musical heritage. It is entirely plausible that religious songs were sung by the laity in the villages or while on pilgrimage, while musical scores remained unwritten.

In a tradition that has long excelled in the literary mode of versification in superb poetry in Pāli and Sinhala, it appears that, at this initial stage of inquiry into this facet of this complex cumulative tradition, one might withhold the opinion that religious music, whether appropriately labeled *bhakti-gī* or otherwise designated, is not indigenous to the history of Buddhist men and women in Sri Lanka.

/34/   This point was made by Professor M. Palihawadana when he wrote, "The 'creative passivity' at the end of the field of possible action serves as the ground for the emergence of salvific change . . ." (1978:190).

/35/   See Perry and Ratnayaka, where the recurrent observation is most recently made again, that the soteriological process does not require entry into the monastic order.

/36/   DhpA:IV,75–76. The English translation is from a forthcoming work, "*The Dhammapada: A New English Translation with the Pāli Text and for the First Time an English translation of the Commentary's Explanation of the Verses with Notes Translated from Sinhala Sources and Critical Textual Comments,*" by John Ross Carter and M. Palihawadana.

SECONDARY SOURCES

Carter, John Ross
    1979a   "The Buddhist Tradition." In *Modern Sri Lanka: A Society in Transition*, ed. by Tissa Fernando and Robert W. Kearney. Syracuse, N.Y.: Foreign and Comparative Studies/South Asian Series, no. 4, Syracuse University.

1979b   (ed.) *Religiousness in Sri Lanka*. Colombo: Marga Institute.
1979c   "The notion of refuge (*saraṇa*) in the Theravāda Buddhist tradi-
                 tion." *Studies in Pali and Buddhism*, ed. by. A. K. Narain. Delhi:
                 B. R. Publishing Corporation. Also in the following:
1982   (ed.) *The Threefold Refuge*, with George D. Bond, Edmund
                 Perry, and Shanta Ratnayaka. Chambersburg, Pa: Anima Press.

Karunatillake, W. S.
1979   "The Religiousness of Buddhists in Sri Lanka Through Belief
                 and Practice." In Carter (1979b).

Nevill, Hugh
1954–55   *Sinhala Verse (Kavi)*. Pts. 1–3. Ed. by P. E. P. Deraniyagala.
                 Colombo: Ceylon National Museums Manuscript Series, vols.
                 4–6.

Palihawadana, M.
1978   "Is there a Theravada Buddhist idea of grace?" In *Christian
                 Faith in a Religiously Plural World*, ed. by Donald G. Dawe
                 and John B. Carman. Maryknoll, N.Y.: Orbis Press.
1979   "Dhamma Today and Tomorrow." In Carter (1979b).

Perera, L. P. N.
1979   "The Significance of the Sangha for the Laity." In Carter
                 (1979b).

Perry, Edmund, and Ratnayake, Shanta
1982   "The Sangha in the Threefold Refuge." In Carter (1982).

PRIMARY SOURCES AND REFERENCE WORKS

Editions used are those of the Pali Text Society unless otherwise indicated.

Abbreviation	Title
A	*The Anguttara-nikaya.*
AA	*Manoratha pūranī: Commentary on the Anguttara-nikāya.*
BGS	*The Book of the Gradual Sayings.*
D	*Digha-nikāya.*
Dhp	*The Dhammapada.*
DhpA	*The Commentary on the Dhammapada.*
DPPN	*Dictionary of Pali Proper Names.*
Dialogues	*Dialogues of the Buddha.*
Itv	*Iti-vuttaka.*
Jā	*The Jātaka Together with Its Commentary.*
Kk	*The Kati Kāvatas: Laws of the Buddhist Order of Ceylon from the 12th Century to the 18th Century.* Ed. and trans. by Nandasena Ratnapala. *Münchener Studien zur Sprachwissenschaft.* Munich, 1971.
M	*The Majjhima-nikāya.*

PsmS	*Psalms of the Early Buddhists I: Psalms of the Sisters.*
PTSD	*The Pali Text Society's Pali-English Dictionary.*
S	*The Samyutta-nikāya of the Sutta-Pitaka.*
Sn (HOS)	*Buddha's Teachings: Being the Sutta-Nipata or Discourse-collection.* Edition in Pali with English translation by Lord Chalmers. Harvard Oriental Series, No. 37. Cambridge: Harvard University Press, 1932.
SnA	*Sutta-nipāta Commentary II: Being Paramatthajotika II.*
Thag	*The Thera- and Theri-gāthā: Part I, Theragāthā.*
Thig	*The Thera- and Theri-gāthā: Part II, Therīgāthā.*
Vin	*The Vinaya Piṭakam.*

On Practicing Religiously:
Music as Sacred in India

Donna Marie Wulff

The religious significance of music in India was first impressed upon me by the avid devotion of an Oberlin College freshman who had studied music in South India. Learning that I was a faculty resident in the college's Asia House, he asked if he might keep in my apartment the large stringed instrument that he had brought back with him. From the moment the *viṇā* arrived I was aware that it was to be treated like no other instrument I had ever seen. Its installation, on a special mat spread out on my living room floor, had the quality of a religious ritual. Subsequently, whenever its owner came to practice, he took off his shoes before touching it; I, too, had to remove mine when he consented to show me how to play a scale. He would never step over the instrument, nor was I to allow anyone else to do so. I found these rituals and proscriptions most puzzling, and it was only after I myself had undertaken the formal study of Indian music that I began to understand the significance of such a religious attitude toward an object that my culture had conditioned me to regard as a mere instrument.

When one studies any Indian cultural form in depth, one comes to realize that the religious and the secular are not discrete realms in India, as they tend to be conceived in the modern West. The arena of music is no exception. Yet it was years before I discerned the roots of such a reverence for music, which lie deep in the Hindu past, and realized that although the study of Indian music shorn of such attitudes may yield insight of a theoretical sort, it is not an adequate mode of studying what an Indian understands by music. Unfortunately, Western scholarly categories have here as elsewhere been far too narrow, with the result that most works on Indian religions hardly make mention of music, whereas works on Indian music have by and large treated only the technical aspects of the subject and ignored its religious contexts and significance. In an article of this scope it is not possible to rectify this situation, but only to point out some of the most fundamental concepts and images and to suggest avenues for further research.

I

My student's attitude toward his *viṇā*, learned from his teacher in Madras, reveals important Indian presuppositions about music that have found expression in images, festivals, and ritual practices. Especially in the South, but also among Hindu and Muslim musicians in the North, music, like all learning, has traditionally been regarded as a sacred endeavor. The goddess Sarasvatī, patron of learning and the arts, is often represented with a *viṇā* in one hand and a book in the other. Once a year, on the days set aside for her worship, *viṇā* teachers and their students in South India assemble all their instruments in front of the household shrine. In ordinary homes, too, instruments and books are gathered together and placed before the family shrine, in which there would typically be a picture or image of Sarasvatī. These are then worshipped as the very body of Sarasvatī: they are offered fruits, coconut, cloth, incense, and lighted oil lamps and garlanded with fresh flowers. For the entire day they remain so arrayed, and on the following day (Vijayadaśamī, the climax of the Navarātrī festival and the most auspicious day on which to begin an endeavor) they are taken up briefly to be played or read./1/ Thus the process of learning music—and indeed all subjects—is sanctified and renewed periodically through ritual.

Such worship has its parallels in practices that are carried out throughout the year. If one accidentally touches a book or an instrument with one's foot, one must ritually touch it to one's eyes and forehead in a gesture of reverent homage (*praṇām*). One must never take either of these into a room that is ritually unclean, nor allow either to come into contact with one's lips or with leftover food. Indeed, one should treat a book or an instrument exactly as one would treat an image of a deity or a great human being who is worthy of reverence./2/ They are, in theological terms, the very *mūrtis* (embodied forms) of divinity.

Even in North India, where a mixed Hindu-Muslim culture of many centuries and the strong British influence of the last three have resulted in the modification and attenuation of Hindu ritual, certain practices of a markedly religious nature persist. As in the South, music festivals and concerts are sometimes opened by a brief ceremony of worship (*pūjā*), in which incense and oil lamps may be lit, flowers and fruits may be offered, and prayers of invocation may be sung./3/ Even if a more elaborate ceremony is not done, the lighting of incense, and perhaps an oil lamp, conveys the sense that what is about to take place has been consecrated and thereby elevated above all that is merely mundane.

Some Hindu musicians in the North also do their own preliminary ritual, touching the stage and joining their palms to touch their eyes and forehead in a gesture of *praṇām* that consecrates the space and time in which they are about to perform. Still more striking is the personal ritual done by

Ali Akbar Khan, a prominent Muslim performer on the sarod, before he starts to play: he does *praṇām* to a picture of Śāradā Mā, the black goddess of Maihar, Ali Akbar's village—a picture he keeps in his instrument tool case./4/ Finally, the way in which the well-known sitarist Ravi Shankar prepares for a performance is reminiscent of the meditation of an experienced *yogī*: "When I myself start to perform a *raga*, the first thing I do is shut out the world around me and try to go down deep within myself. . . . When, with control and concentration, I have cut myself off from the outside world, I step onto the threshold of the *raga* with feelings of humility, reverence and awe" (57).

Likewise indicative of the religious quality of music in India are the initiation ceremonies traditionally conducted in both the North and the South to inaugurate a student's period of formal study with a *guru*. Like a wedding ceremony, such an initiation has traditionally been understood to bind *guru* and disciple together for life, and in the North a red thread is tied around the right wrist of the disciple to symbolize this bond. Fresh white garments and the auspicious time of the ceremony, dawn, represent the fact that this is a new and consequential undertaking. The moment may be further consecrated by the offering of such items as a cloth, flowers, fruits, sweets, and a coconut in *pūjā* by the disciple himself or an attendant priest. It is in the context of such an atmosphere of reverence and eager anticipation that the first brief lesson is given./5/ Thus the whole enterprise is blessed, for in India the study of music, as we shall see, has been understood to lead not simply to technical mastery, but to the highest spiritual goal.

Such attitudes and practices toward instruments, performance, and study have their parallels in attitudes toward the repositories of the musical tradition, its *gurus*. Ravi Shankar laments the passing of the ancient system of *guru-śiṣya-paramparā*, "the continuity of tradition through master to disciple" (13), which he describes in terms that have particular resonance for the scholar of religion: "There was that rare joy and zeal on the part of the *guru* in giving his time and energy to the teaching of the sacred traditions to his beloved disciples; and on the part of the *shishya* there was devotion to the *guru*, and dedication of his life to pleasing the *guru* with his *sadhana* and his service" (14–15). He refers to his own teacher, the legendary Ustād Allaudin Khan, as "my revered *guru*," and summarizes his remarkable life, which he chronicles in fascinating detail, as a model: "From early childhood, Baba was ready and determined to make any sacrifice for music. Indeed, his entire life has been devoted to music" (51). The sacrifices to which he refers include running away from home as a boy of eight and joining a troupe of itinerant musicians in order to learn music, subsisting on next to nothing as a youth in Calcutta, and practicing sixteen hours a day or more, tying his long hair with a cord to a ring in the ceiling at night so that he would be awakened immediately if he nodded off to sleep (51–56)./6/

Although the ideal about which Shankar writes with such fervor no longer represents the norm in India, elements of it survive, especially in the villages but even in the more westernized cities. In his research in Delhi, Daniel Neuman found that the *guru* served not only as a teacher of music but also as an important model for the disciple in learning the social and cultural role of the musician (31; cf. Silver). Attitudes of respect and reverence are still commonly expressed by students in referring to their *gurus*, and these attitudes are conveyed to them directly in the ceremonial presentation of gifts on *guru-pūrṇimā*, the full-moon day once a year set aside for their honor. The very terms *guru* and *śiṣya*, used of those engaged in all traditional learning, likewise refer to spiritual preceptors and their disciples, and certain of the religious connotations of the terms carry over into contexts that a Westerner would regard as purely secular. In writing of the devotional saint-singers of medieval India, the prominent South Indian scholar V. Raghavan uses traditional religious terms to indicate the importance of a *guru* even for imparting instruction that could be learned from books: "For when a thing is taken from a book, it is like a faggot without fire, but when the guru imparts it he transmits also a part of his power and grace" (4–5). Shankar also uses the term that is usually translated "grace," *kripā*, in writing of the necessity of "the favor of the *guru*" (*guru-kripā*) for the achievement of musical mastery by the student (57)./7/

Devotion to one's *guru* and to the ideal of music that the *guru* represents takes first and foremost the form of regular and disciplined practice, and it is striking that it is again a religious term, *sādhanā*, that is used to refer to such practice. Shankar glosses the term in a musical context in a way that makes explicit its religious connotations: ". . . sadhana . . . means practice and discipline, eventually leading to self-realization. It means practicing with a fanatic zeal and ardent dedication to the *guru* and the music" (12). The Arabic and Urdu term *riaz*, used by Hindu as well as Muslim musicians in the North, has similar connotations of discipline and devotion (Neuman:42). Even musicians who hesitate to say that musical performance is religious will often claim that *riaz* or *sādhanā* is religious. Some Hindu musicians, in fact, say explicitly that *svarasādhanā* (the study of music and especially the rigorous practice that it involves) is a religious discipline directed toward God./8/ The metaphysical conceptions behind such assertions and the textual basis of these conceptions form a fascinating chapter in the evolution of the Hindu tradition.

II

To a Westerner the idea that music, or at least some music, is divine is comprehensible. There is, after all, church music, and even when the choral works of Bach are sung in a concert hall, something of their religious power persists. Yet the notion that practicing scales and exercises is a religious act somehow strikes a Westerner as odd. In order to understand this and the other attitudes and practices that we have surveyed, we must explore Indian views of the nature and religious significance of music. We shall focus on those expressed by contemporary Indian musicians of a traditional bent, notably Ravi Shankar,/9/ and in medieval Indian treatises on music.

In his autobiography, Shankar repeatedly calls music "sacred" or "divine." The reasons for his use of such religious terms are made clear in a single paragraph in which he effectively summarizes the classical Indian view of music:

> Our tradition teaches us that sound is God—Nada Brahma. That is, musical sound and the musical experience are steps to the realization of the self. We view music as a kind of spiritual discipline that raises one's inner being to divine peacefulness and bliss. We are taught that one of the fundamental goals a Hindu works toward in his lifetime is a knowledge of the true meaning of the universe—its unchanging, eternal essence—and this is realized first by a complete knowledge of one's self and one's own nature. The highest aim of our music is to reveal the essence of the universe it reflects, and the *ragas* are among the means by which this essence can be apprehended. Thus, through music, one can reach God. (17)

The tradition to which Shankar refers is enshrined in a series of ancient and medieval treatises on the arts and especially on music. The earliest of these, the *Nāṭyaśāstra* ("Treatise on Dramatic Art") attributed to Bharata, is a voluminous compendium dating from perhaps the first century B.C.E. that treats music as one of the arts involved in a dramatic performance. Although this work continues to be quoted and cited by Indians writing on music (Wade:14), the treatise that has been most influential in musical circles is the thirteenth-century *Saṅgītaratnākara* ("Ocean of Music") of Śārṅgadeva (Nijenhuis, 1974:6; 1977:12; Shringy and Sharma:xii). This work, largely devoted to the technical aspects of music, nevertheless contains passages treating the metaphysical status of sound, the divine origin of music, and the power of music for attaining both mundane and transcendent goals. The consonance between the views expressed in these passages and those enunciated by such contemporary Indian musicians as Ravi Shankar suggests a remarkable continuity in the traditions regarding these matters. Certain of the conceptions expressed in these passages thus reward our sustained attention.

In the *Saṅgītaratnākara* and other medieval treatises on music, sound, termed *nāda*, is accorded high metaphysical status. Early in the work Śārṅgadeva identifies *brahman*, the ultimate reality and ground of the universe, with *nāda*, and advocates the worship of this *nādabrahman* (1.3.1)./10/ In the opening verse of the treatise, he has referred to the great God Śiva as *nādatanu*, one whose body is sound, and here claims that not only Śiva, but Brahmā and Viṣṇu as well, are *nāda* in their very essence and may therefore be propitiated through the worship of *nāda* (*nādopāsanā*) (1.3.2)./11/

In addition to asserting the primacy of *nāda* by identifying it with the highest reality in the universe and with the essence of certain deities, Śārṅgadeva attempts to demonstrate this primacy through an analysis of the elements of language. He shows that discourse, necessary to every form of human activity, is based upon words, and words, in turn, upon syllables; syllables, he says, depend on *nāda* for their manifestation, and thus the entire world is based upon *nāda* (1.2.2). Language here clearly means spoken language; this verse is thus reminiscent of much earlier, Vedic conceptions of the power of speech,/12/ to which we shall turn in our third section.

In his initial discussion of music, Śārṅgadeva distinguishes three forms that are designated by the generic term *saṅgīta*: *gīta* (vocal music), *vādya* (instrumental music), and *nṛtta* (dance) (1.1.21). He then shows how all three are inseparably tied to *nāda*: vocal music has *nāda* as its very essence, instrumental music manifests *nāda*, and dance is likewise based upon *nāda* because it is dependent on both these forms of music (1.2.1). This integral relation of music and *nāda* is essential to Indian views of the soteriological significance of music, for music, as a manifestation of *nāda*, is seen as a mode of access to the highest reality.

Śārṅgadeva's statements about the efficacy of music are tantalizingly brief. He extols it in one verse as the sole means of attaining the four aims of human existence, *dharma* (righteousness), *artha* (material prosperity), *kāma* (pleasure), and *mokṣa* (final liberation) (1.1.30)./13/ Elsewhere he gives his purposes in revealing the "Ocean of Music": beside the more mundane one of gaining glory he lists fulfilling the eternal *dharma*, liberating all beings, and attaining the ultimate beatitude (1.1.13–14). He does not, however, explain how music is able to achieve such momentous results. Kallinātha, in his commentary on the *Saṅgītaratnākara*, argues that the technical knowledge of *śruti* and other elements of music gives the insight necessary for the attainment of the soteriological goal of final release (Shringy and Sharma: 110). Yet music hardly seems unique in its capacity to facilitate such insight. The distinctive qualities of music surely lie elsewhere.

Śārṅgadeva is especially eloquent in speaking of the remarkable power of music. He begins by detailing its effects on certain deities: Brahmā is fond of Sāmaveda singing, omniscient Śiva is pleased by songs, Krishna, though infinite, is captivated by the sound of the flute, and Sarasvatī is attached to the *vīṇā* (1.1.25–27). If even the great Gods themselves are responsive to music, he reasons, how much more must this be the case for lesser creatures. The two examples he gives are poignant ones: an infant crying in its cradle, wholly unaware of the pleasures to be derived from objects, on tasting the nectar of a song, knows joy beyond all measure; and even a fawn eating grass in the forest, on hearing the song of a hunter, is so enthralled that it is ready to give up its life (1.1.28–29).

Although he has here used deities and animals as examples of the power of music, it is clear from his next section that Śārṅgadeva is primarily interested in the effects of music on human beings. He there lists four kinds of bodies and explains that he will deal with only one, the human, because it is uniquely suitable for manifesting and perceiving *nāda* (1.2.17). At the end of this section, in which he describes the body and the process of human growth in considerable detail, he expresses an apparent paradox that lies at the heart of the Hindu schools of *yoga* and *tantra*: although the body is filled with all manner of impurities, wise persons gain both worldly enjoyment (*bhukti*) and salvation (*mukti*) by means of it (1.2.163–64). Śārṅgadeva nowhere gives the reason for his elaborate treatment of the genesis of human embodiment, but it may well be in order to facilitate the adept's reversal of that process in the gradual attainment of liberation.

Of central importance for our understanding of the value placed on music for attaining religious realization is a distinction made in the *Saṅgītaratnākara* and elaborated more fully in other musicological texts. The authors of these treatises distinguish two levels or forms of *nāda*, "unstruck" (*anāhata*) and "struck" (*āhata*) (1.2.3). The unstruck *nāda* is a vibration of the "ether" (*ākāśa*) that permeates all space; like the ether itself, it cannot be directly perceived, yet it is the basis of the entire perceptible universe. Alain Daniélou compares it to the neo-Pythagorean "music of the spheres" in that it is understood as forming "permanent numerical patterns that are the basis of the world's existence" (21)./14/ The *Saṅgītamakaranda* pictures the gods as delighting in this ethereal sound and great *yogīs* as projecting their minds into it and thus attaining liberation (1.5–6; translated in Daniélou:21)./15/

In contrast to this imperceptible form, *āhata* ("struck") *nāda* is, as its name indicates, produced by a physical blow. It thus consists of a temporary vibration of the air and is, unlike its eternal prototype, audible to ordinary mortals. Despite its apparently independent origin, however, it is conceived as a manifestation of the eternal *nāda* (Daniélou:21). This fact is clearly of immense significance for Indian views of the religious value of music, for it is musical sounds in particular that form an image of the unstruck *nāda* (Daniélou:22).

The *Saṅgītaratnākara*, designating music as a form of *āhata* ("struck") *nāda*, calls it *lokarañjanam*, "pleasing to people," as well as *bhavabhañjanam*, "breaker of the cycle of earthly existence" (1.2.167–68). It has the latter capacity because it reveals the unstruck *nāda*, thereby bringing persons into contact with ultimate reality. Its uniqueness does not, however, lie simply in its ability to effect liberation, for there are other methods of accomplishing this end, but rather in its power to do so painlessly and even pleasurably. Śārṅgadeva contrasts it in this respect with two other paths, the discipline of yogic meditation leading to a state of inner absorption (*dhyāna*), and the worship of the unmanifest *nāda*. The first he acknowledges to be arduous, but even the second, he says, fails to appeal to ordinary people because it lacks charm (*rakti*) (1.2.165–66). Music, for Śārṅgadeva, is thus an avenue of religious realization accessible and indeed attractive to persons on every level of spiritual development./16/

The theory of the twofold nature of *nāda* and the view that music manifests the eternal *nāda* constitute only one form in which the texts convey a sense of the sacredness of music. A similar point is made by stories of music's divine origin. The *Dattilam*, a compendium antedating the *Saṅgītaratnā-kara*, most probably by several centuries, says that it was Brahmā himself (Svayambhū, literally, "the self-existent one," the world's creator) who bequeathed the art of music to Nārada and the other heavenly musicians (*gandharvas*), and that Nārada in turn took it down to the earth (Dattilam 2, as found in Nijenhuis, 1970:16). Śārṅgadeva goes a step further, asserting that Brahmā and the other gods *discovered* music (1.1.22), and correspondingly describing his own task in composing his treatise as one of *revelation* (*āviṣ-karoti*, 1.1.14). Historical or quasi-historical statements tracing music back to the Vedas, in particular the Sāmaveda, are also indirect claims to its divine origin and sacred status; such statements are found in medieval treatises/17/ as well as in numerous books on music by contemporary Indian musicians and musicologists (e.g., Shankar:19; Sambamoorthy, 1960:71; Prajñānānanda, 1963:12–13; Gautam:1; Gosvami:5).

The theories of the metaphysical status of sound and of the divine origin and salvific power of music that we have surveyed have important implications for traditional Indian views of the role of the musician. It is not only music in general that is understood to have a divine origin and eternal prototype; this principle is also enunciated more specifically in relation to the melodic structures (*rāgas*)/18/ that govern individual performances, and even to the individual renderings of a given *rāga*. Shankar articulates the classical Indian position on this issue when he maintains that *rāgas* are not invented: "Rather, a *raga* is discovered as a biologist might 'discover' a new species or an explorer a new continent" (20). The Indian musical *guru*, who is also a composer–performer, thus conceives of himself or herself as a transmitter and preserver rather than an originator./19/ Indeed, the classical musician in India has traditionally been esteemed as a sort of "priest" or conduit through whom the eternal unstruck *nāda* becomes struck and thereby accessible to mortals./20/ Such a view of music as existing eternally and being periodically revealed by the inspired musician has significant antecedents in earlier Indian ideas of revelation in speech through the agency of the inspired poet-seer. These ideas are expressed in the most ancient "texts" of the Hindu tradition, the hymns, ritual formulas, and commentaries comprising the Vedic corpus, to which we turn briefly in our next section.

In the preceding pages, we have concentrated on what may be termed the classical understanding of music and the musician, in which music is viewed as a means of attaining oneness with ultimate reality (*brahman*) and the musician is seen as the priest or conduit making this reality accessible. Yet parallel to this interpretation is a second major tradition that has been no less influential, at least from medieval times./21/ In this devotional (*bhakti*) tradition, music is also seen as a means of religious realization, but ultimate reality is here envisioned as profoundly personal, and the musician is not so much a conduit as a devotee, singing or playing before God./22/ Unlike the impersonal *nādabrahman*, which is embodied and conveyed to human listeners through the structured sounds of music, the personal God of the devotee is conceived as a listener who is able to respond with enjoyment and appreciation to the performance. Indeed, it is ultimately for God and not for an earthly audience that the devotee plays or sings.

The image of the musician as devotee might seem to imply that music would function primarily as an expression of love and dedication, rather than as a means of attaining union with God. Yet in this devotional tradition, too, music has long been seen as capable of invoking the divine presence. In a frequently quoted Sanskrit verse, Krishna is represented as telling Nārada that he does not dwell in the resplendent celestial abode of Vaikuṇṭha, nor in the sun, nor even in the hearts of *yogīs*, but rather where his devotees sing./23/ In the early sixteenth century, the charismatic religious leader Caitanya and his followers in eastern India utilized the chanting or singing of the names of Krishna as a means of inducing a state of religious ecstasy in which the Lord's presence could be experienced (see Hein:18–31). Moreover, the power of such impassioned singing was not confined to the participants, but could be felt by those who witnessed it as well, as stories like the following tale of the emperor Akbar's response to the singing of Haridās attempt to show: "It is said that once Akbar asked Tansen to bring him to his guru, Swami Haridass. The Saint, who had his hermitage in Nidhban, by the river Yamuna, was singing with such fervour and devotion that Akbar felt enchanted. When the emperor returned to his court, he asked Tansen to sing the same bhajan as had been sung by his guru. Tansen obeyed, but Akbar did not feel the same ecstasy as he had experienced when he heard Haridass sing. Tansen humbly explained that he as a musician sang before a king, while the Saint poured out his soul to God, so his bhajans had an uplifting power that a mere musician could not be expected to produce" (Neuman:59).

In emphasizing the difference between the hermitage and the court as settings for music, the preceding story makes a valid point, but it draws the contrast somewhat too sharply. Tansen himself is the subject of numerous anecdotes attesting to the power of music, not only over persons but also over the elements: it is said, for example, that he caused rain merely by singing *malhār*, a *rāga* of the monsoon season./24/ If a courtly or other audience should be present, an inspired performer may nevertheless become so deeply absorbed in the music that he or she can transcend, to some degree, at least, the limits of the performance setting. As we shall see, such a state of absorption is commonly experienced as a form of union, whether with the reality made manifest in the music, as in the classical view, or with the One conceived in a devotional mode as its ultimate recipient. The musician in either view is therefore understood to exemplify and make available to an audience a profound spiritual experience./25/

What have Indian musicians and musicologists had to say about the nature of this experience? Can we find further clues to their reasons for claiming that music has the power to liberate performer and listener alike from the fetters of worldly existence?

The texts that we have surveyed commonly articulate three significant effects of music. First, music gives ineffable joy. Śārṅgadeva, as we have seen, points to the pleasing quality and enchanting power of music. The great South Indian musician-devotee Tyāgarāja, in a song in praise of *nāda*, says that by losing oneself in music one attains the bliss of *brahman*,/26/ and in another song he similarly refers to the bliss of singing "divine" music./27/

Secondly, music conduces to a state of inner calm. The South Indian musicologist T. V. Subba Rao, interpreting the thought of Tyāgarāja, compares music to *yoga* in that it likewise "brings about that state of mental equilibrium indispensable for contemplation" (206). Swami Prajñānānanda, a Bengali scholar and leader in the Ramakrishna Order, enunciates this effect along with the first one, stating that the human soul finds in music the goal of its journey, and attains through this divine art "tranquillity and ever-lasting bliss" (1973:470). Shankar likewise unites these two elements in a single statement: "The beauty of the *raga* leads the listener to a serene and peaceful frame of mind and brings him joy" (20).

Finally, music brings about an experience of unity. Prajñānānanda speaks of the act of appreciating music as one of meditating on it, communing with it, and ultimately becoming one with it (1973:471). In a similar vein, Shankar expresses his vision of the ideal of music as an "intimate one-ness" of music, musician, and audience: "And when that oneness is achieved, it is the most exhilarating and ecstatic moment, like the supreme heights of the act of love or worship. . . . It is like feeling God. . . . The miracle of our music is in the beautiful rapport that occurs when a deeply spiritual musician performs for a receptive and sympathetic group of listeners" (57–58).

In the West, too, music has long been appreciated for its ability to alter consciousness, to bring at least momentary joy even to those who are most despondent, to confer peace upon those who are anxious, and to convey to all performers and listeners, ideally, a sense of unity with something greater than themselves./28/ Historians of religion would do well to attend to phenomena such as the reverent hush that comes over an audience just before a great symphony orchestra begins to perform, or the awe in which certain of the greatest musicians are held in the West. Yet although music forms an integral part of the religious life of many Christian and Jewish communities, the West has not traditionally conceived it in religious terms. Joy, calm, and an experience of unity have often been acknowledged to be among its effects, but these have not been identified by Western theologians with salvation in the way that they have by Indian writers.

It is noteworthy that each of these three effects of music has long had
strong religious connotations for Indians, especially Hindus. From the time of
the early Upaniṣads, *brahman*, the ultimate reality, has been identified with
ānanda, "bliss, joy" (e.g., *Taittirīya Upaniṣad* 3.6). Meditative calm, achieved
in various ways, has likewise been valued as a state conducive to ultimate
realization by Hindus of all major schools, even by those inspired by such
ecstatic devotees as Caitanya or Rāmakrishna. Finally, unity, conceived either
monistically or in a modified, more personalistic way, is represented as the
final goal by major Hindu texts and teachers from the Upaniṣads and the
Bhagavadgītā to the present. It is no wonder, then, that music, which conduces
to all three states, transporting performer and audience for a time beyond
mundane cares and indeed beyond all ordinary levels of consciousness, is perceived in India as a powerful means of liberation.

III

We have seen that claims for the divine origin and religious power of
music can be found in a series of ancient and medieval treatises on music and
dramaturgy beginning with the *Nāṭyaśāstra*. In making such claims, these
texts and subsequent Indian writers have traced classical music back to the
Sāmaveda, and some have termed music, or the dramatic arts as a whole, the
"fifth Veda" (e.g., *Nāṭyaśāstra* 1.12). Such attempts to find the origin of Indian
classical music in the Sāmaveda have always struck me as somewhat dubious,
for the styles and principles of singing seem quite different. Yet the view of
music as comprised of *rāga*s that exist eternally and are merely discovered
from time to time by inspired musicians is strongly reminiscent of Brāhmaṇical notions of revelation. Whether or not musical continuity can be demonstrated between the Sāmaveda and the classical traditions of North and South
India, a striking parallel can be seen between Brāhmaṇical and somewhat later
conceptions of the nature and significance of sound. I would argue in fact that
the Vedic legacy—a profound sense of the power of sound—has contributed to
a series of developments that have been highly consequential for the entire
subsequent Hindu tradition.

As the *rāga*s of classical Indian music are thought to have eternal proto-
types, so the *mantra*s (verses and formulas) of the Vedic ritual are represented
in Brāhmaṇical literature as being eternal (Gonda, 1963b:66). Moreover, as the
inspired musician was thought to discover the *rāga*s and render them audible
through performance, so the Vedic poet-seer (*ṛṣi*, *kavi*) was understood to
have perceived these *mantra*s and crafted them into poetic formulas for use
in the ritual. These formulas were viewed as having power over cosmic processes: it was imperative that they be uttered—and uttered correctly—if
calamitous consequences were not to ensue (Staal:11; Jairazbhoy, 1968:145).
As we have noted, power over the elements is likewise attributed to certain
*rāga*s in the hands of a great musician: *dīpak*, for example, can cause fire,

and *malhār* can bring rain. Finally, just as the musician must be profoundly perceptive and inspired in order to discern and render the eternal *rāgas*, so the Vedic poet was thought to have fashioned the *mantras* "with the deepest, most profound understanding possible, that is, with insight arising from the heart" (Findly:9)./29/

Although it is not clear from the earliest texts that sound was originally understood to be the medium of revelation, the predominantly oral character of the verses once formulated may be seen from a number of considerations. Several of the terms commonly used in the Ṛgveda itself to refer to these formulas emphasize their spoken nature: *ukthá*, that which is uttered; *gír*, that which is sung; *stóma*, that which is recited (Thieme:101–3). The manner of their use in the sacrifice is likewise significant: they were recited or sung, and their efficacy was in fact thought to depend on their proper pronunciation (Staal:11; cf. Gonda, 1963b:66). Their centrality to the sacrificial performance can be discerned from the fact that they allow of no substitutions, whereas substitutes are permitted for the materials involved in the sacrificial action./30/

Among the most striking pieces of evidence for the oral nature of the Veda are the methods by which the verses have been learned and transmitted with virtually perfect fidelity for the past three thousand years without the aid of writing. In addition to two modes of recitation in which the order of the words remained unaltered, a number of patterns of permutation were developed according to which each verse or segment would be learned. When one reflects on the fact that the Ṛgveda contains roughly a thousand hymns averaging ten stanzas in length, it becomes obvious that memorizing this collection alone in even one mode of recitation is a prodigious feat./31/ The ingenuity and care with which the priests have guarded every syllable of the Vedic corpus attest to the tremendous value that they have placed on these sacred utterances. Indeed, preserving and transmitting them precisely, with attention to every subtle nuance of their intonation, has been regarded as a religious act as well as a sacred duty (Jairazbhoy, 1968:145).

In addition to the fact that the hymns, formulas, and commentaries of the Vedic corpus have been learned and transmitted exclusively orally,/32/ the most common term (together with *Veda* itself) by which this corpus has been known provides further evidence of the religious significance of sound from ancient times in India. This term, *śruti*, means literally "that which has been heard"; it is distinguished from *smṛti*, "that which has (merely) been remembered," tradition, the two terms forming a dichotomy under one or the other rubric of which all Hindu texts have been classified. Although the Ṛgveda itself contains traces of a primarily visual or mental conception of revelation,/33/ the prevalent use of the term *śruti* and its interpretation in the later tradition indicate that sound was early accorded a major role in this process as well as in those of conserving and transmitting the sacred utterances and employing them in the ritual. Aurobindo Ghose, a prominent modern Indian philosopher and interpreter of the Veda, is not atypical in his exegesis of the term: "The language of Veda itself is *śruti,* a rhythm not composed by the intellect but heard, a divine Word that came vibrating out of the Infinite to the inner audience of the man who had previously made himself fit for the impersonal knowledge" (Ghose:11).

We have amassed a considerable body of evidence for the primacy of sound in certain of the earliest layers of the Hindu tradition. One final development of Brāhmaṇical thought merits our attention in this connection. In sources beginning with three late Ṛgvedic hymns, speech is conceived as a female deity, Vāc. Her metaphysical significance is immense: in more than one hymn and frequently in the later literature she is credited with the creation of the universe, and she is even called "the one being" (*ekam sat*) (R.V. 1.164.46), a phrase reminiscent of monistic conceptions that came to prominence in the Upaniṣads. The Vedic poets envision her as residing at the very summit of the universe (R.V. 1.164.10; 10.125.7–8) and as depending on nothing beyond herself (Brown, 1968b:393–94; cf. 1968a:203–5). W. Norman Brown sees her as "representing the ultimate elevation of the magic power which holy sound is considered to possess" (1968b:393). Although she never attained popularity as a goddess, her paramount importance for the priestly circle that exalted her provides further evidence of the sacredness of sound in the Brāhmaṇical tradition.

IV

In our attempt to place Indian theories of the religious significance of music in a broader perspective, we have surveyed a number of earlier conceptions of the power of sound, some of which have had continuing importance to the present day. Limitations of space, however, have precluded a full treatment of certain highly consequential terms. Most noteworthy among these is the term *mantra,* the etymological sense of which, "a tool for thinking," provides the clue to a series of major developments in religious thought and practice that took place especially in yogic and tantric circles (see Eliade:212–16; Gupta et al.:90–111; Gonda, 1963a:273–84). A related term of Vedic provenance that has likewise had considerable currency in later centuries is *akṣara,* "the imperishable one," a term that emerges as the creative syllable of the hymns (Brown, 1968b:394) and evolves to mean that element of a word that admits of no further analysis and is hence considered in grammar to be invulnerable (Gonda, 1959:105). In the later Hindu tradition, *akṣara* came to refer primarily to *brahman* and to the sacred syllable *oṃ,* the most important *mantra* from the time of the Upaniṣads (see Chandogya Upaniṣad 1.1). Finally, the term *brahman* itself, which designates a central metaphysical concept from the Upaniṣads onward, refers in the Ṛgveda to the sacred utterance (Thieme:103; cf. Gonda, 1950:40). Its evolution in meaning from the prayer-word to the ultimate reality in the universe needs to be reviewed with particular attention to the role of concepts of sound in this development./34/

These terms and their interrelations are matters on which considerable work remains to be done. Further research is likewise needed on some of the topics that are discussed more fully in the present article. Most obviously lacking is fieldwork in both North and South India on attitudes and practices of contemporary Indian musicians and their *gurus*. A survey of biographical and autobiographical statements in modern Indian vernacular periodicals and books might well be valuable in this connection. Yet musicians in India have rarely written autobiographically—Ravi Shankar is the great exception—and one thus has no ready textual access to their views and experiences. There is the further problem that explicit statements are particularly inadequate in this area. Music is ultimately ineffable: its power lies precisely in its ability to affect one at a level deeper than any touched by discursive prose.

Finally, further work is needed on the treatises and their commentaries, and on the relation between the earlier Brāhmaṇical and Mīmāṃsaka theories of the perception of the eternal *mantra*s by the poet-seers and the views found in the treatises on the eternity of *nāda* as primordial sound and of the *rāga*s of Indian music. Given the close connection of music theory in India with the science of grammar (Danielou:3–4; Shringy and Sharma:xii), which in turn grew out of Mīmāṃsaka speculation on the ritual, it seems reasonable to posit continuity between the Brāhmaṇical views of revelation in speech and later Indian views of the religious significance of music (see Lannoy:274–80). Yet further evidence is needed before such a connection can be more than a tantalizing hypothesis.

For any period of Indian religious history, it is difficult to ascertain how widely known a given document or conception may have been. This problem is implicit at a number of points in the present article, but it bears most seriously on the musicological treatises discussed in part II. There are several reasons for doubting that these treatises represent the thinking or even the unverbalized experience of a large number of Indian musicians and audiences at any period past or present. First, the treatises are written in Sanskrit, and in medieval as well as modern India this limited their readers to a small minority belonging chiefly to the *brāhman* class. This fact is especially significant for the North, where most professional musicians, unlike the majority of those in the South, have been non-*brāhmans*. Second, we find statements that parallel those in which music is said to conduce to all four aims of life (including liberation) in a wide variety of texts, for example, those on pilgrimage (see Eck, 1982:306). Are such statements in the treatises, then, merely pious utterances without real conviction? Third, one can point to the pervasive Muslim presence in North India from medieval times and the fact that most contemporary North Indian performers are Muslim. How influential, then, could Hindu theories of the nature and significance of sound have been?

Without more extensive and detailed research, it is impossible to refute these objections with finality. Yet the evidence we have surveyed reveals sufficient congruity between the views and practices of a number of North and South Indian musicians (both Hindu and Muslim) and statements found in the treatises to allow at least the tentative conclusion that the treatises represent a living tradition that survives, in some measure, into the contemporary era. Furthermore, although orthodox Islamic writers deny the sacredness of music, the Sūfīs have affirmed this sacredness, and indeed the Sūfī tradition has contributed its own understanding of the divinity of music to the composite culture of North India. Inayat Khan, for example, utilizes characteristic Sūfī modes of expression when he writes the following: "Music . . . is nothing less than the picture of our Beloved. It is because music is the picture of our Beloved that we love music. . . . Our Beloved is . . . our source and our goal; and what we see of our Beloved . . . is the beauty which is before us. . . . All the beauty that attracts us in any form . . . tells us that behind all manifestation is the perfect Spirit, the spirit of wisdom" (1).

We have seen that sound and music have had sacred significance in India from Vedic times. Indeed, it is difficult to avoid the conclusion that "in no [other] human civilization [has] speculation on sound and word . . . played such a lasting and important role as in the Indian culture" (Gupta et al.:90). The Brāhmaṇical legacy is one important factor contributing to this emphasis. However, the conception of music as a means of religious realization and its study as a religious discipline (*sādhanā*) also fit well with several major characteristics of the Hindu tradition as a whole. First is its emphasis on practice rather than on doctrine, a characteristic that sharply distinguishes it from the major forms of Western Christianity. Second, the musical patterns of North and South India reflect the initiatory character of Hindu religious life: the emphasis on guidance by an experienced *guru* accords with the practice prevalent in all Hindu sects and schools. Finally, the sense that a physical endeavor, such as learning to sing or to play an instrument, may be an avenue of liberation from the fetters of the mundane world parallels closely the use of the body as an instrument of transcendence especially in the disciplines of *yoga* and *tantra*. It is noteworthy that initiates of both these schools likewise use sound as a tool to focus the mind and free it from mundane, discursive thought.

We are now in a position to reflect briefly on two important differences between Hindu India and the Christian West in their views of music. First, the Indian discussions of the religious significance of music do not founder on the issue of music's sensuousness, as those in the West commonly do. The body/spirit dichotomy that such Western discussions presuppose is not a feature of Hindu thought. The techniques of *yoga* and other meditative disciplines presuppose a certain continuity: one may seek ultimately to transcend the purely physical, but physical practices, such as breathing exercises, postures, and the repetition of *mantras*, are considered the chief or even the only means by which one may do so.

We have touched earlier on a second major difference between India and the West in regard to the sacredness of music. Sacred music in the West is largely vocal music, whether for solo voice or chorus, and its sacredness is largely or wholly dependent on its text. The organ is the only instrument that has become closely enough linked with church settings that music written for it is typically regarded as sacred. In India, on the other hand, religious music is not, by and large, regarded as merely a setting for a text. In the North, in fact, the words to vocal compositions are often unintelligible, or largely so, for the music contains long melismas on individual syllables. In the South, where the words are more important, instrumental compositions are learned first as vocal compositions with devotional texts that performer and audience alike have clearly in mind during a performance./35/ Thus in neither the North nor the South is instrumental music sharply distinguished from vocal music; either may mark a religious occasion. Sound itself, as we have observed, is viewed as powerful and revelatory; even the musician practicing scales and exercises may therefore be seen as performing a religious act.

A final piece of evidence for the religious significance of music in the Hindu tradition is the pervasiveness of singing and recitation in rituals and festivals of all sorts, both public and private. The ritual use of chanting and singing goes back some three thousand years, for not only the Rgveda but also the more melodically intricate Sāmaveda were essential elements of the elaborate Srauta sacrifices (see Howard:14–25; Jairazbhoy, 1968:140–42). In contemporary Bengal, too, no important religious occasion is celebrated without some form of music or chanting: Vedic recitation and the vernacular musical performance form known as padāvalī kīrtan, together with such forms of communal singing as bhajan and sankīrtan, are major elements of life-cycle rituals such as marriage and funerals as well as of seasonal festivals throughout the year. The often impassioned melodic rendering and interpretation of portions of the epics and purānas, especially the Rāmāyana and the Bhāgavata, and sometimes other devotional texts as well, continue to draw large crowds in city and village alike.

The centrality of sound and music in Indian religious life mandates that students and scholars take these elements seriously. In addition to the classical music traditions of both North and South India, we should give more attention to living forms of explicitly religious music, such as Rāmāyan Gān, Bhāgavat Pāth, and Kathaktā, viewing them in their total performance and cultural contexts. Second, books on the Hindu tradition should incorporate such studies as well as the findings suggested in the present article. Finally, aural materials, such as Staal and Levy's excellent two-record set entitled The Four Vedas, should be used by those wishing to gain a comprehensive understanding of the Hindu tradition, for these resources provide an important corrective to the strong textual bias of the study of religion. Such sustained attention to the aural dimension, utterly central as it is in India, should help us perceive as never before the true richness of the Hindu tradition.

NOTES

Note of Acknowledgement: I wish to express my appreciation to my teachers of Indian music, comparative religion, and Indology, and to the friends and colleagues who have contributed essential information and insights to the present article. To Peter Row, who gave most generously of his time and his extensive knowledge of Indian music theory and practice and who criticized a draft of the first two sections, I owe a profound debt of gratitude. I am also deeply grateful to Jack Hawley, who first suggested that I write this article, gave me invaluable encouragement along the way, and commented helpfully on a completed draft. Veena Das discussed my ideas with me at an early stage, and suggested several valuable sources and approaches; her enthusiasm for the project has also been a great boon. Indira Peterson, Julian Smith, and David Buck, my Oberlin student, have contributed greatly to my understanding of South Indian views and practices. Finally, Ellison Findly, whose fine paper on *mantra* I draw on in section III, has discussed with me some of the ideas that I have begun to explore in that section.

/1/   I am indebted to Indira Peterson and Julian Smith for this description of the worship of Sarasvatī in South India.

/2/   Indira Peterson, personal communication.

/3/   Incense seems to be an invariable concomitant of a performance, regardless of whether any of the other elements are present. According to Indira Peterson, most orthodox *brāhman* musicians in South India do *pūjā* before a performance. In the annual festival of the Music Academy of Madras, there is a *pūjā* ceremony before the first concert of the day; after this, the presence of burning incense and the pictures of the deities on the corner of the stage extend the effects of the ceremony throughout the day. Each performance must be consecrated in the place where it will occur, in order that it go well; this ritual may, however, take place before the audience arrives. A performance also begins with a song or instrumental composition in praise of Gaṇeśa, the Lord who removes obstacles (personal communication). According to Julian Smith, a *vīṇā* player's worshipful gesture of kneeling before the instrument at the outset of a performance serves to establish a reverent mood whether or not there is a ceremony of worship (personal communication). For a characterization of the form of Hindu worship called *pūjā*, see Hopkins:110–12).

/4/   I learned of this practice from Peter Row; the goddess's identity was told to me by George Ruckert, Dean of the Ali Akbar College of Music in San Rafael, California.

/5/   I have attempted to write generally enough that what I have said applies to both North and South India. However, in the North, the *gaṇḍā* ceremony, in which the red thread is tied, is conducted after the disciple has demonstrated his or her loyalty to the *guru* through a period of study lasting generally for two or three years, rather than at the beginning of that study (Peter Row, personal communication). My description is based largely on the perceptive report of his initiation by Julian Smith (personal communication). For Muslim practice, see Neuman:55–58.

/6/   Such a hagiographical account is reminiscent of stories of great Western composers' lives read as inspirational literature by young music students in America and Europe.

/7/   A term or terms that may be translated "grace" were repeatedly encountered by Neuman when he asked what was required to become a performer in North India; the three elements most commonly enunciated were "(1) one's will or discipline, (2) . . . one's guide, and (3) one's spiritual status or divine intercession or grace" (Neuman:30).

/8/   Veena Das, personal communication.

/9/   Because of the dearth of autobiographical accounts by Indian musicians and because I have not had the opportunity to conduct interviews, I have had to rely heavily on Ravi Shankar's book. I am aware that his views have been criticized by certain of the more secularized younger musicians; yet, according to Peter Row, even these younger musicians, whether Hindu or Muslim, share to a remarkable extent his "musical mysticism" (personal communication). I cite and quote him because he represents so well the traditional pattern that I am attempting to portray.

/10/   The commentator Siṃhabhūpāla glosses the compound *nādabrahma* with the phrase *nāda eva brahma*, "*brahman* which is sound itself" (Vedāntavāgīśa and Ghosha: 39; Shringy and Sharma:109).

/11/   The commentators explain that the *tad* in *tadātmakāḥ* ("having that as their essence") refers to *nāda* (Vedāntavāgīśa and Ghosha:39) or *nādabrahman* (Telang:31). What form such worship was to take is unfortunately not specified by Śārṅgadeva. Elsewhere he states that sages worship the unmanifest *nāda* by the procedure laid down by (previous) *gurus* (1.2.165–66), but again he gives no further details.

/12/   This verse appears to be quoted frequently; it is found verbatim in the *Saṅgītadarpaṇa* (1.14). Kallinātha, in his commentary on *Saṅgītaratnākara* 1.3.1, identifies *nāda* with *parā vāc*, Speech (Vāc) conceived from the late Ṛgveda onward as the highest principle of the universe (see section III of the present essay). Utilizing another female conception, one developed especially in tantric circles, he likewise identifies it with *brahmaśakti*, the "energy" of *brahman* (Telang:31; Shringy and Sharma:110).

/13/   See section IV for an acknowledgment of the numerous parallel statements in other sorts of texts. Tantric texts in particular combine mundane and spiritual goals (see Gupta et al.:7, and Gonda, 1963:66).

/14/   The idea that the motion of the planets forms a harmony that parallels musical harmonies, revealing the same numerical proportions, has been attributed to the Greek philosopher and religious teacher Pythagoras (late sixth century B.C.E.). After Plato this theory was often interpreted literally as referring to an ethereal music, perceptible to mortals whose souls are attuned to the celestial harmonies. For a brief article on the development of these conceptions, see James Haar, "Music of the Spheres," *The New Grove Dictionary of Music and Musicians* 12:835–36. A more substantial article by Haar tracing the considerable influence of Pythagorean conceptions through classical and Renaissance writers down to the present day is his "Pythagorean Harmony of the Universe," in the *Dictionary of the History of Ideas* IV:38–42. Haar has written a Ph.D. dissertation on the subject, "Musica Mundana: Variations on a Pythagorean Theme" (Harvard University, 1961).

/15/   According to Nijenhuis, this work, attributed to a Nārada, is of uncertain date (1977:13). She cites Prajñānānanda, who dates the author to the fourteenth or fifteenth century (1977:20).

/16/   The view that music constitutes an easier way to final liberation is expressed in numerous texts. The *Yājñavalkya Smṛti* contains a verse (3.114), quoted with slight modifications in such later treatises as the *Saṅgītadarpaṇa* (1.32), that states that a person who knows the art of *vīṇā* playing and the technicalities of music will proceed without effort on the path to liberation. Such verses are also quoted by some Muslims; the Sūfī Inayat Khan renders in English a Sanskrit verse on the *vīṇā* that expresses the apparent incongruity between the mere physical instrument and its wondrous power to bring about liberation: "That instrument of gut strings! By looking at it, by touching it, by hearing it, you can be made free, even if you kill a Brahmin!" (37).

/17/   The *Nātyaśāstra*, in the passage that served as the prototype of later origin accounts, identifies *nāṭya* (drama), or itself as a treatise on *nāṭya* (of which music is a component part), as the fifth Veda (1.12–18). The *Saṅgītabhāṣya* terms *nāda*, in the sense of music, "the fifth approach to the Eternal Wisdom, the Veda" (Daniélou:21). The *Saṅgītaratnākara*, following *Nātyaśāstra* 1.17, asserts that Brahmā himself extracted and collected vocal music (*gīta*) from the Sāmaveda (1.1.25).

/18/   For an excellent concise introductory treatment of the concept of *rāga* (Hindi *rāg*), see Jairazbhoy, 1971:28–29; his treatments of *tāla* (Hindi *tāl*) and the composed piece in North Indian music (1971:29–31) also constitute a useful starting point for understanding these elements.

/19/   The frequency with which one hears or reads the term "purity" in relation to a *rāga* (e.g., Shankar:57) may be taken as evidence for this conception. A delightful story that forms part of the oral lore of musicians throughout India serves as a particularly graphic illustration. The sage Nārada, regarded as the original *guru* of music among mortals, was very proud of his musical accomplishments. He was invited in a dream to visit the heavenly musicians (*gandharvas*) (of whom he is often represented as originally one), and there he saw a great number of divine beings who were all twisted and deformed. When he inquired who these were, he was told that these were the *rāgas* as a certain would-be musician named Nārada was wont to render them. Nārada, deeply ashamed, resolved to preserve and transmit them properly thenceforward (Peter Row, lecture, November 21, 1982). Raghavan, citing three textual sources, the *Bṛhaddharma Purāṇa*, the *Liṅga Purāṇa*, and the *Adbhuta Rāmāyaṇa*, gives a summary version of the story in his introduction to Ramanujachari and Raghavan, *The Spiritual Heritage of Tyāgarāja* (46–47).

/20/   I am indebted to Peter Row for this insight and for this way of phrasing it.

/21/   According to Neuman, "That music is a means of devotion is perhaps the most common idea expressed by musicians" (60).

/22/   For this perception of a *bhakti* mode as one of two fundamental musical attitudes I am indebted to Peter Row. In the *bhakti* tradition in general, God is conceived as a personal deity, usually Śiva, Viṣṇu (especially in his avatars as Krishna and Rāma), or Devī, the Goddess (especially in her forms as Durgā and Kālī).

/23/   The verse is quoted and translated by Hein (27). It is also given in Sanskrit by Sambamoorthy (1960:71), and paraphrased in gist by Rao (207).

/24/   For references to such a feat, see Holroyde:89; Sharman:166; Khan:54–55; Shankar:28–29. A story to this effect is part of the common oral tradition of musicians in North India; Peter Row has heard such a story many times, in several variant versions (personal communication).

/25/   It is said, for example, that the outstanding *bīn* player Ustad Bande Ali Khan, after fourteen years of assiduous practice, was able to send a certain holy man, beside whom he practiced daily, into a state of deep meditation (Neuman:63).

/26/   Tyāgarāja, "Nāda Lōluḍai," as found in Ramanujachari and Raghavan: 510–11. For another song identifying music as the bliss of *brahman* see his "Garuḍadhvani Kīrtana," as quoted and translated by Raghavan in his introduction to the above volume (64).

/27/   "Intakanna Yānanda," as found in Ramanujachari and Raghavan:508. Many of the songs quoted and translated in this last section of the anthology, on "Nāda Yōga," express the ineffable joy that music brings. For an assessment of Tyāgarāja's views of the spiritual value of music, see chapter II of Raghavan's introduction.

/28/   See, for example, Franz Liszt's essay, "Berlioz and his 'Harold' Symphony," in Strunk:846–73, especially 849–50 (reference supplied by Peter Jeffery).

/29/   In the interest of brevity I have not here separated out discernible layers in the evolution of Brāhmaṇical thought regarding the *mantras*. In the Ṛgveda itself, the insight received in revelation is understood as requiring development by the poet, whose active role in the process is indicated by such verbs as √ *takṣ,* "hew" (Gonda, 1963:106–11). It is in the systematized view of the later Mīmāṃsā school that the *mantras* themselves are explicitly said to be eternal. Yet the Ṛgveda itself contains evidence that the *mantras* once crafted by the poets were regarded as inviolable: Staal attributes the fidelity with which these *mantras* have been transmitted to "the awareness of the transcendence (*apauruṣeyatva,* 'non-human origin') of the sacred word" (11). Cf. Apte:277.

/30/   Frits Staal, comments in response to papers on *mantra* in a panel at the Annual Meeting of the American Academy of Religion in San Francisco, December 19, 1981.

/31/   The feat is even more remarkable than this calculation indicates, for the commentarial materials appended to the Ṛgveda and each of the other three *saṃhitās* ("collections") were also committed to memory. For a succinct characterization of the divisions of the Vedic corpus, see Howard:1–2. Examples together with an explanation of the different modes of Vedic recitation are found in the two-record set of Staal and Levy, *The Four Vedas,* and the accompanying booklet.

/32/ The Veda was not written at all for some two millennia, and even after it was first committed to writing approximately a thousand years ago, the written form was not utilized in the process of transmission.

/33/ Ellison Findly points to the personal hymns of Book 7, notably R.V. 7.88, a hymn of Vasiṣṭha to Varuṇa, as evidence of a face-to-face encounter between the poet and his God: the visual aspects of the poet's experience are expressed in verse 2 (38–40). In R.V. 6.9, however, we find an auditory image alongside the visual and mental ones: "My ears fly open, my eye opens out,/ beyond to this light set in my heart./ My mind (manas) flies up, straining into the distance./ What shall I say? What shall I think (maniṣye)? (R.V. 6.9.6, as translated by Findly:30).

/34/ Gonda (1950:3–4 and passim) rightly points out the impossibility of determining the original meaning of such a rich and complex term, and of constructing a clear chronology of successive meanings.

/35/ Julian Smith, personal communication.

REFERENCES

Āpte, Hari Nārāyaṇa, ed.
1897   *The Sangīta Ratnākara by Śrī Niśśanka Śarngadeva with Its Commentary by Chatura Kallinātha.* 2 vols. Poona: Anandasrama Press.

Apte, V. M.
1943   "The 'Spoken Word' in Sanskrit Literature." *Bulletin of the Deccan College Postgraduate and Research Institute* 4.4:269–80.

Bake, Arnold Adriaan
1930   *Bydrage tot de Kennis der Voor-Indische Muziek* (Sangīta-darpaṇa, text and translation). Paris: Paul Guethner.

Brown, W. Norman
1968a   "Agni, Sun, Sacrifice, and Vāc: A Sacerdotal Ode by Dīrghatamas (Rig Veda I.164)." *Journal of the American Oriental Society* 88:199–218.
1968b   "The Creative Role of the Goddess Vāc in the Rig Veda." *Pratidānam. Indian, Iranian and Indo-European Studies Presented to F. B. J. Kuiper*: 393–97. The Hague: Mouton & Co.

Coward, Harold G.
1976   *Bhartṛhari.* Boston: Twayne Publishers.

Daniélou, Alain
1968   *The Rāga-s of Northern Indian Music.* London: Barrie and Rockcliff.

Eck, Diana L.
1982   *Banaras: City of Light.* New York: Alfred A. Knopf.

Eliade, Mircea
1958   *Yoga: Immortality and Freedom*. New York: Pantheon Books.

Findly, Ellison Banks
n.d.   "*mántra kaviśastá*: Speech as Performative in the Ṛgveda."
                        Understanding Mantra. State University of New York Press,
                        forthcoming.

Gautam, M. R.
1980   *The Musical Heritage of India*. New Delhi: Abhinav Publica-
                        tions.

Ghose, Sri Aurobindo
1956   *On the Veda*. Pondicherry: Sri Aurobindo Ashram.

Ghosh, Manomohan, tr.
1951   *The Nāṭyaśāstra Ascribed to Bharata-muni*. Vol. I. Calcutta:
                        Royal Asiatic Society of Bengal.

Gonda, Jan
1950   *Notes on Brahman*. Utrecht: J. L. Beyers.
1959   *Four Studies in the Language of the Veda*. The Hague: Mou-
                        ton & Co.
1963a   "The Indian Mantra." *Oriens* 16:244–97.
1963b   *The Vision of the Vedic Poets*. The Hague: Mouton & Co.

Gosvami, O.
1957   *The Story of Indian Music: Its Growth and Synthesis*. Bom-
                        bay: Asia Publishing House.

Gupta, Sanjuktpa; Hoens, Dirk Jan; and Goudriaan, Teun
1979   *Hindu Tantrism*. Leiden: E. J. Brill.

Haar, James
1961   "Musica Mundana: Variations on a Pythagorean Theme."
                        Unpublished Ph.D. Dissertation, Harvard University.
1973   "Pythagorean Harmony of the Universe." *Dictionary of the
                        History of Ideas* IV: 38–42. New York: Charles Scribner's Sons.
1980   "Music of the Spheres." *The New Grove Dictionary of Music
                        and Musicians* 12:835–36. London: Macmillan.

Hein, Norvin J.
1976   "Caitanya's Ecstasies and the Theology of the Name." *Hindu-
                        ism: New Essays in the History of Religions*. Ed. by Bard-
                        well L. Smith. Leiden: E. J. Brill.

Holroyde, Peggy
1972   *The Music of India*. New York: Praeger Publishers.

Hopkins, Thomas J.
1971   *The Hindu Religious Tradition*. Encino, Calif.: Dickenson
                        Publishing Co.

Howard, Wayne
1977   *Sāmavedic Chant*. New Haven: Yale University Press.

Jairazbhoy, N. A.
1968   "Le Chant Védique." *Encyclopédie des musiques sacrées.* Ed.
               by Jacques Porte. Vol. I, pp. 135–61. Paris: Editions Laber-
               gerie.
1971   *The Rāgs of North Indian Music: Their Structure and Evolu-
               tion.* Middletown, Conn.: Wesleyan University Press.

Khan, Inayat
1980   *Music.* Lahore: Sh. Muhammad Ashraf.

Lannoy, Richard
1971   *The Speaking Tree: A Study of Indian Culture and Society.*
               London: Oxford University Press.

Neuman, Daniel M.
1980   *The Life of Music in North India: The Organization of an
               Artistic Tradition.* Detroit: Wayne State University Press.

Nijenhuis, Emmie Wiersma-te
1970   *Dattilam: A Compendium of Ancient Indian Music.* Leiden:
               E. J. Brill.
1974   *Indian Music: History and Structure.* Leiden: E. J. Brill.
1977   *Musicological Literature.* Wiesbaden: Otto Harrassowitz.

Prajñānānanda, Swāmī
1963   *A History of Indian Music.* Vol. I: Ancient Period. Calcutta:
               Ramakrishna Vedanta Math.
1973   *Historical Development of Indian Music: A Critical Study.*
               Calcutta: Firma K. L. Mukhopadhyay.

Raghavan, V.
1966   *The Great Integrators: The Saint-Singers of India.* New
               Delhi: Publications Division, Government of India.

Ramanujachari, C., and Raghavan, V.
1966   *The Spiritual Heritage of Tyāgarāja.* 2nd ed. Madras: Sri
               Ramakrishna Math.

Rao, T. V. Subba
1962   *Studies in Indian Music.* Bombay: Asia Publishing House.

Sambamoorthy, P.
1960   *History of Indian Music.* Madras: Indian Music Publishing
               House.
1953–69   *South Indian Music.* 6 vols. Madras: Indian Music Publishing
               House.

Shankar, Ravi
1969   *My Music, My Life.* New Delhi: Vikas Publishing House.

Sharmā, Batuk Nāth, and Upādhyāya, Baldeva, eds.
1929   *The Nāṭyaśāstra of Bharata.* Benares: Chowkhamba Sanskrit
               Series Office.

Sharma, Prem Lata
n.d.   "Music as an Effective Means of Sadhana." Unpublished paper.

Sharman, Gopal
1970   *Filigree in Sound*. New Delhi: Vikas.

Shringy, R. K., and Sharma, Prem Lata
1978   *Saṅgīta-ratnākara of Śārṅgadeva*. Vol. I. Delhi: Motilal Banar-
               sidass.

Silver, Brian
1976   "On Becoming an Ustad: Six Life Sketches in the Evolution of
               a Gharana." *Asian Music* 7 (2): 27–58.

Staal, J. F.
1961   *Nambudiri Veda Recitation*. The Hague: Mouton & Co.

Staal, J. F., and Levy, John
n.d.   *The Four Vedas*. 2-record set. Asch Mankind Series AHM
               4126.

Strunk, Oliver, ed.
1950   *Source Readings in Music History from Classical Antiquity
               through the Romantic Era*. New York: W. W. Norton and Co.

Telang, Mangesh Ramakrishna, ed.
1920   *Saṅgīta-makaranda of Nārada*. Baroda: Central Library.

Thieme, Paul
1952   "Bráhman." *Zeitschrift der deutschen Morgenländischen Ge-
               sellschaft* 102:91–129.

Vedāntavāgīśa, Kālīvara, and Ghosha, Śāradā Prasāda, eds.
1879   *Sangīta Ratnākara by Śārnga Deva with Sangīta Sudhākara, a
               Commentary by Sinha Bhūpāla. (Svārādhyāya)*. Calcutta: The
               New Arya Press.

Wade, Bonnie C.
1979   *Music in India: The Classical Traditions*. Englewood Cliffs,
               N.J.: Prentice-Hall.

NOTES ON CONTRIBUTORS

JOHN ROSS CARTER (Ph.D., Harvard, 1972) is Associate Professor of Philosophy and Religion at Colgate University and Director of the Fund for the Study of the Great Religions and of Chapel House. He has published articles and books on various aspects of Buddhist studies.

JUDITH KAPLAN EISENSTEIN (Ph.D., Hebrew Union College) is retired from the faculty of Hebrew Union College–Jewish Institute of Religion, School for Sacred Music. Among her publications is *A Heritage of Music: The Music of the Jewish People*.

LOIS IBSEN AL FARUQI (Ph.D., Syracuse, 1974) teaches religion and arts at Temple University and has written on visual arts, women, and family in Islamic culture. Most recently she has published *An Annotated Glossary of Arabic Musical Terms* (1982).

BARBARA L. HAMPTON (Ph.D., Columbia) is Associate Professor of Music at the City University of New York. In addition to ritual music, her research interests include problems of change in African urban music. A recent publication is "Toward a Theory of Transformation in African Music," *Transformation and Resiliency in Africa* (Washington: Howard University Press, 1982).

JOYCE IRWIN (Ph.D., Yale, 1972) has taught at the University of Georgia and Colgate University and has written on women and sexuality in the Reformation as well as music and theology in the late Middle Ages, German Lutheranism, and American Puritanism.

BRUCE B. LAWRENCE (Ph.D., Yale, 1972) Professor of History of Religions at Duke University, has written *Shahrastani on the Indian Religions, Notes from a Distant Flute*, and *The Rose and the Rock* and many articles in Islamic and South Asian religious, literary, and cultural history in the pre-modern period.

STEPHEN A. MARINI (Ph.D., Harvard) is Associate Professor of Religion and Director of American Studies at Wellesley College and Adjunct Associate Professor of Church History at Weston School of Theology. He is the author of *Radical Sects of Revolutionary New England* (Harvard University Press, 1982) and is currently working on the Evangelical tradition in America, from the Great Awakening to the Civil War.

OSKAR SÖHNGEN (Dr.phil., Bonn, 1922) is the author of many books and articles on theology and music, including *Theologie der Musik* (1967) and *Musica sacra zwischen gestern und morgen* (1979). He was for many years professor at the Musikhochschule in Berlin.

DONNA MARIE WULFF (Ph.D., Harvard, 1977) is Assistant Professor of Religious Studies at Brown University. Her dissertation, on the dramatic works of Rūpa Gosvāmī, is forthcoming in the AAR Academy Series. With John Stratton Hawley she edited *The Divine Consort: Rādhā and the Goddesses of India* (Berkeley, 1982). She studied sitar for two years in India and is currently researching a contemporary musical and dramatic form of devotion in Bengal, Vaiṣṇava *kīrtan*.